Gordon C. Zahn is Professor of Sociology at the University of Massachusetts at Boston, and a prominent Catholic pacifist. A former Fulbright Senior Research Fellow, he is the author of *German Catholics and Hitler's War*, *The Military Chaplaincy*, and *War, Conscience, and Dissent*.

Another Part of the War

THE CAMP SIMON STORY

Gordon C. Zahn

The University of Massachusetts Press   Amherst, 1979

A note of special gratitude is due Peter Lasauskas
for the use of the photographs included in
this volume.

Contents

To all who were there, and especially to those who were willing to return in memory to a time of discomfort and trial.

To Dorothy Day and the Catholic Worker without whom the witness, such as it was, would not have been possible.

And, finally, to friends and colleagues who spoke the encouraging words that convinced a sometimes doubting author it was really worth the try—this book is gratefully dedicated.

There is little danger that the Second World War—the "big war," the "last good war" as some would have it—will pass unnoticed in the final recapitulation of human history. Enough has already been written to fill entire libraries; and this output, one need have no doubt, will be multiplied several times over as new facts and documents are brought to light and new interpretations (to say nothing of the controversial revisions of old opinions and interpretations now coming into print) are advanced. Massive works of historical scholarship find a more popular echo in the works of journalists and novelists and these, in turn, are given even more immediate expression through the visual media of movies and television. Sometimes the story is told on the sweeping scale of major campaigns and crucial battles; at other times, and no less effectively, in more individual dimensions with the focus upon the experiences and reminiscences of the people, great or lowly, caught up in an event far beyond their ken or control. Tragic in mode, or heroic, or even comic, they all contribute to a fuller understanding of that event now almost forty years into the past. This is an understanding sorely needed if mankind's hopes for a world in which total war will never again be possible are to be fulfilled.

This book addresses itself to another part of that war. For a period of slightly less than six years, approximately twelve thousand men were classified as conscientious objectors under the provisions of the Selective Service and Training Act and assigned to duty in the one hundred and fifty or so camps and special units of Civilian Public Service. In obtaining their IV-E classification they had convinced either their local draft boards or other conscription authorities that they were opposed to all participation in war by reason of their religious training and belief.

The men assigned to alternative service were not the only conscientious objectors to World War II. A much larger number (Selective Service estimates suggest there were between twenty-five and fifty thousand) declared themselves willing to perform noncombatant service in the military forces and were classified I-A-O. Finally, another six thousand or so were sentenced to federal prison either because they failed to convince the designated authorities of the legitimacy or sincerity of their claim to the IV-E classification or because they refused to cooperate with the conscription program even to the point of registering and seeking such classification.

If one compares these modest totals with the millions of men who accepted the national call to military service, it is probably not surprising that so little is known about the conscientious objector and the alternative service program, or that what little is known is so often distorted and misinterpreted. It has been altogether too easy to take the CPS* program at face value as clear evidence of democracy's tolerance and respect for the rights of individual conscience while, at the same time, dismissing those who took advantage of the alternative service option as an unpatriotic, self-centered, perhaps even cowardly dissident minority that was unwilling or unable to respond to the challenge presented by totalitarian tyranny in its drive for world domination. A quite contrary view was held by many, perhaps most, of the men who actually served in the program. In their eyes CPS was punitive in practice and intent, an experiment in the democratic *suppression* of a dissident religious minority in time of war.

There is more to this than a simple difference of perspective. If there is any validity to the participants' charge, it is important that the case be made and put on the record. This is not just a matter of correcting the past. There is abundant evidence that the alternative service camps of World War II are still considered viable models for the possible future handling of the problem of conscientious objection if the Selective Service System, now in the limbo of stand-by status, is ever restored to full operation. It is even possible that, had the half-hearted "amnesty" introduced under the Ford Administration succeeded in persuading a sufficient number of Vietnam-era exiles and deserters to return, a resurrected camp program would have been the vehicle for the alternative service required under its terms. Before there is any repetition of the CPS experience,

---

*Civilian Public Service. In most future references to this alternative service program the abbreviation will be employed.

therefore, it is important that its full story be told.

This study proposes to tell only part of that story. Between late October 1942 and the middle of the following March, seventy-five conscientious objectors were assigned to a forestry camp located near Warner, New Hampshire. Camp Simon, the name selected by the campers themselves, had the distinction of being the only such camp operated under Catholic auspices and intended primarily for Catholic conscientious objectors. To keep the record straight, this only camp was actually two: Warner had been preceded by a smaller camp at Stoddard, New Hampshire, which remained in operation for about a year until it was shut down and its members transferred to larger facilities at Warner. For reasons to be explained later, I have decided to treat these as two separate phases of a single camp experience.

Whether one chooses to regard Camp Simon as one camp or two, some justification is needed for making it the subject of special study and attention. Clearly it was one of the smallest CPS camps in terms of the number of men assigned there, and its early demise made it one of the shortest-lived. If a single camp is selected to serve as an illustration of the CPS program, its weaknesses, and its implications, it could be argued that one of the larger, more representative and more enduring camps operated by the major traditional peace churches would be better suited to that purpose.

Perhaps so. On the other hand, there are some perfectly good reasons behind my choice. The first is partly personal and partly professional. As one of the men assigned to perform alternative service there—my arrival actually coinciding with the official opening of the Warner camp—I can bring the benefit of personal interest and the methodological advantages to be gained from participant observation and insights. I cannot deny that this experiential dimension can be as much a liability as an asset, but in this particular instance the danger is outweighed by the deeper understanding of the events and personalities to be described, an understanding made possible by that more intimate association.

But there are other equally important considerations to be taken into account. Camp Simon was unique in several crucial respects. In the social sciences the analysis of a single case has its greatest value if, on the one hand, it is representative of an entire class or category of phenomena or, on the other, if it is unique in such a way as to illuminate or demonstrate some otherwise unrecognized aspect of the class or category to which it belongs. A social history of the Warner camp, in my judgment at least, meets the latter test. The special problems and privations encountered there were really the magnified expression of faults present but not fully acknowledged, in the structure of the alternative service program itself. Even the most remote possibility that such a system might ever again be brought into being should be cause enough to explore the unhappy experience in some detail.

That reference to special problems and privations touches indirectly upon the effects of Camp Simon's status as the only camp sponsored by Catholics for Catholics. It was, in a very real sense, the first corporate witness against war and military service in the history of American Catholicism. Indeed, the claim might even be made that it was the first such witness in the entire history of the Church. Having said this, I must introduce some basic reservations and qualifications that would seem to negate both claims.

For one thing, to speak of Camp Simon as a corporate witness overstates the case if one takes that to mean that the men assigned there represented anything even approaching consensus in principle or application with respect to their opposition to the war. If anything, the reverse was true. As this record will show in occasionally shocking detail, the Warner campers as a group were extremely individualistic and ever on guard against anything that threatened to limit the intellectual and ideological independence that had brought them to camp in the first place. Partly as a result of this, the camp situation would be marked by dissension and disaffection throughout its brief history and, often enough, these conflicts were provoked by essentially trivial matters and incidents.

On a more positive note, however, there was a least common denominator in the obvious fact that all had rejected service and in the kind of unity that arose from the misery they were obliged to share under the compulsion of conscription. From these most of the men were able to fashion a sense of common identity and an awareness of mutual interest. One might even speak of an esprit de corps that, strangely enough, grew stronger once the Warner camp was closed and the men distributed among other CPS camps and units or returned to civilian life. I find it remarkable that today, more than thirty years later, the memory of that brief and generally unhappy association still serves as a continuing bond for a surprisingly large proportion of the Warner veterans. To this extent, certainly, the designation "corporate" is justified.

But how "Catholic" was that witness? The question raises a more complicated problem and one which accounts in great part for the severity of those shared deprivations. That single Catholic camp was in no sense officially Catholic, nor did its members receive encouragement from their spiritual leaders or fellow communicants. If it is too much to describe the Catholic conscientious objector as a religious outcast, this is only because the general Catholic population took no notice of him. Camp Simon was administered by the Association of Catholic Conscientious Objectors, an impressive sounding organization that was really nothing more than a "front" set up by the Catholic Worker movement. And as for the Worker itself, though it has achieved a considerable measure of respect and admiration today, in the 1930s and 1940s mainstream Catholics tended to view the movement and its radical teachings as being of doubtful orthodoxy if not actually heretical.

Dorothy Day and her associates might be praised and admired for works of charity performed for the derelicts of the Bowery and other "skid-row" areas of our major cities; but when it came to the platform espoused in the penny paper bearing the movement's name, the insistent demands for social justice and a personalist and communitarian restructuring of society fell on deaf or resisting ears. This was particularly true of the Worker's pacifism. After the Pearl Harbor attack its refusal to support the war, coupled with its open endorsement of conscientious objectors and their stand, cost it many of its friends and contributors. There was at least one dramatic instance, in fact, of a formal break with the parent movement by one of its houses of hospitality.

Even in the absence of more official support, however, the men of Camp Simon (or, at least, those who actively practiced their faith) had no doubts as to the Catholicity of their witness. This confidence extended further than the ability to defend the *legitimacy* of their refusal to serve with appropriate theological arguments. Most of them regarded their stand as the *correct* stand to be taken, a binding moral obligation for them and, presumably, for other Catholics as well. This is not to say, of course, that they regarded those who did not see things their way as guilty of sin; instead, they were more likely to make allowances for what they considered a tragic failure on the part of most to think the matter through. When they had the rare occasion to argue the case they would present conscientious objection as the logical and behavioral consequence of the faith they and their detractors alike professed.

There is a time factor to be considered here. Recent developments in the Catholic Church's teaching and practice—most particularly the statements of the Vatican Council and Popes John XXIII and Paul VI

—lend a kind of ex post facto validation to what was then almost universally rejected as a deviant interpretation of Scripture and traditional Catholic thought. Whatever delayed gratification these changes in direction and emphasis may bring now, it really does not have too direct a bearing upon the quality of the witness of the men of Camp Simon at the time. They would have welcomed the added confidence and the respect and support that might have been theirs had those statements been on the record then, but most of them were already totally convinced that they were making a Catholic witness even though their spiritual leaders and fellow communicants did not accept the fact.

As will be detailed at the appropriate time, not all the men of Camp Simon were Catholic and those who were did not agree themselves in their interpretations of the morality of war and opposition to war. However, all the various elements, with the possible exception of a handful of the Warner campers, accepted the Catholic identification of the camp and agreed it was important, if at all possible, to keep the Catholic camp in existence as a corporate witness against the war. It was only after the problems seemed to get completely out of control with no reasonable solution in prospect that some wavered or abandoned that objective. As far as the actively practicing Catholics were concerned, divided though they may have been in theological or ideological outlook, they continued to plead the case for a continued Catholic presence in CPS until the very end.

There is another dimension to Camp Simon's uniqueness, however. Much of the turbulence that marked its brief history must be traced not only to the fact that they were out of place as far as their fellow Catholics were concerned but that they were also (and, moreover, considered themselves to be) out of place in CPS. This enhanced the sense of isolation and alienation that was theirs and served to intensify the hardships and burdens that formed the substance of most of the continuing complaints and protests directed against those held responsible for the defects and injustices of the alternative service program.

And they were outsiders in a number of ways. First, by taking a stand against a war supported by a nearly total national consensus, they justifiably felt alienated from family, friends, neighbors, and the whole of society around them. Even if they were not actually disowned or repudiated, as so many were, there was punishment enough in the sorrowful tolerance encountered in those closest to them and in the knowledge of having disappointed people who meant a lot to them. Add to this, then, the fact that they felt alienated as well from the Church, in a very real sense orphaned by that spiritual mother in whose name they had taken their unpopular stand. Now they found themselves in CPS, outsiders again in a program conceived by and clearly dominated by the traditional peace churches (Friends, Mennonites, Brethren) leaving them a small minority in an almost exclusively Protestant operation.

The time factor is relevant here, too. These were, one must remember, preecumenical days, a matter of no small concern for Catholics whose orthodoxy was already suspect in the eyes of their religious community. It did not help when they found themselves patronized by some of their CPS counterparts who apparently shared the opinion that Catholic objectors were not really Catholic but had somehow freed themselves from the rigidity and narrowness usually ascribed by Protestants to the Catholic Church. In any event, this third level of alienation—from CPS itself—carried the heaviest load of resentment. Rightly or wrongly, many of the Catholic objectors believed they had been trapped into a situation not of their making, obliged to accept deprivations imposed by a set of concessions and compromises arranged without their approval or participation between the military officers who ran the show and the Protestant peace church leaders.

If this sense of alienation was exaggerated and the resentment not altogether justified, the fault lay with the situation as much as with the men themselves. It is because of this that the Camp Simon history provides such valuable insight into the nature and implications of the alternative service program. There is another, more peripheral benefit to be gained. Much of what will be recorded in these pages will stand in startling contrast to recent events that found Catholics— including priests, nuns, and even a bishop or two—distinguishing themselves as leaders of the opposition to the war in Vietnam. If, as has been suggested, this small and short-lived experiment in the New Hampshire woods was the first corporate Catholic witness against war, to what extent can the men of Camp Simon be viewed as forerunners of that "great Catholic peace conspiracy" of the Vietnam years? The question may not find a definitive answer here, but it should be clear that until that earlier resistance becomes more widely known, the question itself can make little or no sense.

Since the principal emphasis will be given to reconstructing the social history of Camp Simon, especially in its Warner phase, the mode of approach will be that of the social sciences to the extent possible. The fact noted earlier that the author was a member of that camp and has something of a personal stake in getting its story told should aid in its telling. It is possible, of course, that this entire venture reflects nothing more than the autobiographical urge often associated with the sobering awareness of advancing age, but every effort will be made to avoid letting this account degenerate into a pacifist equivalent of those old soldiers' tales replete with self-celebratory recitation of wartime exploits and adventures. This should be quite easy to do; exploits and adventures were few indeed at Warner.

The primary source, then, especially as it bears upon the basic orientation and organization of this study, is my own personal recollection of the events and personalities described. Such recollections do not stand alone but will be supplemented and confirmed in many cases by the descriptions and commentaries contained in letters written from camp at the time. These letters were saved at my request and provide occasionally helpful insights even though they are not the thorough and incisive record of my days in camp I intended them to be.

One man's memory, even supported in the manner indicated, is a weak foundation for a serious study. Some effort had to be made, therefore, to reach others whose reminiscences might serve to reinforce or, where necessary, correct my own. The effort was made and succeeded beyond my fondest expectations, considering that for more than three decades there had been little or no contact between me and most of my former colleagues. Following the procedures described in the body of the study I was able to get in touch with almost half of the men listed on the Warner roster, most of whom were willing to cooperate by furnishing the information requested. For the most part this was limited to the respondents' remembered impressions of the Warner campers, but a few additional questions brought other information of interest and value to the study.

There were other sources of a documentary nature. The most valuable by far was the voluminous and highly detailed daily journal kept by one of the men and generously made available to me. Not only did this provide a wealth of contemporary insights and descriptions of events against which to check memories assembled from my own and my respondents' recollections; the journal also made it possible to put those remembered events in their proper chronological sequence.

Another nearly contemporary source was a study made of the Stoddard camp by Harold P. Winchester. Written from the perspec-

tive of the social anthropologist, this, too, relied upon the then much
fresher recollections of men who had served there. One special value
of this incomplete study to my own should be obvious. Because I
had not been at Stoddard myself, the Winchester account becomes
the principal source of material related to that phase of Camp Simon's
history. Since most of the tensions and controversies that were to
disrupt life at Warner had their beginnings at Stoddard, the Winchester account helped fill what would otherwise have been a serious gap.

Documentary sources of a more conventional nature provided
other essential data. The Jane Addams Peace Library at Swarthmore
College is the depository for the records of the National Service
Board for Religious Objectors, the coordinating body established by
the various peace church agencies and other sponsors to supervise
and administer the alternative service camps and program and, even
more crucial a task, to deal directly with the Selective Service System
officials. These records, which include the individual personnel files
of all men ever assigned to CPS, were reviewed to obtain preinduction
social background data relating to the Warner campers as well as the
complete sequence of later assignments and transfers, date and manner of final discharge, and any other incidental information bearing
upon their subsequent CPS careers.

The Swarthmore deposit also includes the administrative files and
records of the administrative agencies and the separate camps, but in
this instance what could have been a source of considerable importance proved to be of only limited value. The fault is easy to trace.
Anyone familiar with the Catholic Worker movement will also be familiar with the almost studied inefficiency of its record keeping operations. That same haphazard approach was carried over to the ACCO,*
not at all surprisingly since the two were, in effect, the same. As a
result very little in the way of organized data was to be found in
these files. So, too, with the *Catholic Worker* newspaper. Every
monthly issue carried a column for each of the ACCO camps and
units. Unfortunately (and for perfectly good reasons as we shall see)
these were usually typical house organ releases and are not too reliable or informative as accounts of Warner events and developments.

One final documentary source of somewhat peripheral value in the
Swarthmore holdings is the diary of Paul Comly French, Executive
Secretary of the NSBRO.† The French diary provides a comprehen-

---

*Association of Catholic Conscientious Objectors. In most future references to
the association the abbreviation will be employed.
†National Service Board for Religious Objectors. In most future references to

sive, detailed, and extremely interesting record of the activities and opinions of this central figure in CPS history. Too lengthy to be read in its entirety in the course of my few visits to Swarthmore, this fascinating document could only be scanned for any entries or references it might contain during the Warner period relating to the problems and issues that dominated the campers' lives and concerns. There were a few entries mentioning the attempts made by ACCO leaders to keep the camp alive, and there were French's own occasional observations and comments about matters of broader concern throughout CPS such as the recurrent demands for pay and government-operated camps or the sporadic protests against specific actions taken by Selective Service. Apart from these entries, there appeared to be nothing of direct relevance to the present study.

When all is said and done, the question of whether or not the Camp Simon story is worth the telling remains. Predictably enough, I think it is—even if it would serve no other purpose than to focus attention on what we might consider a historical curiosity. There is much more to it than that, however. At a time when vast numbers of Catholic men willingly (a great many *enthusiastically*) went off to war, an infinitesimally small number of individuals refused because they felt that war is morally wrong. The significant changes that have taken place in their church's attitude toward war and related issues, changes that have brought the Church much closer to the attitudes and behavior that were rejected as deviant then, merit the serious consideration to be given here to their witness. In another more secular vein, the focus placed upon this one camp—small, short-lived and troublesome though it was—will help define relationships and trace implications that might well be lost in more broadly structured analyses of the alternative service program.

In another sense, of course, even this limited focus is too broad. The real explanation of conscientious objection lies in the individual objector's personal values and motivations. A study that relies entirely upon a group or categorical approach risks missing or confusing that most essential dimension. This danger is minimized, however, when the group is small enough so that sufficient emphasis can be placed upon the uniqueness of character and the specific position of its various members. Camp Simon and the men assigned to it during its Warner phase offers such an opportunity. It is my hope that this account of its brief history will fulfill that promise.

---

this coordinating agency the abbreviation will be employed.

ORIENTATION ANTHEM

This ain't the Army, Mr. Jerk.
This ain't the Army, Mr. Jerk.
            We shun the trenches
            Where all that stench is
            By doing this very vital work.

This ain't the Army, Mr. Gray.
Standing here high above the fray
            We beat the taxes
            By swinging our axes
            And refusing to take any pay.

This ain't the Army, Mr. White.
We always strive to do what's right
            And what's more perfect-er
            Than to be an objector
            And be gay while the other fellows fight?*

Sung to the tune of Irving Berlin's song, "This Is the Army."

It is best to begin on a personal, even autobiographical, note. My arrival at the Warner camp is clearly etched in my memory even though there are some gaps in my recollection of the journey there. One thing, however, does stand out: the trip from Milwaukee to Boston was my first experience with the luxury of sleeping-car rail travel, the last luxury I was to enjoy through the courtesy of the U. S. Government and its Selective Service System. I have a confused impression of some difficulty in negotiating the connection between the two rail stations in Boston, and since I arrived at Warner by bus, I assume there was also a connection to be made at Concord. But, as I said, the memory of being met by Lou Schnittler and Dean Farfether and bouncing the last three miles or so of the road leading to the camp on Mt. Kearsarge is as distinct, more than thirty years later, as if it had taken place over our last vacation break.

This is probably because the event carried with it special implications of a new beginning and an entirely new direction to my life. Not only was this the longest trip I had ever made, but its length and ultimate duration were unknown. Twenty-four years of uninterrupted urban life had suddenly turned into the prospect of an indefinite stay in the New Hampshire wilds; the sheltered, white-collared office clerk was now to be converted into the outdoor woodsman. It was altogether a strange and, if I were honest with myself, somewhat exciting change.

It was that for most of my fellow campers too, of course. In my case these "new life" implications found an added dimension in the fact that the preceding two years had brought the deaths of my last immediate relatives, the second bereavement occurring barely three months before I received the order to report for induction. Though I fully expected to return to the office job from which I had been drafted once the duration had passed, I also entertained the fantasy that this new beginning and the associations it would bring might lead to a new and very different future. In fact, it did: I never would "go home again" in the sense of resuming the pattern of life that had been interrupted.

But my expectations of the more immediate future were not all that pleasant. As a rather naive member of a remarkably naive generation, I arrived in CPS with no clear notion of what I would find. Most of the other men called to alternative service—and this would be especially true for those with a background of pacifist activity— may have known what to expect. My own opposition to the war had developed in isolation and was the product of independent, some would probably say idiosyncratic, thought. This would affect my experiences at Warner—and after—in some rather important ways.

Since the question is frequently asked, I should make it clear that I always have difficulty explaining how I became a pacifist and conscientious objector. The most likely source was the voracious reading to which I was addicted as a child and, even more, to a sentimental aversion to causing injury to other creatures. One of my earliest recollections of this attitude traces back to the primary grades and the shock, even horror, I found in my best friend's delight over receiving a B.B. gun with which he hoped to shoot squirrels. Although I always enjoyed adventure stories in books and movies, I was most impressed by the tragic finality of death and, in the war stories at least, by the senselessness of it all. By the time I reached high school, I was writing amateurish antiwar poems and, on one memorable occasion, became embroiled in a controversial exchange of letters to the editor of the local newspaper sparked by my protest against hunting as a sport. It is strange, in this connection, that I do not recall being influenced greatly by the movie, *All Quiet on the Western Front*, which converted so many (including Lew Ayres, its star) to pacifism. I suspect this may have been because I was already fixed in my personal commitment before I saw the film.

That commitment was essentially religious, but here, too, it derived more from a personal and highly sentimentalized version of Christianity than from any formal introduction to Catholic theology. The product of a religiously mixed (and religiously inactive) household, I had very little direct contact with the faith into which I had been baptized as an infant. Catholic friends of the family would occasionally—usually on the major Christian holidays—take me to Mass, but that is about as far as my religious experiences went. My primary and secondary education was received in the public school system, a fact which may have contributed more than anything else to my ultimate arrival at the Warner bus stop. After all, had I been exposed to parochial school training and education, chances are good that I would have gone off to war like most of their other products.

For all of this, however, I always insisted upon my Catholic identity and nonviolently defended the Church and its history in discussion with my non-Catholic peers. It was not until I was in my teens that one of those family friends insisted upon enrolling me in a formal course of religious instruction and I became a regular (perhaps even a bit too rigorous) practicing Catholic. Nothing I learned there affected my already fixed pacifist commitment. I knew that the official teachings of the Church upheld the duty of the individual to obey established authority and that this carried over into a duty to perform military service when called. I was familiar, too, with the general notion of the "just war" though it would not be until I was involved in camp discussions that I would discover how limited a concept that was. I just assumed that the term referred to *any* war declared by the authorities, a misunderstanding that conformed more to the Church's practices than to its theology. Finally, my public school education had probably made me more aware than a parochial school equivalent could have done of the Church's involvement—often enough, *culpable* involvement—with wars of past history. It is not surprising, then, that even as a youngster when I entertained heroic fantasies of making a dramatic refusal to take part in war, I pictured myself as being the only Catholic to do so.

Fantasy this may have been, but it was not as unreasonable as one might suspect. World War I produced only one definitely known Catholic conscientious objector, though more recent research suggests there may have been at least three others.[1] And when conscription did become the law of the land, that fantasy was given a measure of empirical validity in the indignant statement by a prominent member of my draft board (the local Catholic pastor!) that anyone who claimed to be Catholic could never be a conscientious objector. Nor was he alone in that interpretation of orthodox teaching, as we shall see in due course. In my case, registered letters sent to Milwaukee's archbishop elaborating upon my reasons for refusing to serve and seeking his support with the draft authorities went unanswered. This may have been nothing more than standard chancery practice of ignoring inconvenient appeals, but as far as I was concerned it was a sign that I was indeed the only Catholic to take a position against war and military service.

The first indication that I was not alone came from Protestant pacifist friends *after* I had received the IV-E classification on appeal from the initial negative decision of my local board. While discussing my prospects for alternative service, they called my attention to the existence of a Catholic camp in New Hampshire. As readers of the *Catholic Worker*—a paper and a movement of which I had never heard despite the fact, as I would learn soon enough, that there had been a very active house of hospitality in Milwaukee—they had come across the monthly report of Stoddard activities.

When the time for actual induction neared, I indicated a preference for assignment there, and the request was approved. Assignment policies being what they were, I would probably have been sent there in any event. The camp's chronic inability to attract enough campers of a Catholic background meant that anyone not associated with one of the traditional peace churches had a fairly good chance of being sent to Stoddard and, later, Warner. Anyone who identified himself as Catholic was almost certain to be.[2]

My expectations of alternative service at the beginning included grim visions of some kind of prison or concentration camp, complete with armed guards, barbed-wire enclosures and all. Though this, too, is evidence of my ignorance and naivete, it seemed to have empirical support in the extensive FBI investigations, including direct surveillance,[3] conducted on men who sought the IV-E classification. Both the expectations and the investigations found some justification in the temper of the times. The nation, after all, was at war; there was reason enough to assume that conscientious objectors were subversives in a sense and, as such, might be subject to severe restrictions on their activities and freedom. There were restrictions, and they were devastatingly effective and punitive, as later chapters will show. They did not, however, take the direct or crude forms I had anticipated.

There is a point to be made here, though, that is deserving of some consideration when the conscientious objector of World War II and

his witness are reviewed and evaluated. Despite the fact that these
men were not punished or incarcerated in the usual sense of those
terms, it is more than likely that most of them took their stand
expecting some such treatment. If so, the readiness to pay that price
is significant and should merit respect even though it was not exacted
in the manner anticipated. This should be borne in mind when we
turn to the discussion of what might otherwise be dismissed as petty
complaints and evasions that came to dominate so much of Camp
Simon's later history. Heroes and martyrs the men of CPS were not;
yet this does not mean that the capacity for a more heroic witness
was lacking.

My darker forebodings were dispelled by the welcoming letter
received from the camp's administration once my induction notice
was issued. If anything, the descriptions it gave of camp life and
obligations seemed too good to be true—which, in fact, is what they
turned out to be in most respects. The guiding philosophy, the neo-
phyte was assured, envisioned the camp as "a training school for
Christian pacifists." To achieve this would require "constant attention to detail, to the little things" as well as "self-sacrifice and hard
work"; but it would be worth it as "a labor of love." "We can try
to learn to be real pacifists . . . real Christians."

The description of the campers' obligations and rights as far as
Selective Service was concerned was brief and to the point: forty-
four hours of Forestry Service work would be required, with the
added warning, "they may extend the work hours at any time";
leave and furlough time would be granted on the same basis as in
the military service but here, too, this was "a privilege to be granted,
not a right to be demanded. This is conscription." Apart from this,
camp maintenance duties and other jobs around camp were necessary, but for these the rule was to be one of voluntary acceptance of
a shared responsibility—"you will be free to refuse."

A more detailed description of the actual work program, on project and in camp, will be given later along with the sad account of the
decline and ultimate abandonment of the all-is-voluntary principle.
Given the tenor of my almost paranoid expectations, the tone of the
welcoming letter and the pacifist philosophy it expressed made it
welcome in more than the sense intended. If it did not yet induce me
to look forward with joy to induction and camp life, it did at least
give promise that the CPS experience, and the Warner camp in partic-

ular, would be one that offered a real opportunity to effectively oppose war and advance the ideals of peace. This promise, alas, was not to be fulfilled.

My arrival on October 27, 1942, coincided with the official opening date for the Warner camp. As I have already mentioned, before Warner there had been the smaller camp at Stoddard. Officially established in June 1941 under the auspices of the ACCO, this predecessor had teetered on the edge of extinction for several months with a population consisting of six assignees, the camp director, and a woman who had volunteered to serve as a combination cook and camp nurse. Since an approved work project required a minimum work crew of ten men, the camp was put on notice in August that it would be shut down unless more men were assigned to it without delay. An appeal for volunteers from other New England camps under Quaker jurisdiction produced eight transfers, and Stoddard became a fully functioning camp on October 8, 1941.

Though I cannot speak from the perspective of experience, it is clear that the controversies and issues that were to disrupt life at Warner had their beginnings in the Stoddard phase of the Camp Simon history.[4] Some hint of this may be seen in the upbeat tone of the announcement made by the camp's acting director in the November 1942 issue of the *Catholic Worker* (the move had already been completed before the announcement appeared in print) that Stoddard's "little world is preparing itself for a change. The whole camp—250 chickens, two cats, two pigs, 60 cords of wood, 100 bushels of vegetables, 45 men and their belongings—all these are going to be moved 50 miles to a new home."

In that issue he went on to acknowledge:

We have our troubles here. Consider our circumstances: 45 men forced together for a year in a crowded place doing what we think is comparatively unimportant work and living in what for most of us are pretty rude quarters and at a pretty cold temperature.

Thus we have our arguments, our feelings that others are selfish or are not considerate, our weariness of seeing the same faces every day, our jealousies, our irritations at the idiosyncracies of others, and so on—the whole catalogue of minor sins.

The new beginnings were not all that was hoped for. The spaciousness of the promised facilities—the "bunk rooms, recreation rooms, classrooms, artists' rooms galore"—was somewhat oversold, and this would become all too clear in the first weeks of the Warner experience and would lead to new and almost violent dissension because the rosy expectations went unfulfilled. Those, like myself, who began our alternative service in the new setting in innocent ignorance of the troubles of the past found ourselves at a disadvantage when it came to making ostensibly minor decisions that, unknown to us, carried implications of past controversies.

The two men who picked me up in Warner and helped get me settled in camp (one of them a fellow Milwaukeean) were leading members of the camp's intellectual set, and this initial exposure probably accounted for the fact that I would henceforth be associated with that clique and its interest. My acceptance was enhanced once word got about that I was carrying a copy of Proust's *Remembrance of Things Past* when I stepped off the bus—though I must confess that I had not then, nor have I since, read more than a portion of that work. There is every possibility that, had I been met instead by members of the chapel set, my earliest orientation and associates would have been quite different. Though I would not suggest that the divisions were so wide that membership in one set excluded close association with members of others, one's initial identification with one or the other tended to define his place in camp. Here again, a full description of the various factions must be reserved for later.

Even so trivial a matter as a preference for either the "cold" or "hot" bunkhouse, the first decision I was called upon to make, had factional overtones of which I was not aware. Fortunately enough, my preference for the cold was received with favor by Lou and Dean, my two new-found friends, and I was given a bunk directly across from theirs. Only later would I hear tales of the previous winter when arguments raged over how much heat was to be permitted, how many windows were to be opened at night and how wide, and who were imposing their preferences upon the other campers. This, at least, was one problem that *was* solved by the additional space: one whole barracks was to be cold and a second was partitioned with its larger part designated warm and the remainder warmer to the point of being hot.

Not *completely* solved, however. As temperatures sank far below the zero mark in the cold winter of '42, new and, if one may use the appropriate term, "heated" controversies developed over just how cold the "cold" bunkhouse should be permitted to get. One difference of opinion on a particularly frigid night ended with a boot thrown through a window someone insisted upon closing. Shortly after this dramatic episode, I moved over to the more moderate bunkhouse, but this was as much an effort to break the monotony of camp existence as it was a surrender to the rigors of the New Hampshire winter. It did not reflect—though there were some who read the move as such—a transfer of allegiance from the group with which I had become identified.

I have no definite recollection of my first impressions, favorable or unfavorable, of the physical layout of the Warner camp. Possibly because I had expected things to be much worse, I know I did not share the despair of others. One former camper, looking back at his own reaction, writes that it was a less than happy homecoming. The camp was an old abandoned Civilian Conservation Corps facility reactivated to house conscientious objectors for the duration of the war. The only difference, as he saw it, as a veteran of the conservation program, was that his freedom was now more seriously curtailed since the only way he could leave was to go to jail or (as he ultimately did) join the army.

The note of depression in his recollection may have been due in part to the fact that he arrived in March with the dregs of winter everywhere in evidence and a badly disorganized and disillusioned camp already preparing to disband. I arrived in glorious October when the camp was new and hopes were high. Some hopes, though, had already been weakened if not shattered. George Selmon's diary includes two entries that reveal the extent of his own disappointment when he arrived from Stoddard. On October 26 he tells of the "dismalness, the utter depressing character of the new camp" that inspired "a fit of depression the like of which I have seldom known." That sentiment finds an echo the following day with the comment, "The mess hall is very dingy and dismal in lighting, a truly horrible place to be in."

I soon learned that another and more crucial issue dividing the campers was the appropriate, or recommended, attitude toward work. The welcoming letter had defined the limits of the required service to be performed under government supervision and had also stressed the voluntary nature of additional work around camp. Included in what the camp director referred to as "a certain minimum amount of required work" was the maintenance of the health and sanitation standards set by Selective Service. The camp "as a group has decided that any work that cannot be done by the regular maintenance crew will be done on rainy days or before we leave on Saturdays." In addition to the assigned alternative service and other necessary maintenance work, Camp Simon offered the opportunity to do still more. "We are voluntarily poor and so we must do much to support ourselves. Feeding the pigs, keeping the chickens, caring for the garden, etc. is voluntary work. We continue to emphasize in most things this principle of volunteerism because we want to learn to be really charitable. We want to do things when we don't enjoy them. To work for love. To save and do without and give away what we save."

A few days on the scene were enough to show that these elevated ideals were not shared by all; that, in harsh fact, they were explicitly rejected and ridiculed by some. This was not simply a matter of shirking one's fair share of these tasks (which, of course, was true enough in some cases). What seemed to be self-indulgent laziness was for some a kind of principled malingering, at once a form of resistance to a government work project deemed unimportant and a protest against grossly inadequate living conditions. Though the explicit statement of such noncooperation was left to the articulate few who came to be regarded as disrupters by the camp administration and its supporters, the pattern was followed by the majority of the men. Those campers who did make a serious attempt to put their personalist ideals into effective practice and who, by so doing, deserve most of the credit for keeping the camp going as well as it did for as long as it did were likely to be rewarded for their pains with the highly uncomplimentary labels of "200-percenter" or "second-miler" and treated accordingly.

In my own case, I came close to slipping into that latter classification in the innocence of my earliest days at Warner. The first four or five days following arrival were normally to be set aside for orientation purposes to give the newcomer time to adjust to the situation, get his required inoculations, and the like. Shortly after I arrived, I met the acting director and the suggestion was made that I might want to assist in getting the camp settled after the move from Stoddard. Still operating under the influence of the inspirational tone set in the welcoming letter ("It is hoped that each man will see that the atmosphere in camp is up to him and that he will do his part to make it what it should be. You will be encouraged to pitch in and help on the jobs around camp. But you will be free to refuse. You will not be

punished if you don't"), I rose to the occasion and made myself
available for a work assignment the next morning. It was one of the
few instances—quite possibly the last—in which I would voluntarily
pitch in. Though I never went to the extreme of openly refusing a
work assignment (an offense equivalent on the records to the military's AWOL) or was agitator enough to earn disrupter classification,
I soon became adept at knowing where not to be when the opportunities for voluntary work presented themselves.

Be that as it may, my tasks of those first few days scarcely fit the
description "work of national importance." For the most part they
consisted of hours spent at an old coffee grinder reducing kernels of
corn to scatter feed for those 250 chickens that had accompanied the
men from Stoddard. Once that task was completed (and while still in
that presumably free orientation period), I found myself sharing the
far more disagreeable chore of picking through a veritable mountain
of potatoes in search of the very rotten few that were imperiling the
lot. The utter boredom of the one and the nauseating stench of the
other made for a rather inauspicious beginning to the peace witness
I had visualized in such dramatic, at times even heroic, terms. In can-
did retrospect, however, these admittedly ignominious assignments
may well have represented the most significant work I was to perform in my days at Warner.

Surprisingly enough, another aspect of camp life that fell short of
the expectations raised by the welcoming letter was the matter of
religious practice and commitment. That vision of the camp as "a
training school for Christian pacifists" which would "encourage the
study of the Church, its teachings, its doctrine, its history, and its
liturgy" and "make it possible for Catholics to live a fuller religious
life here" never came close to being realized. From my own point
of view, of course, this was not too great a disappointment. Given
the limitations of my religious background and training, I came to
camp not at all sure I could maintain or even adjust to the life style
those elevated standards of religiosity seemed to imply.

I need not have been worried. For one thing, I discovered the camp
roster included a sizeable proportion of non-Catholics. Of even greater significance, many of those who were recorded as Catholics were,
in fact, nonpracticing (or, as one was wont to say in those more tri-
umphalist days, "fallen away") Catholics. The remainder, by now no
more than half of the total camp population, was divided between
those who, like myself, would fit Fichter's classification as "modal"

parishioners and a smaller number, including several former seminarians, who could be classified as "nuclears" and who assumed the responsibility of initiating and maintaining a liturgical program of morning and evening worship at camp in addition to the weekly trip to Contoocook for Mass. In the first flush of good intentions formed in the enthusiasm of arrival, I was a chapel regular for the first week or so; after that, as my good intentions faltered and my enthusiasm waned, I slipped from regular to not-so-regular and, finally, to merely occasional participation in the chapel devotions.

Passing reference has already been made to the fact that these differences in affiliation and practice did not exhaust the range of religious divisions within the camp population. The active, or practicing, Catholics were sharply divided among themselves with respect to the correct interpretation of the morality of war, the one point on which one might have assumed a group of Catholic conscientious objectors would be in basic agreement. Leaving aside the few purely idiosyncratic positions—one man, for instance, described a vision, or personal visitation, in the course of which he was instructed not to go to war—there were three Catholic positions against war and military service represented in camp.

The first, largest, and most orthodox position was based on the traditional theological distinction between the just and unjust war. Applying the conditions developed in the writings of Augustine, Thomas Aquinas, and the neo-Scholastics, those who professed this position had reached the conclusion that World War II could not pass this test and, therefore, that service in the war should be refused. In their eyes, however, pacifism as generally understood—and as incorporated in the teachings of the historic peace churches—was a serious error bordering on heresy; in a Catholic this could only reflect a misguided attempt at individual interpretation of Scripture by the theologically illiterate. A few expanded this interpretation into a kind of "Thomistic pacifism," holding that no *modern* war could ever meet the conditions of the just war. But even these dissociated themselves from the perfectionism of the Catholic Workers and the more humanistically oriented Catholic liberals who did profess and accept the pacifist premises and terminology they disdained.

The Catholic Workers, those men who had either been active in the movement before coming to camp or sympathetic to its philosophy, did not reject the just war/unjust war distinction; they were more inclined to dismiss it as irrelevant. The Christian, they argued—

and it is well to remember that in that time and place the term meant "Catholic" to a Catholic—was called to nothing less than spiritual perfection. Not only did this goal require complete personal dedication to a life of voluntary poverty and the performance of the corporal and spiritual works of mercy, but such commitment and service was to be based on the principle of all-encompassing love, including even (or, perhaps better, especially) love of the enemy. After all, they regularly reminded their more orthodox brethren, the Natural Law from which the conditions of the just war had been derived was simply the standard of behavior required of the good pagan. Christians were called to the higher standard of perfection and could never condone the hatred and the fratricide of war, just or unjust.

The third major faction, in which I was included, claimed to be both Catholic and pacifist, that combination many of our fellow campers rejected as a contradiction in terms. We represented what has since been described as an evangelical position. In some respects it was close to that held by the Catholic Workers though it did not insist upon the same behavioral, or what some would prefer to call life-style, obligations. The pacifists' arguments against war were based less on specific Scriptural injunctions (and certainly far less on Natural Law precepts) than on the logical incompatability between the spirit of the Gospels and the spirit of war. All war, and this includes the Crusades and all the other wars condoned or initiated by Christians, sometimes even by responsible leaders of the Church, were condemned as a direct violation of Christ's teaching and example and as an abandonment of the standards set in the early centuries of Christianity, the "Age of Martyrs." This willingness to criticize the Church and its record brought the Catholic liberals close to the positions taken by the non-Catholic peace church and humanist campers, a fact that only made us and our arguments more suspect in the eyes of our more traditional Catholic brethren.

One other Catholic faction must be mentioned here, though the position they represented was only peripherally theological in nature. A number of the Camp Simon Catholics, probably no more than a half-dozen or, at the most, ten, were dedicated followers of Rev. Charles E. Coughlin, the famed Detroit radio priest, and of the Christian Front movement inspired by his leadership. In a strictly legalistic sense, one might argue that these men did not belong in CPS since their conscientious objection was essentially political, directed against the nation's alliance with the Soviet Union rather than against the war itself. One of their number, in fact, delighted in confounding the other campers by insisting that, had the United States been allied instead with the anti-Bolshevist Axis powers, no Catholic could legitimately claim conscientious objector status! To make matters worse, this position was infused with sometimes hidden and sometimes openly expressed anti-Semitism. In the camp setting the members of the Coughlinite faction were usually staunch participants in the chapel devotions and usually reliable supporters of the camp administration. Even though they did not share the Catholic Worker philosophy or accept its rigorous life-style implications, there were many occasions in which they emerged as the most militant defenders of the camp and its Catholic character against what they viewed as the threat posed by non-Catholic elements acting in concert with the Catholic liberals. In their eyes, needless to say, that latter term was anathema in both its political and religious connotations.

My naive illusion that I was the only Catholic to refuse to accept military service for religious reasons had been dispelled by the discovery that there was an entire camp operated by Catholics for Catholic objectors to World War II. Now, having arrived at that camp, I was confronted for the first time by the fact that there were several different Catholic positions. In the months to follow, these differences in interpretation would be the subject of almost endless discussions, discussions in which I would be a frequent participant if only because I shared that least orthodox position. I enjoyed these discussions and learned much from them, but as a first impression, the lack of unity on what I presumed would be the camp's very raison d'etre was disconcerting to say the least.

In many ways, the most telling first impressions had to do with the men who were to be my companions in service for an indefinite duration. That I was predisposed to favorable impressions here was natural enough if for no other reason than that people are always sympathetic toward those who share their point of view on important questions. In this case that affinity was intensified by the knowledge that these men not only shared my opposition to war but, like myself, had been prepared to carry that opposition into action at some cost to themselves.

There was another dimension to my readiness to be favorably impressed, a kind of inverted snobbery. My modest origins—today, as a practicing sociologist I would rate them as upper lower-class—combined with intellectual interests and aspirations made me particularly susceptible to the aura of superiority I associated with a collegiate background. I was, therefore, somewhat awed by my expectations that the people I would meet in camp would be the college-educated intellectuals, artists, writers, and the like I had always associated with liberal, even radical, movements of dissent.

In this I was partly right and partly wrong, probably more the latter though I never did abandon my exalted stereotype of the conscientious objector completely. The men of Camp Simon, as it turned out, were comparatively well educated as a group, and the camp roster did include a significant number of college graduates, even a few with advanced degrees. On the other hand, it also included many, again like myself, whose formal education had ended with high school graduation, not to mention a few who had not gone that far. There were artists and writers, yes, and some of them fit the stereotype of the avant-garde bohemian perfectly; but these were more than balanced by factory and office workers, equally perfect representatives of the "common man" or petit bourgeois outlook on life. Though on first impression I must confess that I took their very presence in camp as proof of the idealism of their motivation, as time went on and I got to know the individual campers better, I would even discover that for some CPS was more an escape than a witness.

A later chapter will concentrate on thumbnail descriptions of a representative assortment of the campers in terms of their association with the various cliques or divisions which contributed so much to the tensions of camp life. At this point, however, it is appropriate to introduce those few who dominated my first impressions of Warner. First in logical sequence are Lou Schnittler* and Dean Farfether, the two who met me at the bus stop. Lou, as I described him in a letter written at the time, was tall and slim to the point of appearing frail and effeminate. This latter impression was strengthened by his affected mannerisms and supercilious drawl, especially in his ready characterization of things or opinions he did not accept as being "just *too* ridiculous." He presented himself as a poet of sorts and dabbled a bit in pen-and-ink sketches and water colors—in short, he

---

*To preserve the anonymity of the campers, fictitious names will be employed throughout this study. Where reference is made to articles or other material published under their real names, however, these will be indicated in the appropriate citations.

was very much the gifted bohemian I had expected to encounter in the camp setting. His poetry was abstract in content and experimental in form, and as I recall, totally devoid of capital letters or punctuation. I was tremendously impressed.

Dean, for his part, was the very personification of the scholar-intellectual, an impression that was intensified by his remote and reflective expression and characteristic walk, a kind of loping gait with shoulders hunched together. His hair was already thinning to the point of baldness, lending accent to an already high forehead, that classic mark of a superior intelligence which, in Dean's case at least, was validated by the fact. He, too, was a writer, but more of a serious essayist with none of Lou's pretensions and frills. Many of the more profound treatises and carefully structured protests addressed to CPS officialdom were products of his pen.

Lou and Dean, even today, remain paired in my mind. They were all but inseparable until Lou was transferred to a detached service unit at his request. Different though they were in temperament—Lou, voluble and effervescent; Dean, calm and soft-spoken, shy and hesitant lest he inflict his thoughts upon the listener—they, along with perhaps two or three others, formed the core of the intellectual set, the group to which I frankly aspired in the earliest days of camp. It is no accident, then, that I would rate them as my closest friends in that period of first impressions. Even though I soon gravitated to what will be described later as the Catholic liberal faction, I retained my close ties with them—in Dean's case until he left for military service from Rosewood a year or so later. Only Lou was nominally Catholic (Dean was a Quaker) and made much of really being an agnostic and an incessant critic of the more orthodox Catholics and their camp activities and attitudes.

Two distinctly different characters must also be included here for the sheer impact of their personalities upon this new arrival. Both were practicing Catholics and regular participants in the religious life of the camp, though neither would fit into the chapel-set classification to be described later. Pat Rafferty, a boisterous extrovert, introduced himself almost as soon as I arrived on the scene. This sprightly Irish-American from Brooklyn may not have been given to the more esoteric liturgical niceties of the other chapel regulars, but he was the very model of Irish Catholicism, almost aggressively devout. Indeed, on one occasion, he was ready to put his considerable amateur boxing skills to the defense of the Faith in a situation where he felt it was being put to ridicule. Pat was the most openly committed of the Coughlinite Christian Fronters and took distinct pleasure in flaunting his anti-Semitism, much to the discomfiture of the more liberal fellow campers.

It was Pat who insisted upon stressing the distinction mentioned earlier between conscientious objection and pacifism and who insisted that a Catholic could take neither stand in a war against the Soviet Union. It would be difficult to imagine a cluster of positions less compatible with those of the majority of the men at Warner, yet Pat's vibrant personality, in combination with a thoroughly outrageous sense of humor, made him one of the most popular men in camp. In those earliest days, I had some difficulty separating his clownishness from his politics and mistakenly assumed that his openly professed admiration of Mussolini and Hitler was a magnificent put-on. Only later did it become clear to me that he was deadly serious.*

Where one could enjoy and make allowances for Pat, my first impression of Leonard Mattano was one of almost reverential awe. And I was not alone in this, as I was to learn from the recollections, thirty years after, expressed by other former campers. There is little doubt that he was well liked and respected: an accomplished artist, Warner's resident philosopher, an inveterate storyteller. He was a big man, soft-spoken, a romantic figure with a luxuriant moustache. His almost studied air of deep melancholia would give way, almost without warning, to the wildest excesses of hearty laughter and rowdy exuberance. It was Mattano who presided over most of the heroic binges that periodically rocked the settled peace (or entrenched boredom, if you will) of camp life and that caused so much annoyance to those who considered such drunken outbursts inconsistent with a true commitment to the cause of peace. Strangely enough, however annoyed people might have been, Leonard himself would be easily forgiven and his preeminence reigned undiminished once the storm had passed.

---

*At least I *think* he was serious, and his admiration for them seems to have endured. In his response to my questionnaire, Pat's self-description notes that he still believes "the greatest HERO of the 20th Century died in the Berlin bunker" —and the emphasis is his. It may be a reflection of that original and still lingering impression that, once the shock of reading that response passed, I found myself questioning whether he was indeed serious or once again giving expression to his wild sense of humor. But I fear the former is most likely true.

   Dave Komiker and Jimmy O'Toole were camp characters, a not
particularly complimentary classification that was to be expanded
considerably as the camp roster filled in the months to come. Dave
was my work companion in those earliest days, in a very real sense
my mentor in the disgusting potato-sorting ordeal. A short, swarthy,
exceedingly simple fellow, he gave the impression of a medieval men-
dicant caught in a time warp. Almost embarrassingly pious in his
unsophisticated way, he wore a heavy rosary around his neck and
would often go out of his way to force religious discussions by raising some obscure or pointless theological question in a loud and insistent voice. There was no subtlety in his appearance, style, or manner; yet he was generally accepted, even by those who were most
embarrassed or annoyed by his presence, as one would accept an unruly but affectionate puppy. One of the all too many who probably
should never have been conscripted but were sent to CPS anyway,
Dave was the idiosyncratic objector referred to earlier. His refusal
to accept military service, as he explained it to me on that stinking
heap of rotting potatoes, was an act of simple obedience to instruc-
tions he had received in a personal revelation, or visitation, from the
Virgin Mary.
   In Jimmy's case, I never was to learn even that much about the
reason for his being in camp. He certainly did not match Dave in
religious awareness or commitment. I remember him as being regular
in his weekly Mass attendance and probably more regular than I at
chapel devotions, but he never gave the slightest indication of being
spiritually engaged to any significant degree. Intellectually, however,
the two seemed pretty much at the same rather low, possibly even
subnormal, level. Jimmy appeared to be much younger than his
twenty-two years, and this impression of immaturity was reinforced
by his behavior. He walked with a strange rocking gait, asked endless
and usually irrelevant questions, and responded to any criticism or
rejection with an indifferent shrug and supercilious snigger. Because
of his addiction to cola drinks he was nicknamed "the Pepsi Kid" although, despite his preference for that particular brand, he was more
open-minded on that score than his nickname might suggest. It was
not at all unusual for him to be seen with a bottle of Pepsi in one
hand and "the Real Thing" in the other, alternating his swigs from
both.
   Blessed with doting female relatives, he received regular and generous packages of good things from home which, as far as one could

tell, he never considered sharing with others. In speech he affected a British accent and this, in combination with his profession of admiration for Winston Churchill and "the Empire," led to a pattern of exchanges with Pat Rafferty that endures in memory as classics of high comedy. The apparent inconsistency between his Anglophilia and his refusal to support the war effort seemed not to trouble him at all. Dismissed by most, including myself, as obviously retarded in personality and intellectual development,* Jimmy was often the butt of ridicule and harsh, if not cruel, sarcasm and practical jokes, to which he would respond with a condescending smile, the shrugged shoulder, and that snigger. For the most part, however, he was treated, albeit with undertones of strained exasperation, in a paternalistic, protective fashion by his fellow campers. If it was obvious to most of us that O'Toole should not have been called into any kind of service, he never gave the slightest indication of feeling out of place in the Warner camp setting.

These, then, were my first impressions of Camp Simon, and for the most part they were favorable. My early letters to friends are full of praise for the lovely setting and the autumn foliage which, though it had passed its peak, was still glorious enough in its decline to dazzle this urban Midwesterner. Even the food drew no criticism; I noted it was "very plain" but "fair," a first impression that changed drastically as the true state of the camp budget and dietary shortcomings became more evident to me. And since the camp was still in the throes of getting organized, no government work was being done and none would begin until the second week in November, so I had no complaints on that score.

It was a time for learning the ropes, for discovering the lines of division among the campers and the nature of the issues dividing them and, in the process, for finding my own place in the over-all pattern. The two major concerns with which I had arrived, the fear that the life in camp would be too restricted and subject to direct military control or that the camp might turn out to be an oppressively pious monastic community, were proved false from the very beginning.

*This may be wide of the mark. The personnel records show that O'Toole had attended college before entering CPS. Also one of the former campers went so far as to include him as one of the "more intelligent" men at Warner in his response to my questionnaire. I was to serve with Jimmy until May 1945, however, and never found cause to change my first impression.

All of which is not to suggest, of course, that religion and religious expectations would not be an important factor in camp life. True, the camp director's idealistic view of CPS as the occasion for striving after perfection may not have been shared by the majority of the practicing Catholics and most definitely was not shared by the others. Nevertheless, there was general agreement on such things as the need for a chapel (and, though this was never achieved, the services of a priest on a regular basis) and on the importance of establishing and maintaining the specifically Catholic character of the camp.

For most of us this objective, if achieved, would have been justification enough for whatever sacrifice the effort might entail, but opinions differed as to how it could best be implemented in view of the large proportion of the camp membership that was either non-Catholic or nonpracticing. Still even these outsiders were ready to support that objective. Warner, almost everyone agreed, was more than just a camp at which alternative service was performed. It was to be special in the sense that it was the only Catholic camp and, to that extent, represented a corporate witness with implications extending beyond and above the individual witnesses of the campers themselves. If for no other reason, this expectation and the extent to which it was met, or not met, make the story worth the telling.

2   *A Witness Unheard and Unwanted*

As noted in the Introduction, any sustained reference to a corporate witness could be misleading. Conscientious objection is always a personal rejection of war and participation in training for war. This is true even for members of the so-called peace churches which endorse or, in some cases, impose a doctrinal pacifism. In that latter instance, however, it can be said that the religious denomination also gives witness as a body, so that the individual Quaker, Mennonite, or member of some similarly identifiably pacifist religious community is both expressing a personal conviction and representing the approved or required church position.

This was not the case with the Roman Catholic Church and its members. Not every Catholic assigned to CPS may have pictured himself as a possibly solitary example, but none could be unaware of the fact that he was part of an extremely small and not particularly well-regarded minority within the Church. It is important to put the issue in the perspective of the time. Today, in the backwash of the widespread and remarkably effective Catholic opposition to the war in Vietnam, it is all too easy to forget that such opposition was extremely rare and would have found neither endorsement nor even tolerance during the Second World War.

Examples abound. The Selective Service files contain the letter of one Catholic layman who, upon learning that a camp for Catholic objectors had been established in New Hampshire, urged that they not be permitted "to get away with this." "A Catholic," he wrote, "can consistently hate war (as I do) but this thing of claiming exemption is contrary to the practices of the Church and all these people should be MADE to serve, as well as all the other religious nitwits." Less emotional but, considering its official status, much more significant is the protest voiced by the chief clerk of a Michigan draft board in reaction to a successful appeal from one of its negative decisions: "We feel sure that the classification of IV-E is a mistake as it is impossible for anyone who is a member of the Roman Catholic Church to be a Conscientious Objector."

The prevalence of such attitudes undoubtedly contributed to the conviction on the part of the Camp Simon men (at least the practicing Catholics) that their presence in camp was something more than just an individual witness against the war. For them, the very existence of the camp itself became a witness *for* the Church and, even more, *to* the Church. Since they viewed their stand as the most authentic expression of the true meaning of Christianity, neither the obvious fact that they constituted a ridiculously small and insignificant segment of the Catholic population nor the scorn and criticisms they received from their fellow communicants (including, all too often, their spiritual leaders) could weaken or destroy that commitment. Instead, the experience of rejection strengthened their determination to establish and maintain a corporate witness at almost any cost in personal discomfort and hardship.

This determination was reflected in the name chosen for the Stoddard-Warner camps: Camp Simon. The most direct link to the "man of Cyrene named Simon" (Matt. 27:89) lay in the obvious fact that he, like they, had been conscripted. But the point was not lost that the task the man they had selected as patron was drafted to perform was that of sharing Christ's burden on the way to Calvary.

For the majority the assignment to service at the Warner camp was already proof of a considerable measure of determination and perseverance. In any war, and especially in a war as popular as World War II, it is never easy for a man to gain recognition of his conscientious objection unless he happens to be a member of one of the traditional peace churches and, often enough, not even then. At that time the law required a convincing statement of reasons for objecting to military service along with supporting evidence of sincerity; it also required proof that the objection was to *all* war and was based on religious training and belief.

Catholics found themselves in difficulty on both counts. Since traditional Catholic teachings on the morality of war included that distinction between just and unjust wars, they were technically ineligible for the CO classification. At least a strictly legalistic interpretation virtually assured that they would be obliged to go through the appeals process before their claim was recognized and approved. This process involved that comprehensive investigation by the FBI in the course of which the registrant's family, friends, and pastors would be interviewed to establish the sincerity of his convictions.

It was at this point that the second obstacle was encountered. Rare indeed was the priest who was willing to support a claim for conscientious objection on the basis of Catholic religious training and belief. Even where one was prepared to testify to an individual's sincerity, he would probably describe the man as a victim of an erroneous conscience and assure the investigator that a refusal to bear arms was not supported by orthodox Catholic teaching. In one case, the FBI investigator reports receiving such assurances from no less than five priests, only one of whom was prepared to grant that the individual under investigation could be acting "in good faith"! In another case the registrant's pastor described him as "a splendid Catholic type" only to add that no Catholic, presumably not even so splendid a type, could be a conscientious objector on the basis of his religious training and belief.

Sometimes, as in my own case, such adverse judgments were made in the registrants' presence. The transcribed minutes of a meeting of another local board includes the verbatim testimony: "I am a Catholic priest, and they are sending them away right along. There is no choice, and our lives and freedom are at stake; if you have been reading the Scriptures, you must have been misinterpreting them."

To multiply such examples would serve little purpose. Most Catholics sent to camp must have encountered such opinions somewhere along the way and would carry the memory of such official repudiations as part of their emotional and spiritual baggage throughout the days and years spent in alternative service. The continued existence of a Catholic CPS camp, then, assumed added importance as irrefutable evidence that a Catholic *could* be a conscientious objector. More than this, it provided a welcome assurance to the objectors themselves that they were not alone, rejected though they might be by the overwhelming majority of their fellow Catholics.

It would be difficult to exaggerate how crucial this could be to the psychological well-being of the men whose consciences had led them into this particular form of social deviance. If most of my unpleasant anticipations of locked gates, unfriendly guards, and all the other imaginings of direct oppression at the hands of military authorities proved unfounded, there was no escaping the more subtle, but no less destructive, penalties of alienation and ostracism all had to pay to some extent. Faced with a published opinion of a priest in a missionary magazine that "if a conscientious objector is found among our Catholics, it is not because of the moral teachings of our Church but because he is afraid of his hide—he is a coward," it was gratifying to be able to publish a rejoinder in a paper issued under the auspices of a CO camp operated by and for Catholics.[1] True, very few outside of the camp's own membership might ever read that rejoinder, but at least it was on the record.

The burden of alienation and rejection went beyond the lack of support from church authorities. In far too many cases, these same attitudes reached into the most intimate family circles. Most World War II COs could probably tell of strained and broken friendships and of the scorn or ridicule encountered among casual associates at school, fellow workers, neighbors, and the like. There was no way, in a society totally geared to the winning of a war ostensibly dedicated to defending the highest ideals—or, as many saw it, a crusade against evil incarnate—for the deviant minority to escape the awareness of general disapproval for refusing to join in the common effort. Nor would one be entirely free of his own nagging twinges of doubt and uncertainty, as friends and relatives were drawn more completely into the national consensus or into situations of personal involvement and danger.

For Warner's Catholics the cruelest rejection of all, however, was that suffered at the hands of the religious community of which they were a part. After all, the failure of friends, even family, to grasp the full spiritual dimensions of the refusal to accept military service could be understood and even accepted. But, considering the essentially religious character of the CO stand, the condemnation by priests and the studied unconcern of their bishops was, for some, enough to constitute a serious test of faith. It did not help to compare this rejection with the tolerant respect and direct encouragement given by other religious communities to their members in CPS. This applied not only to the traditional peace churches with their historic stance of favoring, in some cases requiring, conscientious objection of their draft-eligible men, but other denominations (e.g., Methodist, Presbyterian, Congregational) pursued a policy of benevolent neutrality. While they may not have been completely evenhanded, favoring the soldier over his alternative service counterpart, they at least made the effort to keep in touch with the latter and sustain the bond of fellowship. Some could boast of formally organized peace groups operating within the broader religious community (e.g., Episcopalian Pacifist Society) to give moral and material support to the men of their faith who refused to go to war.

The Catholic CO, in contrast, had to contend with a frankly hostile religious community.[2] The hostility manifested itself less in forms of open repudiation (though, as we have seen, there was enough of that) than in more pervasive, even though silent, signs of disapproval. At a time when every possible evidence of spiritual and material support was lavished upon his Catholic brothers in uniform, the CO and his problems were ignored. Every parish had its honor roll, listing men called into service by the draft, but men conscripted to work in the woods of New Hampshire would not be included in that list. Our new fellow-parishioners in the Contoocook church attended by the Warner campers—at no small sacrifice, I might add, since it involved a Sunday morning hike of almost ten miles to get there and back—received us with a chill completely unrelated to the inhospitable winds that raged outside.

This is more than a complaint, valid though it may be, of unfair treatment. After all, the lot of any dissident minority is never a happy one, and to expect otherwise would be a folly of which few, if any, of the Camp Simon men were guilty. Strictly speaking, they were the lucky ones if only because they had overcome the obstacles of sadly ill-informed clergy, prejudiced local draft boards, scandal-conscious relatives, and the like. They knew full well that other Catholics who were just as convinced of the immorality of war and the incompatability between their moral commitment and the acts demanded of them by the warring state had not been successful in gaining the IV-E classification. Many were forced to compromise their consciences and accept military service because they were denied encouragement or support from those charged with the responsibility for providing spiritual guidance and counsel. Still others, unwilling to make that compromise, ended up in prison. The sometimes shocking entries in the CPS records and FBI reports on the men who did get to camp are a measure of the pressures those others must have suffered as well, pressures that led many to abandon their equally legitimate claims to recognition as conscientious objectors.

Martin Zorick's file illustrates the point I am trying to make. Former Warnerites remember Martin as a quiet, friendly, hard-working fellow, neither a flaming radical nor a troublesome bohemian intellectual. On his original Selective Service questionnaire he indicated his opposition to military service in simple and direct terms: "The dictates of my personal conscience forbid me to participate in war in any form because by Divine decree man was destined to increase and improve, not to decrease and destroy which war does." His problem with the draft board, however, centered on the fact that he had checked the box indicating a *limited* conscientious objection (a willingness to serve in noncombatant status under a I-A-O classification) even though his statement clearly implied the more total refusal that should have merited a IV-E status.

The inconsistency is explained in a letter from Zorick to the editors of the *Catholic Worker* seeking their assistance in correcting the mistake. His initial indication of a willingness to accept the I-A-O classification was based on the advice of his pastor who had told him he would "be granted the right of a conscientious objector providing I would be *only* opposed to *combatant* service. That was against my belief, but I checked one 'X' on the questionnaire." The pastor, he went on, explained the purpose of providing the other option on the form was to identify the "men who were totally no good to the country" and advised him that "being opposed to all types of military training would be altogether out of the question and I would be picked up and put into an actual combatant unit. . . . I sought counsel from others but they either didn't know anything on the subject or refused to give it."

There is no way of knowing how many similar instances of faulty spiritual guidance one could uncover, but it is probably safe to say that the priest as military recruiter was no isolated phenomenon. In Zorick's case there was some concession to his conscience in that he was being pushed into noncombatant service and not, as was the more general practice, talked out of conscientious objection altogether. The I-A-O classification, carrying with it the promise[3] of assignment to medical corps or some other duty that did not involve the bearing of weapons or actual killing, was a tempting half-way house for the Catholic. It offered some measure of recognition for the war-rejecting conscience while still making it possible to fulfill one's obligations to legitimate authority, a civic virtue of no small importance in the Catholic value system.* Nevertheless, for anyone who, like Zorick, sincerely believed that any direct involvement in the war effort subject to military authority was immoral, I-A-O status could only represent a compromise of conscience little better than accepting full military service.

As noted, the men who succumbed and spent years of their lives in service they believed sinful were not the only victims of this Catholic hostility toward the CO position. At the other end of the scale were men who, failing to convince the draft authorities of the legitimacy of their claim to the IV-E classification, chose prison rather than accept induction into the armed forces. Altogether somewhat over six thousand men went to prison for this reason, a deceptively small number when one realizes that they constituted approximately one-sixth of the total federal prison population at that time. Inaccessibility of the relevant data makes it difficult to determine how many of these men were Catholics, but it is safe to assume that, given the general lack of ecclesiastical understanding and support, their proportion was significant. Efforts were made by the ACCO and other pacifist groups to establish and maintain some degree of contact with the objector-prisoners, but with only minimal success at best. Theirs is a story yet to be told.

One such case did come to my attention later in the war, and it illustrates the difficulties these men faced. Two Catholic men—brothers, I believe—serving a sentence for refusing to report for induction into the military, were denied consideration for parole because they were unwilling to volunteer for the service they had been imprisoned for refusing. This does not appear to be unusual; in fact, men who had completed their sentence were often called up by their local boards and, when they refused military service as they had done before, ended up in jail again for this new violation of the Selective Service and Training Act.

At any rate, in the case in question an appeal was directed to the bishop of the Baltimore-Washington diocese asking that he intervene on the brothers' behalf. The appeal brought a prompt and blunt letter of rejection from the chancery office. With Catholic men risking

*It should be unnecessary to point out that alternative service, since it was provided for by the conscription law, also fulfilled the obligations to legitimate authority. Few, other than the IV-E objectors themselves, recognized that fact and even those who did would not see it as equivalent, or comparable, to a military service classification.

their lives on battlefields all over the world, so the response went, the bishop could not be bothered about the fate of the few who refused to do their duty. Deciding to pursue the matter further, the authors of the original appeal obtained a personal audience, not with the bishop but with the chancery official who had written the letter. After an extended and remarkably friendly discussion, it was agreed that he would submit the issue to a prominent moral theologian for an opinion. In due order this opinion led to a significant modification of the diocesan position in the form of a new letter admitting:

Now it may be that while the overwhelming majority of the citizenry consider a specific war to be a just one, there would be some who, including perhaps even Catholics, *would be sincerely and honestly convinced that the conflict was not just. If, regardless of any personal considerations or selfish interests, a Catholic were so persuaded,* he would not only have a right to be a Conscientious Objector, but he would be bound to be one.

The indicated emphasis is mine. To those involved in making the original appeal this was a great victory indeed—though, unfortunately, there is no evidence that this new classification succeeded in getting the prisoners the parole to which they were entitled. Yet the very fact that what should have been an uncomplicated application of traditional moral teachings to an actual situation could be regarded as a victory and a significant theological breakthrough merely testifies to the generally unsympathetic attitudes encountered from those in ecclesiastical authority. Victory or not, even the revised opinion was not to be taken as endorsement. The most to be said for it is that it expressed reluctant recognition of what the official clearly regarded as a very remote possibility, and one for which the Church assumed no responsibility.

It would be an exaggeration, of course, to say that the men of Camp Simon had no support at all. Their non-Catholic compatriots elsewhere in CPS provided what encouragement they could, but this was often of dubious morale value. Too often it took the form of expressed admiration for courage displayed in freeing themselves from the rigid authoritarianism of Rome; thereby demonstrating that, in Protestant eyes as much as in traditionalist Catholic eyes, the stand they had taken was not really a Catholic position at all.

Considerably more aid and comfort was drawn, in fact, from Rome. Our conviction that opposition to the war was the authentic Christian witness and, therefore, completely orthodox in the most meaningful sense of that term was strengthened with each new statement issued by Pope Pius XII from the Chair of Peter. Every fervent appeal for an early negotiated peace and each new protest against the ever escalating horrors of the war found a ready audience in the New Hampshire woods. The gratification may have been tempered by dismay that these pronouncements were not accompanied by more specific condemnations—naming names and citing incidents—but this failure was usually attributed to weakness of papal style and not to any ambiguity of principle.

Subsequent scholarship suggests we may have been more right than wrong in this interpretation. It is clear that Pius carefully avoided giving any public sign of preference for either warring side lest by so doing he risk his eligibility for the role of mediator and peacemaker to which he aspired. Some interpreters, in fact, have treated him harshly on this score, reducing the Pope's cherished neutrality to little more than a display of devious political and diplomatic machinations. Others have gone further, interpreting his studied evenhandedness as a personal fault of cowardice or ego-centered ambition. Whatever criticisms the Catholics of Camp Simon may have had to offer were all in the other direction. It was not enough that he chose to remain neutral; instead, they looked to him for the kind of statement that would have called upon all Catholics on both sides of the conflict to cease their warring ways.

Such a statement was never forthcoming. Indeed one suspects (and this suspicion is confirmed by some of the Pope's postwar statements and actions) that Pius XII, had he known of Warner, would have had no more understanding of, or sympathy for, Catholic conscientious objection than did those priests who were so confident and emphatic in the misinformation and false guidance they provided to draft boards and FBI investigators. If this is true, and all the comfort and encouragement his words gave to those who had taken their stand against the war he so regularly condemned were at best incidental and certainly unintended, this would still not diminish their importance as a major contribution to the wartime morale of the men of Camp Simon.

Other occasional support of a more direct and tangible nature came from sources closer to home. There is some evidence that at least three American bishops made some financial contributions to the Catholic camp, but how much or how often is not known. Nor is it clear whether any of that support was furnished after the attack on

Pearl Harbor. Whatever ACCO financial records may have existed then have long since disappeared. Even were this not the case, given the Catholic Worker record-keeping procedures, they would probably not be of much help.

One of these episcopal contributors, presumably, was Archbishop John T. McNicholas of Cincinnati.[4] He deserves special mention here as a figure of considerable importance to the men of Camp Simon who regarded him as theological patron as much as financial angel. It was a 1938 pastoral letter issued by McNicholas that included the statement most frequently cited by them as an explicit endorsement of the stand they were to take.

There is the practical question for informed Christians who acknowledge the supreme domination of God and the divisive toleration of governments that reject and ignore God: will such Christians in our country form a mighty league of conscientious noncombatants? The organization of such a league deserves the serious consideration of all informed Christians who have the best interests of America at heart. . . . *Governments that have no fixed standards of morality and consequently no moral sense can scarcely settle the question of war on moral grounds for Christians who see and know the injustice of practically all wars in our modern pagan world.*

Again the emphasis is mine, but even without it, it should not be necessary to stress how important it was to have a prominent member of the American hierarchy citable in this fashion. Such a call was encouragement enough to last the duration. And it had to be. No similar call would be issued or sentiments expressed by McNicholas or any other American bishop once the war began. His subsequent contributions to the war debate had a contrary thrust. In 1944 he was the principal speaker at a massive Holy Name rally which brought 65,000 people to New York City's Polo Grounds to pray, as the *New York Times* would report, "for victory in the war and for a lasting peace."[5] Even earlier he had gone on record in support of aid to the embattled Soviet Union. One observer indicates that he may have been chosen for this by the Pope himself to counteract possible Catholic reticence on this score.[6]

To return to the matter of financial contributions, however, even lacking adequate records it is certain that episcopal donations were small, occasional, and discreetly unofficial. Anything more would have been celebrated with an enthusiasm far exceeding whatever improvement they might have brought in material living standards for the men in camp. The desperate hunger for even the most indirect hint of official support or encouragement finds tragicomic illustration in the January 1942 issue of the *Catholic Worker*. Featured front-page placement is given a brief letter from the Archbishop of Manila in which he praised a retreat he had attended at the Worker farm in Easton, Pennsylvania, and included a promise to pray "for your works at Harlem and Stoddard." Whatever the good Archbishop intended by that pious thought, it probably did not justify the exuberant headline, "Archbishop Writes, Promising Prayers for War Objectors." Such overblown coverage of a routine courtesy testifies to the rarity of any occasion for even borrowed gratification.

This discussion of the lack of support available to the men of Camp Simon must not end without acknowledging the few Catholic clergy of lesser rank who did provide open and consistent encouragement to the Catholics in CPS and prison. Three are particularly deserving of mention for their significant wartime support. Monsignor Barry O'Toole of the philosophy faculty of Catholic University was present at the creation of the Catholic peace witness. While the peacetime conscription proposals were before the Congress, he appeared to testify in opposition to them. Later he wrote an extensive discussion of the issue under the title, "War and Conscription at the Bar of Christian Morals," which would receive more than its share of reverent quotation in camp debates.[7] Beginning with the May 1943 issue of the *Catholic Worker*, John J. Hugo, a Pittsburgh priest closely associated with the movement's retreat program, contributed a series of articles under the general heading, "Catholics Can Be Conscientious Objectors," which was so well received that it was reprinted as a ten-page supplement to the November 1944 issue with a stronger title, "The Immorality of Conscription." The third priest in this small group was Paul Hanly Furfey, the highly respected sociologist at Catholic University. Furfey's opposition to war and conscription antedated both of the other priests', and had already found expression in a 1935 article (also in the *Worker*) which McNeal credits with giving birth to the American Catholic peace movement.[8]

There were others, less well known, who made contributions. Even though the basic pattern was, as described, for priests and other spiritual counsellors to dissuade young Catholics from becoming conscientious objectors, there were occasional exceptions to the rule. These recognized a contrary obligation to assist and defend the men whose consciences would not permit them to make war. A few priests even undertook to register their own protest by repudiating their ministerial deferments and returning their draft cards to Selective Service, an impressive anticipation of a practice that was to become a common form of protest against the American war in Vietnam decades later. These protest actions, of course, were ignored.

As the reader must certainly have inferred by now, the most important and consistent support came from the Catholic Worker movement and its monthly paper. Without that support, moral and material, there would have been no viable Catholic witness against American participation in World War II. Individual Catholic witnesses there might have been, as there were in World War I, but without the funds, insufficient though they were, provided by Dorothy Day and her co-workers and, equally important, the opportunity to bring their existence and their arguments to the attention of a Catholic audience, such individuals would never have become aware of each other and a corporate witness, even on the limited and imperfect scale of Stoddard and Warner, would not have been possible.

From the very first it was Miss Day who spoke out in opposition to conscription and then, when these objections failed, proclaimed the right of the Catholic layman to refuse to take up arms in war. Miss Day recalls her appearance before the Congressional committee and the indignation her testimony provoked from the church dignitary who had come to argue for deferment of seminarians. It was this exchange which brought Barry O'Toole into the fray; so infuriated was he by Day's account of the dressing down she had received for suggesting that laymen, too, might claim exemption that he appeared before the committee the very next day to lend his scholarly prestige to her cause.

The beginnings of what was to become the Association of Catholic Conscientious Objectors can be traced back to 1935 when members of the Worker's New York staff formed a study group, PAX, to explore the pacifist dimensions of the movement's philosophy and program. When war and conscription became more immediate possibilities, that study group became a more activist "Catholic Worker Peace Group." When the ACCO finally emerged in a full-page announcement in the September 1941 issue of the *Catholic Worker*, it represented little more than a final change in name "for purposes of convenience and propaganda value in dealing with the Government." That, at least, is how it was described by Dwight Larrowe, author of the article announcing the change and the man who would later become the director of the Stoddard and Warner camps.

Though the original letterhead carried an impressive list of outside sponsors, the ACCO was entirely dependent upon the parent Catholic Worker movement and would remain so throughout its history. This had both positive and negative impact upon Camp Simon and the two detached service units operated under ACCO jurisdiction. Regardless of how one calculates the final balance between the plusses and minuses, however, one thing should be clear: without the Catholic Worker and its ACCO "front," the Catholic peace witness during World War II would have been limited to isolated individuals putting in their time and performing their alternative service in camps operated by and for the traditional peace church denominations.

Apart from the theological differences and distinctions discussed earlier, several other themes and currents contributed to Catholic rejection of military service, some of which may have struck familiar chords in broader segments of the Catholic population for a time. Even though the majority of Catholics of German or Italian descent had little or no sympathy with the fascist powers, some residue of emotional attachment to the places and traditions of the mother countries was still present, and limited their enthusiasm for the more extreme war aims proclaimed by the nation's leaders. The long-standing animosity toward the British among American Catholics of Irish descent played an even more obvious part, especially when taken in context with isolationist interpretations of American involvement in the war as the prime objective of British diplomacy. Finally there was the deep reservoir of anti-Communist sentiment characteristic of American Catholicism which stood as an obstacle to wholehearted acceptance of a common cause with the Soviet Union. This latter theme found its most virulent expression in the extremism of the Coughlinite Christian Front, a movement which, in addition to anti-Communist and anti-British isolationism, touched yet another base by attributing American involvement in the war to the workings of an international Jewish conspiracy.

One or another of these themes may have played some part in forming the decisions that brought some men into CPS. Even so, except for a very small minority, the dominant and decisive factor common to them all was a firm moral conviction that war is immoral and contrary to Christian teachings. This was certainly true of the Catholic Worker movement and its leadership. Theirs was a message of Christian pacifism, pure and undiluted. It was a position not taken or held without cost. As Miller shows in his fine history of the movement,[9] maintaining that pacifist commitment in time of war meant the loss of many friends and supporters. To cite but one particularly serious example, the June 1941 issue of the *Catholic Worker* published a lengthy letter from the Seattle House of Hospitality dissociating its members from the pacifism proclaimed by the movement's leaders. Henceforth, the Seattle group announced, it would no longer distribute the paper; but they also expressed the hope they could continue to be regarded as part of the family nonetheless. Other readers and financial contributors were more thorough and much less friendly in making their break.

Indeed, though no poll was ever taken, it is most probable that the majority of the paper's readers had serious misgivings concerning its controversial policy line on war and conscientious objection. The lack of adequate response to the urgent and repeated appeals for assistance and support for the men of Camp Simon seems to support this assumption. If so, this fact would only reinforce the point developed here, namely that the Catholic conscientious objector to World War II was rejected, not only by the secular community whose orders he refused to obey, but by his religious community as well. What little support or encouragement he did receive, welcome though it was, could not counteract the general atmosphere of indifference, scorn, and resentment surrounding him and his stand.

This is not to dismiss or diminish the contributions made by the Barry O'Tooles, the Hugos, the Furfeys, and, above all, by Dorothy Day and the Catholic Workers. If anything, the debt of gratitude owed them, not only by the men who benefited most directly but by all who would associate themselves with today's more impressive Catholic peace witness, is magnified by the futility of their efforts to turn the overwhelming tide of alienation and rejection in those years of that "last, good war."

Although the Catholic Worker provided the only material and ideological support Catholic men in CPS could count on throughout the
war, Dorothy Day made no effort to hide the fact that she did not
entirely approve of the stand they had taken. As far as she was concerned—and her position has not changed since—a truly authentic
witness against war and conscription called for total noncooperation,
beginning with a refusal to register for the draft. She did not, however, object when others in the movement organized the ACCO as a
vehicle for participation in the alternative service program. For better
or worse, that participation would continue until October 1945
when, in response to the initiative of the Catholic men in the two
ACCO special units still in existence at the time, supported by the
Warner remnant then serving in the Friends' camp at Trenton, North
Dakota, the ACCO withdrew from the National Service Board for
Religious Objectors, thereby terminating its formal relationship with
the Selective Service System and CPS. Needless to say, with the war
over and demobilization already in progress, this was little more than
a symbolic gesture. It was not, however, an empty gesture.

It is essential that the reader have some understanding of the complicated CPS structure and the sometimes even more complicated relationships between the various administrative levels. Civilian Public
Service was established to provide the men excused from military
service on grounds of religious training and belief with the mandated
opportunity to perform alternative service consisting of work of national importance under civilian direction. As the program developed,
it would become only too evident that much of the work was any-

thing but important and that the direction was civilian in only the narrowest technical or legalistic sense. One can assume that the pacifist leaders who participated in the original planning acted in good faith and did not anticipate those developments. Even so, once the shortcomings became obvious, the religious sponsoring agencies (and this would include the ACCO) decided they had little choice but to continue on the basis of a prudent judgment that these known disadvantages were still preferable to the greater disadvantages of the probable alternatives. The most compelling argument to support this judgment was the sad record of mistreatment and abuse to which objectors to World War I had been subjected.[1]

Civilian Public Service came into being in December 1940 and continued in operation until March 1947. The three historic peace churches, acting through a special coordinating agency (NSBRO), concluded an agreement with the officials of the Selective Service System under the terms of which the religious agencies were to assume full financial and administrative responsibility for the support and operation of alternative service work camps to which men classified IV-E were to be, as the Selective Service assignment forms put it, "delivered." Altogether, before the program was terminated, a total of 151 work camps and special service units were established at which the 11,887 men assigned to them would perform 8 million man-days of work at a cost to the religious agencies of more than $7 million.[2]

The three peace church agencies dominated the program throughout its history and bore most of these costs. The largest number of units (slightly more than sixty) were operated by the Mennonite Central Conference; the American Friends Service Committee and the Brethren Service Committee assumed responsibility for about forty each.* Late in the program (1943) five government camps administered directly by Selective Service were established, and these were augmented by approximately twenty-five others that became the government's responsibility when some of the founding religious agencies terminated their support.

Individual camps and units were administered by a scattering of other religious or pacifist agencies: the Methodist Commission on World Peace assumed responsibility for two; the Disciples of Christ,

*In most future references the designation MCC, AFSC, and BSC will be employed for these religious sponsoring agencies.

the American Baptist Home Commission, the Evangelical and Re-
formed Church, one each. The ACCO accounted for four in all: the
Stoddard and Warner camps (only one, actually, since the former
closed as the latter opened); a general hospital special unit at the
Alexian Brothers Hospital in Chicago; and another special unit at the
Rosewood State Training School near Baltimore. Although the ACCO
was one of the four original founding agencies, its financial limitations and the small number of men it brought into the program reduced whatever influence that status might have given it within the
councils of the NSBRO.

For the first year of CPS all alternative service was performed in a
camp setting. After May 1942 special (or detached) service units
were opened in hospitals (usually mental hospitals), training schools,
reformatories, and the like. Men ordinarily became eligible for assignment to these only after completing a period of basic service in a
camp. The more glamorous projects—the "guinea pig" health experiments, rural development projects in Puerto Rico, and "smoke-jump-
ing" (fire-fighting parachute units)—remained relatively few in number
and were highly selective in the personnel assigned to them. Although, largely in response to the agitation and demands of the
campers, the later years of the program featured a continuing shift of
emphasis to special unit assignments, the camps continued to serve as
induction and processing centers and remained for most their only
CPS experience.

The actual work projects were administered by a variety of federal
agencies. The Forest Service dominated the field with thirty camps;
the Soil Conservation Service ran a poor second with eighteen; and
other agencies involved included the National Park Service, eight;
Bureau of Reclamation, three; with one each for the Farm Security
Administration, the Fish and Wildlife Administration, and the Government Land Office. Men assigned to a given camp or unit were under the authority of a camp director appointed by and representing
the religious agency responsible for its operation. The men were then
turned over to the project superintendent or other employee of the
respective federal agency in the morning and returned to the director's authority at the conclusion of the work day. To this extent, in
that strictly literal sense, the alternative service was performed under
civilian direction.

Once we move outside the context of camp and work project to
the more significant and policy-setting levels of administration, the

relationships become more complicated. Logically the chain of authority should have led from camp director to the officials of the religious agency whose employee he was; and this was the pattern as far as immediate budgetary arrangements, official visitations, educational and recreational programs, and other local operational matters went. However, with respect to authorization of transfers or discharges, the introduction and application of disciplinary regulations, and other more general policy decisions, the greater measure of control over the director and, through him, the men lay with the NSBRO in Washington. The various religious sponsoring agencies had official representatives at that office, of course, and furnished much of its staff, but this central coordinating agency was the principal channel for all major operational and policy decisions, and these were usually promulgated by Paul Comly French, its executive secretary.

It was here, at the Washington level, that the civilian nature of the direction was diminished if not lost altogether. Even from the CPS beginnings in peacetime—and increasingly so as the war progressed— the relationship between the NSBRO and the Selective Service System was one of petitioner dealing with none-too-receptive master. Before too long the NSBRO appeared to degenerate into little more than a one-way channel of communication through which the edicts from on high were transmitted to the camps and special units. This may be a slight exaggeration. It is possible that there were instances when Selective Service decisions were modified or even withdrawn because of NSBRO intervention, but if this occurred the news of such successes did not filter down to the camp level. Assuming there were such instances, failure to make them known would imply a prudent decision to avoid forcing a loss of face upon the military officers on whom future similar concessions would depend. Unjust or not, this impression of NSBRO impotence and futility (and stronger critics spoke of collaboration and complicity!) was widespread throughout CPS and certainly dominated the perceptions of the men of Camp Simon.

In the strictest sense, this and even more direct and complete authority in the hands of Selective Service could have been construed as fulfilling the "under-civilian-direction" mandate of the law since, technically at least, the Selective Service System was a *civilian* agency despite the fact that it was headed by an army general and staffed in large part by uniformed officers. As far as CPS was concerned, final authority lay with General Lewis B. Hershey, but actual responsibility for CPS Camp Operations was delegated to Colonel Kosch of the field artillery. In addition, other positions of special responsibility bearing upon the life and welfare of the men in alternative service were filled by military officers of lesser rank. Thus, though much of the correspondence and bureaucratic minutiae issued with respect to the day-to-day operations of CPS was signed by civilian appointees, everyone knew that the real authority, especially that relating to substantive policy, lay with General Hershey, Colonel Kosch, and the other uniformed "civilians."

It is easy enough to understand that officers, who had chosen the military as a life career and who were engaged in the overall effort to provide as many men for the armed forces as efficiently as possible, would not be overly sympathetic to the few thousand who rejected all military service and who, moreover, openly rejected its values and objectives. Taking this into account, Paul Comly French went out of his way at several places in his diary to praise the friendship and respect shown him by the military men with whom he had to deal, and even to marvel at the cooperation and consideration he felt he received from them.[3]

It is perhaps just as well that French kept his complimentary observations to himself and his diary. Wider circulation could only have served to confirm the already strong conviction held by many that this chief spokesman for CPS was so easily impressed by the tolerance exhibited by the war-making authorities that he may not have been sufficiently committed to supporting a truly effective witness against the war. The men at Warner and other camps had learned from bitter experience the impossibility of getting any kind of hearing on issues of crucial importance to them. Those who had seen rejected out of hand every attempt to right the injustice of requiring them to work without pay had quite a different view of the attitude of the officers in question.

A more disturbing perspective on Selective Service's own definition of the authority structure of the CPS program may be drawn from remarks made by one of its civilian officials at a meeting with the men of the ACCO Alexian Brothers Hospital unit in October 1942. Some of the men there had become a problem by engaging in a protest against racial segregation in the Chicago area. The Selective Service trouble-shooter sent to handle the matter spelled out in no uncertain terms the agency's view of the situation. Notes taken by one of the participants record these statements:

an assignee loses all of his civilian rights upon entering CPS;

even though a man's work record is perfect, anything he does which differs from the authorities may subject him to discipline;

an assignee should be neutral on controversial issues in which opinion is even-ly divided, even to the point of not expressing opposition to something like the poll tax;

In response to a question as to precisely when the assignee lost his constitutional rights to free assembly, the answer was blunt and to the point: when we tell you these things, when we set up these units, all your movements on and off the project are under the direction of the Selective Service System, every hour from the time you left your home.

"The supreme law of the land is Selective Service then, and not the Constitution?" "At the present time it is."

Shocking as this direct exchange may be, the Selective Service representative did not stop there. As he stated the case, the religious agency was no longer the assignees' representative; that relationship ended once the man left camp for service in a special unit. In this he was factually in error, of course. The NSBRO continued to maintain administrative jurisdiction over such special units just as they did over camps. Nevertheless his assessment of the weight accorded that jurisdiction was not too wide of the mark. There is no reason to doubt that the procedures for possible disciplinary action were just as he described them: Colonel Kosch, not the NSBRO, would decide whether and when a troublemaker was to be returned to camp.

The civilian direction over the CPS program, in short, was equated with the arbitrary exercise of power by Selective Service officials. This extended even to the point of overruling medical board recommendations for physical or psychological discharges for campers with seriously disqualifying or incapacitating ailments or conditions. This is over and above the general laxity of interpretation of physical standards and the careless manner in which they were applied routinely to all conscientious objectors. The fault there lay with local draft boards. But this initial injustice was compounded several times over in those cases where men who had suffered serious breakdowns were kept in camp, sometimes at the risk of their lives, because Selective Service officials chose to ignore professional diagnoses.

In this, perhaps, one finds the most compelling evidence of the total vulnerability of the conscientious objector to the abuse of authority by the military officers placed over him. One such case involved a Warner inductee some months after that camp was closed and he had been transferred to the Trenton camp. The file includes a report of a psychiatric examination that declared, "One can see no reason why this psychoneurotic personality should be continued in camp; certainly he is not fit for military service. . . . A personality condition with a frustration neurosis. Unfit for military or camp service and should be classified as IV-F."

The recommendation was explicit enough. Unfortunately, in reviewing the clinical factors leading to that recommendation the examining psychiatrist made a comment which caught the attention of the Selective Service officials at headquarters, a reference to the camper as "a spoiled boy who always had his way." This was reason enough for Colonel Kosch to reject the recommendation on the grounds that, as he put it, "He is a camp problem. These do not warrant discharge." *Six months later* another medical report on the same individual was more desperate in tone: "He is definitely schizophrenic at this time and very close to the breaking point. He should be discharged without delay." This report was more successful, and the man was discharged, but not "without delay." *Three more months* were to pass before his release was approved.

There will be more to say at a later point about this dangerously frivolous approach to physical standards and medical discharge policies and procedures. What is particularly relevant here, however, are the hidden implications of Kosch's dismissal of a serious personal breakdown as "a camp problem." There is little doubt that the camp director, backed by the religious agency and the NSBRO, concurred in that judgment; indeed, this is why such matters were brought to Selective Service's attention in the first place. An individual undergoing a mental breakdown, or approaching the brink, was certain to be a camp problem if only in the sense that the camp and its sponsoring agency had assumed responsibility for him and his well-being. Beyond this, he and his condition would introduce a disruptive element in the over-all camp situation, constituting at the very least a morale problem and, in more extreme cases, a potential threat to the health and safety of the other campers. This is no exaggeration. The Warner files include a report of yet another camper's mental condition as having reached "such a point that he is no longer capable of taking care of his physical needs and, in some instances, his bodily functions. His presence in camp has become a problem of health and sanitation which affects the entire group." In this case there was a delay of two months before *he* was discharged—actually a total of almost four months following an earlier psychiatric report which had found him to be suffering from "psychoneurosis, severe, which is of a permanent nature."

The civilian nature of the direction represented at the camp level or even at the higher level of the religious agencies presumably empowered to administer the alternative service program was evidenced in minor matters only. Any issues of consequence were decided by military officers staffing the Selective Service System; and there was no effective appeal from their decision, no matter how capricious or vindictive their motivation. It is important that this be borne in mind in connection with the issues and controversies which contributed so much to the divisions among the men at Warner.

These will be treated in detail in a later chapter. Here it is enough to note that it was entirely predictable that the awareness of their vulnerability would provoke internal dissension among the men in CPS. Less predictable, but in the long run much more significant, it also introduced a note of generational conflict between them and the older pacifist leaders who had assumed responsibility for initiating and maintaining the program. These older pacifists, always mindful of the hardships and abuse suffered by the few who had dared to refuse military service in World War I, tended to accept CPS, shortcomings and all, as an advance in tolerance and respect for the individual conscience. No less important in their eyes, CPS as it was structured provided the opportunity for the objector to demonstrate his sincerity by "going the second mile," in this case by contributing to the welfare of the nation and society as a service of love rather than by devoting his efforts and talents to the destructiveness of war. Viewed in this idealistic context, the incessant demands for improved living conditions in the camps and for pay for services performed was seen by some as selfishness and a lack of appreciation, even as a weakness in commitment.

For their part, many of the men in the program, increasingly resentful of the de facto domination of the military over their lives and witness, extended that resentment to the pacifist leaders. As *they* saw it, the pacifist leadership and the religious agencies were guilty of temporizing and collaborating at the expense of the individual CO's rights and interests. This suspicion that they and their cause were being betrayed added one more layer of alienation; and since the betrayers were men whom they had respected for their past contributions to the cause of peace, it is possible that this was the most traumatic alienation of all.

By purely objective standards, CPS may have been the great advance in understanding and opportunity its founders and supporters held it to be, but before the program came to its end, it would be rejected by the ACCO as "a system of punishing a minority under the guise of a democratically given opportunity to fulfill alternative service and, in so doing, establishing a precedent whereby other minorities could conceivably be similarly punished by enforced and unpaid labor under the actual direction of those most interested in silencing their voices."[4] This, again, was in 1945, long after Camp Simon had ceased to be.

At Warner in the autumn of 1942 the punitive nature of CPS was not all that clear, or at least not everyone was ready to admit it. The Camp Simon story had its beginning in an April 1941 letter from Arthur Sheehan of the ACCO to Paul Comly French accepting the latter's telegraphed offer of the Stoddard camp. Sheehan's response had been delayed pending the outcome of the Catholic bishops' annual meeting; now, having received word that one bishop ("to remain unidentified") would be providing financial aid, Sheehan and the ACCO decided to assume the responsibility.

The acceptance letter also referred to a governing council, the "National Service Council for Catholic Objectors," which was being organized to serve as a watchdog over the financing and auditing of ACCO operations. Since there is no further reference to this, it appears that this seemingly impressive body failed to materialize. The ACCO became and remained (until the withdrawal action of 1945) a full member of the NSBRO and had a representative on that agency's national headquarters staff. The watchdog never watched, probably because there were never any finances to oversee or audit. An internal NSBRO memo dated August 23, 1945, records what it described as "the Catholic dope": the total cost of the Catholic men inducted from the beginning to that date amounted to $44,973.17; the total contributions received toward their support, $3,760.54; the "uncared for" balance, $41,212.63. That ninety-plus percent deficit serves as the most fitting summary of the Catholic CPS experience.

But there was much more disillusionment involved than the financial debacle these figures reveal. Expectations were high in the initial announcement published in the April 1941 issue of the *Catholic Worker*. Readers were informed that the camp would provide for fifty objectors at an annual expenditure of $12,000. The various houses of hospitality and farm communes were asked to set up local cells to assume responsibility for contributing "several dollars a week" toward the support of the camp and to encourage Catholic draft eligibles to avail themselves of the CO option. There was no great concern about the prospects for filling the fifty-man roster. After all, the ACCO had been registering potential Catholic COs for the previous eight months and already had about 400 names on its list; adding the other Catholics whose names would be passed on to them by the NSBRO as they received the CO classification from their local draft boards, a rough estimate of the number to be serviced that year alone was set at between 700 and 800! At that the estimate was modest. A November 1939 survey of 54,000 Catholic students in 141 Catholic colleges and universities had shown 36 percent indicating they would become conscientious objectors if the United States entered the war.[5]

If these expectations proved grossly exaggerated, so also did the quality of the anticipated commitment. The same article that announced the opening of the camp looked forward to receiving men who would be "something more than objectors." That term was overly negative and was likely to win no sympathy and very little understanding. But by accepting work of national importance of a constructive nature, under civilian direction, those presumptive assignees would show "that they have the common good of the country far more at heart than those who differ with them on this issue of military service." That was the philosophy behind the CPS experiment, an idealistic vision that would all too soon become a sour disillusionment and a continuing source of dissension in the grim reality of the Camp Simon experience.

In fairness, though, this should be put in broader perspective. When that article appeared, the issue was set in terms of a *peacetime* draft involving a twelve-month obligation of alternative service. This was extended to eighteen months in August 1941 and with the declaration of war in December of that year to "the duration plus six months." The exalted ideals of a voluntary "second mile" of unpaid service to demonstrate the sincerity of the conscientious objector may have made sense as a relatively short-term commitment; as an open-ended obligation stretching no one knew how far into the future, it was something else.

The *Catholic Worker* and those associated with the movement would continue to profess the high ideals stated in this initial announcement, if only because those ideals conformed so closely with the principles on which the movement itself was based. This, too, became a source of considerable misunderstanding as the months dragged on. Since the ACCO was a creation of the movement, most of the camp's administrative positions were given to men who had been associated with one or another of the Catholic Worker houses of hospitality. This naturally led to charges that the movement's perfectionist philosophy and life style were being imposed upon the entire camp population. The charge was not entirely without justification. In the second (April 1942) issue of the camp newspaper, *Salt*, the director proposed that the camp, then located at Stoddard, be known as Camp Simon. He supported the appropriateness of the suggestion with an argument that would probably not have won the wholehearted endorsement of the majority of the campers then or later. The name, he felt, would be a reminder "that we who are conscripts can do more than is asked, take less than is offered, give freely and humbly." Perhaps, he added, imprisonment would have been the better choice, but since they had chosen alternative service instead, "Let us hope we can be Christian slaves and work, not because of fear, but for the love of our neighbors and for the greater glory of God."

The September 1941 *Catholic Worker* article referred to earlier reflects the same ideological dependence upon a particular interpretation of Christian ideals and obligations. Still operating under the expectation of a large number of Catholic objectors, the need was seen to establish "a camp in which we might lead as full a Catholic life as possible," one in which the members could practice and learn more about the liturgy of the Church and which would be "a center of Peace and Prayer in this war torn world." The hope was voiced that such a camp might obtain the services of a chaplain—a hope, incidentally, that would find repeated expression throughout the camp's history but one that was never to be fulfilled—so that "we could offer daily Mass, the most important part of Catholicism, with him."

These hopes and ideals offer striking illustrations of the extent to which the Worker's values were intended to find tangible expression in the Camp Simon experience, but their most explicit expression was given in the statement of "Fundamental Principles" formulated by Director Larrowe for the opening of the Stoddard camp and in the welcoming letter sent to each new member at the time of his formal notice of assignment. Thus, in the "Principles" we read: "Conscientious objection for Catholics is a precept of perfection. . . . Those who become objectors must earnestly strive after the perfection of love; otherwise there is no justification for their stand. This means a constant, an extreme stress on those aspects of Christian perfection: charity, humility, patience, sacrifice. We must pick up the Cross." Personalism, the foundation of Catholic Worker philosophy, was to govern the relationships within the camp. "Because of our faith in the basic goodness of every man, we strive to appeal only to the man's conscience, by example and discussion, to do the thing which is right. (Note: this would apply to our refusal to allow imposed discipline, emanating from the camp meeting itself; the principle of a minimum of rules and regulations.)"

To anticipate again what must be reserved for detailed discussion later, the failure to achieve these lofty ideals was recognized in January 1943 in the introduction by this same Director Larrowe of a new principle of "functional authoritarianism" under which he, being ultimately responsible for the whole camp, would henceforth exercise "supreme authority." Under this new order, he would explain then, "discipline is essential and must, where necessary, be enforced." Although the personalist credo is still present in the new policy's provision for voluntary assumption of responsibility and authority, the change in tone tells much about the unhappy experiences of the intervening months.

Some of these experiences are described in Harold P. Winchester's unpublished study of the Stoddard camp. Since they relate directly to, and were continued in, the Warner experience, they will not be treated in any detail at this point other than by noting that the form and composition of camp governance and the extent to which it could assure compliance with its policies and decisions were problems that defied resolution to the very end. And one continuing source of aggravation which did much to maximize those problems was this resentment by campers who were of widely disparate religious and ideological persuasions of what they interpreted as an unwarranted intrusion of Catholic Worker philosophy, ideals, and life style under the duress of conscription.

Most historical references to the Catholic peace witness of World War II miss this crucial dimension of the CPS experience and for a simple enough reason. The most available source of information—virtually the *only* available source, in fact—is the *Catholic Worker* and the overly idealized account of camp life and events published in its pages. What is reported there is true enough, but the events selected for mention and the manner of presentation always manage to accentuate the positive while issues and controversies, which dominated camp life, tend to be played down or ignored altogether. The insider could read between the lines and often find enough there to reconstruct the true situation, but the casual reader (and, apparently, historical researchers as well) can easily be taken in and thereby gain the impression that the men assigned to the Stoddard and Warner camps were moral heroes eager to bear the hardships and inconveniences of camp life in a perfect spirit of Christian resignation and self-sacrifice. Such, I fear, was only rarely the case.

This is not to say that these monthly reports are of no value. They do provide the basis for a sequential history, however superficial, of Camp Simon. The July-August 1941 column notes the arrival at Stoddard of the first two assignees and Director Larrowe, and speaks of another on his way from Los Angeles and a fourth, a wheat farmer from North Dakota, who was being transferred from a Colorado camp where he was the lone Catholic among 180 Mennonites. By August about ten more men were expected to arrive.

Apparently these expectations, too, went unfulfilled. There is no further mention of the man from Los Angeles or the wheat farmer; their failure to materialize would have been consistent with Selective Service's policy of restricting new camp assignments to the registrants' respective sides of the Mississippi. At any rate, the October 1941 report admits the difficulty of getting enough men and reports the welcome arrival of four volunteers recruited from other nearby camps following the camp director's personal appeal. These volunteers saved the Catholic camp by providing it with the minimum work force needed to meet Forestry Service requirements.* The presence of a voluntary cook who was prepared to fill in as camp nurse as well was gratefully noted, as were the donations of foodstuffs that had been received. The shape of future turbulent argu-

---

*The four volunteers were the first of the eight who would transfer from the Royalston and Petersham camps. Director Larrowe and one of the volunteers had visited these camps to explain Stoddard's precarious status and solicit such transfers. Two of the transferees were discharged shortly after arriving at Stoddard, but the total group included four men who would make important contributions to the Warner scene: Ron Baxter, Alvin Manton, Angus MacNeill, and Robert Dunfey.

ments over the inadequacies of diet and the lack of medical care is
hidden in these generally optimistic reports.

The next month's column featured a discourse on the differences
between CPS and an army camp, a reference to the extensive use being made of donated apples, and a report on progress being made
with respect to the farming plans for the fall. This, of course, illustrates a lead time problem for which allowance must always be made
in references to the *Catholic Worker* as a source: news of camp hap-
penings seldom reached print until a month or more after the events
reported or anticipated had already taken place. That passing reference to apples holds more significance than one might think. Recalling her visit to the Stoddard camp, Dorothy Day is still impressed by
this. "I know that they were living mostly on apples: apple pies and
apple fritters, applesauce, and apple pancakes, and things of that sort.
However, Mrs. Hower was a good New England cook."*

That farming project, of course, was the voluntary camp work described and promoted in the welcoming letter and other official pronouncements. This, too, held major significance for the future. The
anticipated produce from the farm, the chickens, and the pigs were
all part of the plan to make the camp as self-subsistent as possible.
Considering the ever precarious finances of the parent Catholic Worker movement, a passably successful farm venture was recognized,
even then, as essential to Camp Simon's survival. The failure to
achieve this goal was a major cause of the food crises that were to
develop over the course of months.

All things taken in balance, that November account was strictly
up-beat in tone. In that comparison with an army camp, Director
Larrowe presents it as a matter of contrasts.

*. . . We do not believe in war, we believe in peace. We are not here to learn the
arts of war. We are here to do useful, helpful work. And we are learning at camp
the arts of peace. We do not believe in destruction; we believe in growth. We do
not believe in hate; we believe in love. And so we are working to restore the
forests. We are working to safeguard and improve their growth. We are giving our
work to the neighbors. We want to help and to serve.*

*One former camper, in reviewing an earlier draft of this manuscript, comments
that this is Miss Day "at her most romantic." As the camp cook's assistant for a
time, he recalls a more varied diet including "splendid" New England baked beans
and brown bread. Romanticized or not, the apple-diet impression is also recorded in Miss Day's volume, *Loaves and Fishes* (New York: Harper & Row, 1963),
p. 64.

From my own perspective as one whose experience was limited to
the Warner phase of Camp Simon's history, this description of attitudes supposedly prevailing at Stoddard seems overidealized to the
point of being deceptive. On the other hand, Winchester's study of
that earlier period does indicate that work production, and presumably camp morale, was at a peak in those months of October and
November 1941. Confirmed or not, it seems fair to conclude that
these reports in the *Catholic Worker* could be counted on to put the
most favorable construction on whatever happened. It was, after all,
the house organ of the ACCO and the camp in a very real sense. Since
one important objective of these monthly columns was to impress
the readers and persuade them to contribute to the support of the
men who were engaged in what was presented as so laudable (even
heroic?) a witness for peace, some distortion on this score can be understood and even forgiven.

This note of sacrifice and the appeals for aid were standard features of the monthly camp reports. Thus the December 1941 issue
included a letter of appreciation signed "The Men of the Camp" for
gifts received, and provided a list: "a wash machine, candy, soap,
books, money, mimeograph, pig, cat, magazines." And this was followed immediately with a list of other needs: "a typewriter, flat
irons, sweaters, winter underwear, and sox. We will need more band-
ages and soap and perhaps some overshoes. But we have faith that
what we really need will be provided—what we need, you will give."*

That same November issue exulted over "the greatest of all gifts"
received from the Bishop of Manchester. "He has given us permission
to have Mass said at the camp. That will mean that at last we are really a Catholic camp." But this, too, seems to have been a boon over-
stated. It appears the privilege granted merely permitted a Hillsboro
priest to "occasionally" celebrate Mass there "if he is free and chooses

*These, again, were the needs at Stoddard. More than a year later, Dorothy Day
would write about her impressions following a visit to Warner. "It is 27-below
zero. . . . They need socks, sweaters, mufflers at the camp. The men on our
breadlines need them too. We hope some of our readers are knitting for them."
Two things should be noted here: the needs of the campers were a constant; that
is the first and most important fact. However, the linking of those needs with
those of "the men on our breadlines" could only serve to confirm the belief
held by many of the campers that the two operations were really fused together
in the minds of the people responsible for the administration of the camp whether they, the campers, liked it or not.

to do so." There is no way of knowing how often the privilege was exercised;[6] but the emphasis placed on closer proximity to church as one of the advantages to be gained by the transfer to the Warner location would suggest that it was very occasional indeed.

The attack on Pearl Harbor brought the formal entry of the United States into the Second World War. One of the lesser effects of that historical event, as noted in the January 1942 *Catholic Worker*, was the addition of special prayers and devotions for peace to the daily schedule for the Stoddard camp. The major news in the February column was the minus-22-degree weather and the appearance of the first issue of *Salt*. The camp roster was now up to thirty-one.

The April 1942 column reported the opening of the Alexian Brothers unit and the transfer there of twelve of the Stoddard camp- ers.[7] There is some special significance here in that Alexian was one of the earliest such units to be approved by Selective Service and, as it turned out, one of the very few general hospital units ever to be established. That the ACCO was given administrative authority over this pioneer effort is undoubtedly due in great part to the fact that it was a Catholic hospital. It should be noted, however, that the unit's membership was never restricted to Catholics or even to "graduates" of the ACCO-sponsored camps. From this point on, future issues of the paper would now include a monthly column of news from Alex- ian as well.

That same April issue included, as a kind of Lenten homily, the *Salt* contribution of Director Larrowe's cited earlier in which he pro- posed the Camp Simon name and sounded the call for "Christian slaves." There was probably more to this than the ordinary reader would suspect, for, according to Winchester, there was a steady and apparently drastic decline in camp morale and discipline at about this time. From that high point of the preceding October and Novem- ber when work production levels had met the ¼-cord-per-man-per-day expectations, the output had fallen off until, by mid-December, loaf- ing had become a real problem. By mid-January, still according to the Winchester study, loafing was the practice for all but a few (though, it was noted, some loafed more than others) and in February morale reached its nadir.

The purported cause for this decline was a growing dissatisfaction with the work project, the subject of the next chapter. Though a change in the project seems to have brought a slight improvement in mid-March, there is reason to believe that the director's little homily was really addressed to this deteriorating situation. If so, his recommendations to "do more than is asked" and "take less than is offered" were Lenten thoughts intended more for his in-house audience than for the *Catholic Worker*'s readers at large. This again suggests it is a serious error to assume, as so many who have used his monthly columns as the source for their analyses of the Catholic opposition to World War II seem to have done, that his comments can be taken as a representative expression of the attitudes or the idealistic commitment of all, or even most, campers.

What appears to be a passing thought—the suggestion that "perhaps jail is better"—almost certainly echoes the type of discussion and debate that flourished in the camp setting. It may also be an acknowledgement of the tempered approval voiced by Dorothy Day and other more absolute pacifists to the very idea of cooperating with the conscription program, even to the extent of accepting

classification as a conscientious objector. This dissatisfaction found dramatic expression in the May 1942 report that one of the Stoddard campers, a man closely associated with the Catholic Worker movement, had walked out of camp in protest. The full text of his protest statement was published as a special item, undoubtedly a sign of support and approval on the part of Miss Day and the other editors. As it turned out, the protest was short-lived. After further reflection and reconsideration, the rebel returned to camp, a fact duly noted in the June column. One other item of note in that latter issue was a complimentary reference to the camper who had volunteered to take the place of the "good New England cook" who had departed the Stoddard scene. "He keeps us satisfied—or almost so—at a cost of about 12¢ per meal."

Not until the July-August issue were the internal problems that so disrupted the highly idealized portrayal of camp life publicly acknowledged, and even then the troubles were given an up-beat presentation by Director Larrowe. First addressing himself to the more profound consideration of the nature of freedom and tracing the evils of war and totalitarianism to the tendency of nations to act like rugged individualists, he turned from this to what he felt were instructive parallels to be drawn from the camp and its problems.

In its essence we have the same problem at Stoddard. So we try to educate ourselves to our responsibilities. We try to learn again the proper relation of Man to God and Man to Man. . . .

We have our failures—men who loaf on the work project, the camp is not as neat and clean as it should be, we are inconsiderate of each other, a few are left to bear the burden of the thoughtlessness of others, nerves are frayed and tempers are lost occasionally. These things seem small, yet they are the seeds of war.

The litany of failures continued with specific applications that assume special significance when placed in the context of the Fundamental Principles set forth with such optimism in the early days of Stoddard.

In encouraging freely given cooperation and charity we have allowed injustices to exist. We ask for contributions to the camp—if they are not given then all the assignees must suffer whether they believe in our ideals, our convictions, or not. We ask for freely given help around the camp—if not enough is given, then those who give are fools—suckers—(from a natural viewpoint). They labor and others benefit. True, but we are learning. I am convinced that many of us are happy to serve others, even to receive ingratitude. Happy for supernatural reasons. And that is the lasting growth, the real progress.

"Happy" though he may have been, there is no mistaking Larrowe's tone of deep disillusionment that events had taken so unsatisfactory a turn. And, though he could not know it then, the worst was yet to come in the grim and dark days of Warner.

September 1942 brought a "good news/bad news/promising news" kind of report. George Selmon's chicken-raising venture was mentioned as an acknowledged success, and an abundant blueberry and apple crop was hailed as another blessing. That was the good news. The bad news was that Selective Service had refused permission to use the government trucks to transport the campers to church, sixteen miles distant! Apparently the hopes for some arrangement to have Mass regularly in camp had vanished completely by then. It is the promising news, however, that has most direct relevance to us. A formal request had been submitted to transfer the camp to Warner. Several advantages were seen for the new location: increased size (200-man capacity); nearness to supplies, doctor, and rail transportation (2 miles); and above all, nearness to church ("only about 8 miles, and many of us could walk that"). Once again the importance of corporate witness was stressed: "The principal reason for the existence of a Catholic camp is, after all, the hope of encouraging a fuller Catholic life than would be possible in another camp."

The *Catholic Worker* was forced to skip its October 1942 issue because, as the editors explained the following month, there was "not a penny around." It was left to the November issue to report as an impending change the critical event that had, in fact, already taken place. The Stoddard camp—the forty-five men and their belongings, as well as the chickens, cats, pigs and all the other items listed in the report cited earlier—had already settled into that new home at Warner.

Some extremely important items had been omitted from that moving inventory. Prominent among them were the continuing stresses and strains within the various cliques and divisions that had long since begun to develop into acute personality clashes. The widespread and increasingly bitter disillusionment with the alternative service program itself and its religious sponsors could not be left behind. The acute frustration over the perceived unimportance of the required work fed upon the campers' awareness of an ever-widening alienation from a society welded into consensus in support of the total war they had rejected. All of these provided a generous, but as yet partly hidden, supply of seeds of future and bitter discord for the transplanted men of Camp Simon.

Nevertheless, the note of optimism struck in the announcement of the "impending" move was probably authentic enough. After all, it was a new beginning; and the prospects must have looked good at the time, certainly better than they had been those last few months at CPS #15. Now in its reincarnation as CPS #54, Camp Simon could continue on a grander scale and, if that was not cause enough for optimism, there was the excitement of the change itself to provide a welcome break in the monotony of camp existence. That is the way it must have looked to the old-timers at least.[8] As for me, Warner is where I came in.

PART TWO

THE WOODSMAN'S LAMENT

Oh! for the life of a woodsman
Whose axe on the frosty wood rings,
Surrounded by wedges and sledges,
Great cross-cuts and other odd things.

Oh-ho-ho for the life of a woodsman,
The thrill as the tall timbers fall;
We go for the life of a woodsman,
For it's better than no life at all.

(Chorus)
Yes, its better than no life at all,
So much better than no life at all—
We go for the life of a woodsman.
It is better than no life at all.

Sung to the tune (loosely adapted) of "Columbia, The Gem of the Ocean."

So you want to know our schedule? Well, if you have tears, prepare to shed them now. We are awakened at 3:30 A.M. This is only a trick, and if anyone moves, he is hit on the head with an axe for making noise. At 6:45 we are called and if we are not out of bed by 6:46, we are again slugged. After breakfast (if we get any—the pigs are so much bigger than us and can easily push us out of their trough), we are packed into trucks and taken out to project. As we are thrown off the truck, we are beaten with a whip-lash for one hour. Then we have two hours rest (working in the woods) to permit the blood to clot. After which we are again beaten to work up an appetite for lunch (no lunch). The beating privilege is raffled off to local Legionnaires. In the afternoon we again do the chopping until we are again packed into trucks. When we get back to camp the trucks are driven about at a high rate of speed, and we are forced to jump off while they are still moving. As a penalty for this, we are sent to bed without supper. From 9:30 to 11:00 we are again beaten. It is pleasant, and I am having a fine time and wish you were here.

This attempt at a humorous account of the typical day at Warner was given in a letter I wrote a month or so after my arrival at camp. Almost as fanciful, although obviously more serious in intention, is the official Stoddard schedule published in the *Catholic Worker* for December 1941: "5:45—arise; 6:05—breakfast; 6:35—make bed; 6:50—meditation; 7:15—work project; 12 noon—lunch; 4:30—free time; 5:30—dinner; 6:00—free time; 7:00—rosary; 7:30—recreation and classes; 10:00—lights out." The following month's issue had that war-inspired change mentioned earlier; the St. Francis Prayer for Peace and the Proper of the Mass for the day would be recited at 6:40 A.M. and be followed by meditation, while the 7 P.M. session would be expanded to include the reading of the Oration of the Mass for Peace, a chapter from some spiritual writing, and Compline.

This schedule was undoubtedly followed by some of the men, but given the disparity of their religious commitment, one can be confident that it was not adhered to by a majority of the campers. But, here again, too many scholars in researching the Catholic CPS experience have accepted this published schedule and the overidealized impression it gives of the spiritual tone of camp life. The conclusions they have drawn are complimentary, of course, but not really accurate.

It is perhaps best to separate the work project hours from the free time spent in camp since the campers were subject to different jurisdictions for each, a matter that will assume greater importance in later chapters. The workday *normally* began at 7:30 with the departure of the men assigned to the forestry detail. Lunch was scheduled to begin at noon and end an hour later, after which the men returned to their assigned tasks until 4:15 when it was time to board the trucks for the trip back to camp. Occasional rest or smoke breaks were permitted; but these were made redundant by the actual work patterns exhibited by the men. At first Saturdays were half-days with weekends free following the return at noon—except for those campers who were assigned by alphabetical rotation to weekend kitchen duty. In January 1943, when all government employees were put on a full six-day week, Selective Service officials were quick to extend this ruling to the unpaid conscientious objectors under their control.

In actual practice, the workday was much more flexible. Although the morning siren was sure to sound five or ten minutes before the scheduled departure time, there was always enough time lost in milling about or in getting the necessary work tools to assure a departure closer to 8 A.M. It was the practice, too, for the men to gather for lunch as much as fifteen minutes to a half-hour early (not to mention the other visits to warm up at the camp fire), and they were not at all compulsive about leaving the area when the lunch hour was over. As a result, the average day on project was considerably shorter than announced in the formal schedule.

Some of the campers did not go out on project, being assigned instead to such tasks as camp maintenance and kitchen work, clerical duties in the camp director's and project superintendent's offices, infirmary duty, and similar inside jobs. These were counted, of course, as project work equivalents and, theoretically carried the same forty-four-hour (later forty-eight-hour) obligations. Most of

the men sent out to work in the woods regarded the camp assignments as cushy jobs reserved for the favored few; for their part, the
men with these various administrative assignments were likely to insist that their tasks involved more actual work responsibilities and
time. Strangely enough, both were probably right.

Life at Warner was the greyest of existences. The daily routine began with the call of the night watchman. Depending upon who had
the assignment at any given time, it was usually accompanied by
either loud banging on a pan or what passed for cheery morning
jests and banter. Unlike the bugler's reveille, neither approach could
assure better than a mixed reception. Some men paid no attention at
all, leaving their bunks only at the sound of the work siren. Roger
Tennitt, for one, is still remembered for his much-admired perfection
of timing: he always managed to put his work clothes on over his pa-
jamas and emerge from the bunkhouse just as the trucks were revving
up to leave.

Most campers managed to get breakfast, which was the one regular
meal that, in my memory, was not so bad as the others. George Selmon's carefully tended chicken flock provided eggs with sufficient
regularity, and the bread produced by the camp's amateur bakers,
though repeatedly and loudly denounced by our only honest-to-
goodness woodsman as "pig bread," was quite acceptable when
toasted. My early letters from camp, in fact, were mildly complimentary about the food, a judgment I adjusted drastically downward as
the weeks dragged on. Others remember breakfast much less favorably. Bill O'Flaherty still speaks of the wormy oatmeal and of the
need to stir it rigorously once milk was added so that the worms
would float to the top where they could be skimmed off easily. (This
is a somewhat unsettling thought to me. I have no similar recollection and, worse still, cannot remember whether or not I ever ate
the oatmeal.)

After breakfast there was a half-hour or so free, during which time
the regularly devout took to their prayers and meditations, while the
others occupied themselves with letter writing, reading, bunkmaking,
and similar incidental chores until it was time to leave for the project
site. The ride there, a matter of forty-five minutes or more spent
bouncing around in the back of a canvas-covered military truck, was
memorable mainly for the hardness of the benches, the coldness of
the air, and the ever-present conviction that the insane recklessness
of the driver, a fellow assignee, would surely have the truck careening

off the road at the next sharp turn. The trip was enlivened by considerable needling and teasing back and forth. Pat Rafferty and Jimmy O'Toole in particular provided a source of continuing hilarity in their daily thrust-and-parry verbal exchanges about the Irish and the British in general or, often enough, O'Toole's outspoken admiration for Churchill in particular. O'Flaherty, perhaps the loudest man on the camp roster, made a point of saluting the ubiquitous statues marking the various New Hampshire towns and villages along the route and raising his voice in less than gracious comments about the countryside and its inhabitants.

When the trucks finally reached the actual work site on Shadow Hill, the various tools of the woodsman's craft were distributed, and the men set off in groups of four to perform their work of national importance. Lunch was usually a misfortune and quite frequently a disaster. There were times, for instance, when the night watchman whose task it was to prepare the sandwiches forgot to do so because he became too absorbed in his personal interests. (The job was much sought after for the opportunity it gave for painting, reading, writing, and, of course, sleeping.) On other occasions someone merely neglected to load the lunch onto the trucks. Annoying though this was, it can also be said that the absence of lunch was often less a cause for serious complaint than its presence. Thus, the soup might be burned, a recurring mishap for which the kitchen force would be roundly condemned, though in fairness it must be confessed that the fault may have occasionally rested with whomever was assigned the task of keeping the project campfire going and getting lunch ready. Even at its best (that is, unburned), the soup was a mysterious concoction that drew heavily upon the Catholic Worker movement's experience with Bowery soup lines and, no doubt, used their favorite recipes. On one memorable occasion, word circulated that the next day's soup contained fishheads and other equally exotic components. This rumor led one anonymous irate camper to add a boot to the kettle simmering away in the kitchen—an act of sabotage not in the least amusing to the kitchen crew.

When lunch was over, the men scattered back to their chosen locations until the call sounded to return to the trucks. The ride back was essentially a repeat of the morning trip except that more men were now more awake. None would be particularly tired, however, for few had given themselves much cause to be.

The rest of the day was that "free time," though technically the men were still subject to the authority and direction of the camp director. It was this half-hour or so before dinner and the early evening hours after the meal that camp administrators had hoped would be used to perform the farm chores and other voluntary services. However well this expectation might have served to distinguish cooperator from noncooperator at Stoddard, it was not too good a test at Warner. The first few weeks were devoted to the mechanics of getting the new camp into full operation. After that the New Hampshire winter settled in and left little opportunity for farming or other outside work. As a result, the men were left pretty much to their own devices.

The only group-centered free time activities were those centering upon the chapel group or the creative and social activities of the artists congregated in their bohemia. The number of individuals regularly involved in the former is at best a hazy recollection, but a fair estimate would be a core of nine or ten regulars, supplemented by a dozen or more occasional participants. The evening Compline service probably drew the best attendance; Prime in the morning attracted only the most dedicated. The chapel itself was the handiwork of a group of volunteers who, under the gifted direction of our one liturgical artist, converted a section of the former CCC barracks "school" building into a tasteful center for worship. Though hopes for a resident or regularly visiting priest to serve as chaplain were never fulfilled, it was an occasion of considerable joy when an Irish priest attached to the New York Catholic Worker house of hospitality paid an extended visit in the camp's closing days and finally put the chapel to the use that had inspired so much effort and determination in its building and decoration.

The other end of the same structure was set apart as a studio for the ten or so men who had been artists and writers before coming to camp and for the aspiring few who blossomed after their arrival. A cluster of nonartist friends were also privileged to join this select company. For the rest, the studio was generally recognized and respected as a forbidden precinct. In the studio the lights would burn to all hours while the occupants sketched, painted, talked, and often (to the intense dismay of the camp's peace-and-quiet elements) drank. It was generally assumed that most of the roistering binges that upset the deadening calm of camp existence found their origin here, though in point of fact they were just as likely to begin in the mess hall and bunkhouses. Not all, perhaps not even most, of the camp's artistic production took place in the studio. A substantial part of the sketching and water-color daubing was accomplished during work hours on project when the supervisory personnel were out of sight or otherwise occupied. It is nonetheless true that, while in camp, the artists and their hangers-on disappeared into the studio for most of their free time and stayed there long after most of the other campers had retired for the night.

The middle third of this building was set aside as the camp library, a happy arrangement if only in that it served to keep the two otherwise not entirely compatible uses and groups apart. The full implications of the division between the two will be made clear in due course. At this point it is enough to say that the chapel group, intensely devoted to the importance of establishing and maintaining a Catholic corporate witness against the war, represented the most consistent and most vocal body of support for the ACCO and the camp administrators. The artists, free spirits all, included some of the most consistent critics of the camp, its administration, and, indeed, the entire CPS program, so much so that the studio was regarded by many as a veritable hotbed of dissidence and disruption.

Another form of collective activity, the camp meeting, deserves to be considered in this context. Under the most recent of the several metamorphoses of Camp Simon governance arrangements, the meetings were supposed to be regularly scheduled. In actual practice, however, they occurred on more of an ad hoc or demand basis. A special meeting might be called to deal with some immediate or imminent camp problem or to discuss issues involving CPS in general. More often than not the latter was linked to the latest protest or proposal originating from some other camp. On the increasingly rare occasions when there was no salient issue or problem to be discussed, the tendency on the part of most campers was to ignore the regularly scheduled meetings. This usually made it necessary to reschedule them as special meetings, and even then the attendance would be light unless, of course, some crisis had erupted in the interim to shatter the general apathy.

The problems associated with governance, and the source of much of the normal apathy toward camp meetings, will be discussed in chapter 7. Even so, it is appropriate to report in some detail on the first meeting at Warner, which took place three evenings after my arrival. In many ways it was representative of those that were to follow in the months ahead if only because the issues, though unique in specifics, reflected the continuing strains within the camp community that were to find repeated expression in various contexts and forms throughout its brief history.

The meeting was called to settle, among other things, that issue of space allocation in the school building. An advance contingent of artists had established a squatters' claim to the two best rooms, leaving only one large and two small rooms for all the other purposes that had been so grandly anticipated at Stoddard (e.g., chapel, library, reading-and-quiet room, typing room). Even the bohemians were divided to the extent that the writers and the artists accused each other of imperialistic designs. Tempers grew shorter and voices louder until the climax was reached when John Luzon, one of the artists who was already conceded to be the most disruptive member of the Stoddard camp, advanced the opinion that the chapel should not be too near the artists' studio because the sounds of chanting and singing associated with liturgical practices would be an obstacle to creative activity.

The comment was greeted with general laughter, but to everyone's surprise, Pat Rafferty, who had himself been joking and kidding throughout the argument, rose in indignation to express shock and dismay that supposedly committed men would consider religion a laughing matter. Luzon, a nonpracticing Catholic not known for nicety of language, responded with a shout of "Horse shit!" This provoked Pat, ordinarily a friend of John's and, often enough, a partner in some of his more disruptive actions, to challenge him to an immediate fist fight to settle the matter. John prudently declined, reminding him that Pat had been a "pro" fighter.* The exchange ended with Pat's stalking out of the meeting in a fury, and the meeting ended soon thereafter.

The incident, in retrospect, is comic. But to this newcomer it was an unsettling display, and not at all what I had expected in a community supposedly dedicated to the Christian ideal of peace. One may still confess to disillusionment that so wide a gap between professed values and actual performance could exist, but placed in the broader context of the total Stoddard-Warner experience, it is easier to understand what was happening.

For one thing, the transferred campers were suffering the collapse

---

*This was not strictly true if my memory is correct. Pat had achieved considerable success as a boxer, but as a Golden Gloves amateur and not as a professional.

of high expectations. One of the strongest arguments in support of the move had been the promise of a great increase in space that would be suited to the widest range of special needs and interests. This was in contrast to the crowded conditions at Stoddard that were felt to have contributed so much to the strain and unhappiness there. This disappointment in its turn awakened all the temporarily suspended conflicts and suspicions, in particular those existing between the artists and the chapel group. All may have welcomed the new beginning, but all were determined to make sure that these new beginnings would not work to their personal or group disadvantage. That John Luzon, the archdisrupter at Stoddard, would play a central role in this flare-up was perhaps foreordained. That his performance would be greeted by a strong response from more committed Catholics was no less predictable.

Tension-filled camp meetings were the rule, though few produced such high drama. Fortunately, though the essential divisions were relatively fixed throughout the camp's history, they did not produce the degree of personal animosity that might be expected. Thus, the morning after this particular contretemps Pat was his customarily jaunty self. Lou Schnittler, another nonpracticing Catholic who had supported the artists' claims to the rooms they had already commandeered, met him with the greeting, "Hello, you emotional Catholic." To which Pat responded in exaggerated Brooklynese, "Whaddya mean 'emotional'? I'm *poifectly* calm, *poifectly* calm"—all the while advancing on Lou and brandishing a hatchet in mock threat.

To some extent this controversy, like many others, proved to be much ado about nothing. Except for the chapel enthusiasts at their end of the school building and the bohemians at the other, the rest of the building was put to little use. At Stoddard in the earliest months there had been ambitious visions of an educational program that would utilize the special competences and training of the more educated campers for the betterment of those who had not enjoyed similar advantages. On another plane, as the welcoming letter had put it, the program would seek to "encourage the study of the Church, its teachings, its history, and its liturgy."

The closest these plans came to realization at Stoddard was in the effort to explore the causes of war in the hope that those who participated in the study sessions might be prepared for more effective peace activities once their days in CPS were over. No sooner had the program begun when it bogged down in extended polemical exhanges between the intellectuals with their mainly socialist commitment and the defenders of the Catholicism of those preconciliar days who were given to citing the explicit papal condemnations of all forms of socialism as intrinsically evil. By the time Camp Simon moved to Warner, these dreams had long since collapsed, leaving nothing but an occasional nostalgic reminder of the original hopes or, more frequently, scarcely hidden envy and even resentment of the more elaborate and well-funded programs of the Friends camps. However, from the few accounts of the educational program that have come to me second-hand, it seems the coup de grace was administered by the campers of the Coughlinite persuasion who began to use the study sessions as a vehicle for expounding their own rather peculiar explanations of the causes of World War II.

The failure of such structured efforts should not be taken to mean that no education took place. Quite the contrary. Informal discussions of these and all sorts of other topics provided the principal form of diversion open to us. Such discussions would develop spontaneously on almost any occasion or in any context and often seemed destined to continue without end. Men who might have ended up in angry confrontation in a more organized study group setting found themselves spending hours in relaxed philosophical, political, or religious debate in the bunkhouse, on project, or wherever they might be whenever someone introduced the topic of the moment. What may have been lost in the absence of ordered presentation and exploration was more than compensated for in this manner.

One remaining group activity not to be overlooked was the publication of the camp magazine, *Salt*. At least two issues (January 1942 and April 1942) appeared at Stoddard, and there may have been a third produced there as well. Only one issue was prepared at Warner and, once it became the focus of one of the major camp controversies, it was never released for circulation. *Salt* was mainly the work of the intellectuals (Lou Schnittler, Dean Farfether, Alvin Manton), but it also served as a convenient forum for chapel group leaders like William Grandman and Louis Swanson to expound the Catholic position against war and voice their support for CPS and the camp administration. Cover art and illustrations were provided by the camp artists, some of whom (Leonard Mattano, Roger Tennitt, LeRoy Torto) also contributed to its literary content from time to time.

Compared with the impressive publications turned out at other camps, *Salt* was a very crude effort in almost every conceivable respect. There was none of the slick professionalism, for example, achieved by some of the magazines published in Friends camps, at least one of which would expand after the war into the prestigious Pacifica news and radio outlets.[1] Still, whatever the publication may have lacked in journalistic class, these few issues of *Salt* did provide a vehicle of expression for the various, or at least the dominant, cliques on the Camp Simon scene. Only the Coughlinite campers seem not to have had much opportunity to present their case. Whether this was because the anti-Semitic positions they were likely to take were offensive to the editors or because they disdained participation in any venture involving so many non-Catholics and similarly suspect liberals is not clear. Again, both are probably true to some extent.

Salt's self-description as "a magazine of voluntary contributions which does not necessarily represent the views of the Association of Catholic Conscientious Objectors or of the camp as a whole" suggests that the camp intellectuals and others who assumed responsibility for its publication anticipated a measure of internal disapproval and opposition; and they were right. Even this prudent disclaimer was not enough to save the Warner issue, but that is a tale for later telling. Its literary quality, to put it kindly, was unimpressive. With only one or two exceptions, the fiction and poetry were marked by obscurity of style and self-conscious artiness; the essays were either ponderously profound or excessively pietistic in tone.

Apart from these few and limited cooperative ventures, any free-time activities of a recreational or educational nature were individual and spontaneously engineered. Chuck Sterner and the few others who shared his athletic inclinations might round up enough campers for an evening softball game or, once the New Hampshire winter settled in, an equally makeshift basketball game in the empty barracks building used as a recreation hall. Small clusters of men might decide to hike the three miles or so to the town of Warner, even though there was nothing to do once they arrived other than to purchase a candy bar or something at the drugstore and begin the hike back. The heavy snows brought opportunities for skiing, sledding, or skating for those having access to the necessary equipment or the ingenuity to devise some adequate substitute.

Most free time, however, was spent in more sedentary and private pursuits: reading, letter writing, and journal keeping. And always there were those endless discussions in the mess hall or around the bunkhouse stoves, mostly centering upon the differing philosophies or theologies of war but sometimes spilling over into critiques of music, literature or even, in more mundane moments, concerns related to past experiences and future hopes and prospects. Strangely enough, although these were the months of the tide-turning battles in Russia and North Africa, few discussions centered on the actual progress of the war itself. If it was mentioned at all, it was to express concern over the accelerating costs in death and destruction and voice predictably unfavorable judgments of what the campers regarded as the hypocrisy in the statements of high moral purpose issued by political and military leaders.

Weekends for most were merely more of the same. Campers fortunate enough to be within convenient travel distance from home and sufficiently solvent were able to escape the camp setting. John Canory, the only man in camp with a car, was especially favored in this respect and operated what was known as "the Canory Express," driving himself and a few regular paying passengers to New York City almost every weekend. Occasionally space was found for an outsider as an extra or replacement for a regular who had to stay in camp on kitchen duty when the Express was scheduled to run. Tony Saunders, for instance, made at least one trip riding in the trunk, a striking example of the lengths to which we would go to get away.

For those who had the money, Warner was more accessible to the outside world in that winter of '42 than it is today.[2] The Boston and Maine railroad had passenger connections in both directions, and bus service was also available to carry one away from the grey existence of camp. The restrictions on pleasure driving notwithstanding, the more adventurous could always resort to hitchhiking, accepting the calculated risk that any kindly motorist could turn into an indignant patriot upon discovering why the beneficiary of the highway hospitality was not in uniform. Even so, news of a dance somewhere in the vicinity, the opportunity to visit friends or relatives, or simply the compulsion to break the awful monotony made that risk of inconvenience and unpleasantness worth the taking.

Most campers had come from greater distances and were obliged to spend their weekends in camp, only occasionally savoring the excitement of a day's foray to Concord in the "White Ghost," the camp's panel truck. Assuming it was not dismantled for emergency repairs to put it into shape for the next Sunday's trip to church in Contoocook, this erratic vehicle could accommodate a number of excursionists on its regular trips to obtain provisions or transport recent

arrivals to their required induction examinations, inoculations and the like. This usually required some reason—the opportunity to shop for personal necessities or a desire to go to confession—but it was generally acknowledged that the real reason in most cases was simply to have a brief respite on the town.

In the six months of my stay at Warner, I recall making two or three such trips to Concord and one weekend visit to Boston. Others managed to get away more often, at least until the work week was extended to include the full eight-hour Saturday. Since project work depended on the state of the weather, a bad Saturday morning was the fervent wish of all who had liberty plans. When fate frowned and clear skies denied them their early start, they went out on project with street clothes under their working garb so that they might shed these outer garments in the truck and jump off as it passed through town on the way back to camp.

Work records reveal that the effect of the extended week on the leave/liberty pattern was dramatic. The two months of November and December, when the forty-four-hour week was still in force, show 17 percent of the camp personnel away on the average Sunday; the months of January and February saw this drop to 7 percent. Severe

weather played a part in the decline, but it is clear that the camp's
isolation was the major factor. (Another contributing element was
the campers' financial limitations which made a one-day leave much
harder to justify than a full weekend leave might have been.) Even
the Canory Express was forced to operate on a greatly reduced schedule, though this would have resulted anyway because of the increased
restrictions on pleasure driving.

It is time now to turn to a more extended discussion of the work
project itself. The reader is asked again to remember that CPS was instituted as a program of "work of national importance under civilian
direction." The preceding chapter established that the actuality fell
far short of the description as far as the civilian direction part was
concerned. Now we shall see that the claim to national importance
was equally fraudulent and misleading.

Like Stoddard before it, Warner was a forestry camp. The task assigned to it was clearing away the effects of a major hurricane that had
devastated the New England area a few years before. Dead trees and
leaners were to be felled and cut into cordwood. (Most of this cord-
age was intended for camp use, but was left in the woods, neatly
stacked and destined to rot away after the camp was closed.) At
Stoddard there had been some seasonal variation in the task and there
were times spent in seedling planting, waterhole digging, or firelane
clearing, but the Warner project was destined to come to an end before such variety of tasks could be introduced.

The expected quota of one stacked cord of wood each day for
each four-man crew was a production goal rarely, if ever, approx-
imated by even the more dedicated and cooperative campers. The
majority of the men distinguished themselves by their ridiculously
low levels, qualitative as well as quantitative, of production. The reasons for this poor record are not hard to find. Except for Bob
Dunfey, the one authentic Maine woodchopper in the crowd, and a
few others who had come to camp from a rural background, none of
the campers had previous experience with the kind of work expected
of them or with the tools they were supposed to use. Thus, though
the quota presumably made allowance for this inexperience, it is
doubtful that the true level of inefficiency could be imagined, much
less anticipated. Since these were the men who, after a few weeks of
experience on project, were given the responsibility for instructing
later newcomers in the techniques of woodsmanship, it was inevitable that the over-all efficiency would show a steady decline as the

months went on. Back-handed recognition of this situation may be inferrred from a letter written by the camp director to NSBRO headquarters commenting favorably on the attempts of a new government foreman to hold instructional sessions with some of the campers. As the director put it, educational efforts of this type were "absolutely necessary to break down the city man's prejudice against manual labor and his lack of understanding of the farmers' and woodsman's needs."

Ignoring the less than charitable assessment of the "city man" and his attitudes toward work, Larrowe's basic point was valid enough. The great majority of campers did indeed come from an urban background and were neither qualified for, nor particularly interested in, this "work of national importance" thrust upon them. In retrospect, we must have presented a comic sight, stumbling our way into the woods in a strange assortment of work outfits (assembled largely from donated items in the camp's clothing grab bag*) and loaded down with unfamiliar gear much of which would be lost, in spite of the foreman's repeated warnings against setting tools down where they might sink into the snow and out of sight until the following spring.

My own first day of project work provides dramatic illustration of the perils of incompetence. I had welcomed assignment to the project crew as an escape from those voluntary orientation-period chores of preparing chicken feed and sorting out rotten potatoes. The anticipation was heightened by the invitation to join the work crew of Alvin Manton, one of the camp intellectuals and a man who shared my almost obsessive admiration of the writings of Thomas Wolfe. As one of the more experienced campers, Alvin undertook to give me a few useful pointers about the best way to use an axe, how to notch a tree for a good fall, the proper rhythm to maintain on the two-man cross-cut saw, and the relative ease of splitting the various types of wood, as well as how to recognize them. It was this latter lesson that would be fixed indelibly in my mind. Maple, he informed

* The grab bag consisted of the clothing donated by readers and friends of the *Catholic Worker*. In my own case, having come to camp with no clothing suited for forestry work or the New Hampshire climate, I was fortunate enough to find a fleece-lined woman's coat left behind by a "pleasantly buxom" (Miss Day's description) young lady who had helped out for a time as assistant to Stoddard's volunteer cook. Serviceable despite its quaintness, wearing it made me the object of much camp humor as "the ghost of Polly."

me, was a delight to split but difficult to chop; special care was required in the winter since the hardened sap made the trunk so hard that an axe might easily bounce off at considerable hazard to its wielder. Whereupon he selected a maple of modest size and gave his axe a mighty swing. As he warned, it did indeed glance off, cutting deeply into his foot.* So graphic an example of "teaching by doing," however unintended, made its point with the result that I became one of the most cautious of the Warner woodsmen from that time forward. In all honesty, I must confess that I was also, though only partly for that reason, one of the less productive as well.

But it was not simple inexperience, excessive caution, or failings in manual dexterity that accounted for the abysmally poor production record of the Warner camp. The real explanation lay in the prevailing patterns of work evasion, patterns every newcomer learned to respect and adopt as his own even before he learned to recognize and use the woodsman's tools. Not everyone shirked his duties completely, though a few did. Similarly, not everyone goofed-off, but most did to some extent. The frequently sounded cry of "Timber!" was not a sign of industrious activity but, rather, the signal that the government supervisory personnel were somewhere nearby. Hearing that call, men who had been standing around in friendly discussion or debate, or had wandered off to do a bit of sketching, or had stretched out to take a little nap would now go through the motions of work, only to resume their preferred inactivities once the supervisor or his foremen had passed out of sight.

It is unlikely that these latter were ignorant of what was going on; the ever-so-slow accumulation of stacked cordwood was damning evidence enough. The very half-heartedness of their occasional complaints might be taken as recognition on their part of the essential

---

*My first day on the Warner project was also Manton's last. After a short stay in a Concord hospital he was transferred to the camp infirmary. Whether it is evidence of the inadequacy of the medical care provided there or not, he was soon back in the city hospital under treatment for pneumonia. Following recovery and recuperation, he was transferred to a special service unit in North Carolina. Predictably enough, it is for this accident that Manton is best remembered. One former camper writes, "He could really wield an axe—put him in the hospital." Another suggests he "should never have been permitted to handle an axe." This latter is a somewhat ironic note since Alvin had established himself as one of the better workers at Stoddard. In another sense, though, that latter judgment could have been applied to all of the men on project at Shadow Hill that day or in the days that were to follow.

unimportance of the work. The superintendent's major concern with respect to work production, apart from the need to justify his own employment and that of his two foremen, was that the campers were not producing enough cordwood to keep themselves from freezing in the cold weeks he knew were yet to come. He need not have worried too much about that. The camp would be closed before the supply of wood transported from Stoddard was exhausted.

This widespread malingering was not motivated by laziness alone or even primarily. It was, instead, a principled malingering, in effect, a statement of an ideologically based objection to this specific work project and, for many, to the CPS program itself. Dean Farfether put the case in an article in *Salt*. "Since most of the work is either long-time forestry or soil conservation work and could be done by 'a healthy moron,' he [the CO] feels that his talents, his training, and the needs of the present are being horribly neglected. CPS appears more as an isolated detention camp than as any genuine Selective Service." The overtones of snobbery are unfortunate, but the criticism is no less valid. Even if the superintendent's concern is seen as realistic and compassionate, and it was probably both, any program that finds its justification in having fifty or so healthy and relatively well-educated men engaged in nothing more substantial than cutting enough wood to keep themselves warm scarcely merits classification as work of national importance.

More serious than the squandering of talent was the deleterious effect the double dishonesty—that is, the obvious unimportance of the work and the patterns of evasion—must have had upon the morale of men whose idealistic commitment had brought them into the program in the first place. The Selmon diary provides an unintended and somewhat amusing illustration. Early in his Stoddard experience, George recorded his personal disapproval of the failure of some of his fellow campers to live up to what he felt was a moral obligation to perform an honest day's work. By the time he gets to Warner, however, he is noting, "I worked with the Luzon brothers as a crew, and we fiddled about most of the day, creating our own skits of foremen, jobs, tree-cutting, and Work of National Importance—all parodies."

No parody could be quite as devastating as the cold, hard figures. The 143 days between the camp's official opening (October 27, 1942) and its rather inglorious end (March 18, 1943) represented, on paper at least, a gross total of more than 8,500 man-days of alternative service. The several categories of sick status accounted for just under

1,200; and another 900 were lost to inclement weather. Fully a quarter of the total was taken up by leaves, furloughs, orientation time, and, in a few instances, disciplinary entries (absence without leave or, more rarely, refusal to work).

This leaves about 4,200 man-days devoted to actual work assignments. But even this figure is misleading. The greater proportion of these were taken up by camp operations details: clerical and administrative duties, kitchen and maintenance crews, and the like. In actual fact, then, less than 1,500 of that gross total of 8,500 man-days were spent on project, an average of ten men for every day the camp was officially in existence. And this time, as we have seen, was largely frittered away.

This does not mean, of course, that the actual project work force was ever that small. It is here that the weather factor played its part. It was the practice not to work in the woods if the temperature fell below the zero mark or if enough snow or rain fell to make the axe handles wet and slippery. I do not know whether this policy reflected established forestry regulations or was an ad hoc concession to the patent inefficiency of this particular assortment of woodsmen. I seem to recall that there were several days of sub-zero or otherwise inclement weather when the trucks did roll on schedule. Be that as it may, complete work weeks that winter were rare. More than a third of what should have been project time found the forestry detail excused from work and left pretty much to their own devices. One stretch showed ten successive workdays cancelled by weather conditions; counting the intervening weekends and holidays, this meant that no one went out on project between noon of December 26 and the morning of January 8! There followed a week in which the crews were able to return to Shadow Hill, but the New Hampshire weather intervened again with another nine-day layoff from January 14 to 23.

Workdays lost when the project trip was cancelled altogether is only part of the story. There are no records of the delayed departures while waiting for the weather to clear or early returns to camp when it turned inclement after the men had arrived at the project site. It goes without saying that the men on the project crew who benefitted from such weather cancellations were not at all displeased by the reduced opportunity to engage in their work of national importance. The situation did make for some tension in camp, however. The men who held the various indoor administrative and operational jobs resented being obliged to continue typing, cooking, baking, or mopping, while the reprieved lolled about in their bunks, read, sketched, or just did nothing at all. The frequent appeals for voluntary assistance on special housekeeping details that were issued periodically by the camp director had limited success at best. Only those campers most closely aligned to the camp administration and the ACCO were likely to come forward in answer to the call. The others — the chronic malcontents, the noncooperators, and, of course, the simply lazy — stayed at ease or made themselves scarce.

The latter did not find it at all difficult to rationalize their unwillingness to share the camp burdens. As they saw it, the men with the in-camp assignments had volunteered for them because they considered these jobs desirable, which, in fact, they were. Now that the ball had bounced the other way, in favor of those who had to go forth and face the daily discomforts of project work and the perils of the ride there and back, they saw no good reason not to fully enjoy the unanticipated "better" that came along with the expected "bitter."

The argument from fairness, then, worked both ways and, in the process, placed yet another strain upon the already stricken state of camp morale. The situation was worsened rather than improved when Director Larrowe decided to make an issue of camp authority and discipline by assigning the full project complement to special detail duty on two of these so-called weather days. Few could deny that the general housecleaning he ordered to keep the whole camp occupied was needed, but the resulting improvement in neatness and cleanliness of the bunkhouses and utility areas was probably not enough to balance the intense resentment his arbitrary work edict provoked. Surely it is significant that this single episode of authoritarian display remains so vivid in the memories of many of the men who were involved. One former Warnerite, asked for his remembered impression of the camp director, writes, ". . . to me he represented 'Catholic Quakerism'—the second-mile business to which I was opposed. I remember once he assigned me to cleaning out a latrine and came around to inspect it and pointed out minute spots which I had missed in the cleaning." This respondent is not the only one to still resent having been obliged to perform "made work," putting in time dusting window sills and roof beams for no other reason than to keep the men busy during the normal work hours and away from the activities they considered more satisfying and much more meaningful.

Perhaps, when we consider that for the 143 days of the camp's recorded existence only the period from November 9 through

March 6 represented days that could have been available for project work (weather notwithstanding), the question of whether or not the Warner project could be considered work of national importance is of little moment. Before the earlier date all personnel were involved in getting the new camp into operation; after the later date, all were engaged in preparing for shutting it down. It could be argued, then, that Camp Simon in its Warner phase never reached the state of viability. Had it endured and become more firmly established, it is possible the record of work performance might have become more impressive. After all, it can be argued that other camps in the CPS system did not have Warner's problems, or at least not to the same degree.

This is probably true. Warner *was* different, and this conclusion can be extended to include the Stoddard phase as well. But Warner's brief history counts among the most tumultuous of all the camps. Its problems became a continuing source of urgent concern, not only for the ACCO and the NSBRO but, much more troubling for the latter, for the Selective Service officials with whom that agency had to deal. It is this very difference, I submit, that provides much of the justification for this study.

While acknowledging these differences, however, it would be a serious error to dismiss the Camp Simon experience as so unique that it cannot serve the broader purpose of assessing the over-all merits and demerits of CPS as an alternative service program. On the contrary, it can serve as the extreme case that most clearly illuminates the essential failings of the whole. This is of no small value if only as a corrective to the easy willingness of many to look back and take CPS at its face value. Too many are too inclined to judge the program favorably as an acceptable, even laudable, expression of democratic respect for the rights of a dissident minority in time of war. The Camp Simon experience argues it was not.

None of which is to deny the contributions of men in other camps where something more lasting was accomplished than a few uneven and incomplete stacks of cordwood haphazardly scattered along the slopes of Shadow Hill. There were camps where dedication and morale were high and probably few, if any, where they were as low as at Warner. The Mennonite camps, it was generally taken for granted, were filled with men earnestly committed to a witness of labor under the Biblical "double yoke." These, it is well to remember, accounted for the majority of men assigned to CPS. On a strictly numerical basis at least, it was the willing cooperators, not the disgruntled men of Warner, who were most truly representative of the men inducted into alternative service.

How much of this is stereotype and how much truth is difficult to establish at this remove in time. The men of Warner had the same general impression of the Brethren-operated camps, dismissing them as hotbeds of "200-percenter" enthusiasm. William E. Stafford's moving volume of CPS reminiscences[3] suggests this may not have been entirely true. Stafford tells of a fellow camper's decision to leave CPS for reasons that reveal a measure of disaffection strikingly similar, even in the terms employed, to that expressed by the severest of Warner's critics. As Stafford's friend put it in a letter to the Attorney General, CPS was "a precedent for slave labor, not a place for constructive service in crucial times, a dictatorial program administered, in spite of the wording of the law, by military men." To which most of the men of Warner, had they known of it, would have added their hearty "Amen."

Few would insist that the eight million man-days of work in CPS constituted a *total* waste of talent and human effort. Even in the camp setting, one must assume that many usable ditches were dug, firelanes cleared, forests replanted, farmland conserved and restored. Certainly much of the service performed by men in mental hospital and training school units, as experimental guinea pigs, and in other more exotic special assignments did approach the ideal of "work of national importance." Having granted this much, however, one must also say that all of these worthwhile accomplishments taken together represented an extremely small portion of the whole, and that the whole fell far short of meeting that description.

Even Director Larrowe, a man honestly disposed to see CPS in its most favorable light, was not entirely oblivious to the merit in the objections raised by his Warner rebels. In *Salt*'s second issue, he had written:

So we are doing this forest work—work which will be of great benefit to future generations. But there are other works, perhaps more immediately important to do. There are the broken victims of the war itself—there are the millions in Europe and Asia who need food, clothing, shelter—there are the evacuated Japanese in California who need homes and work—there are the sharecroppers of the South who still need help. There are innumerable works of mercy to be done, works of justice really, since the suffering is the result of injustice right

here at home. Sometimes we would rather be doing these works than chopping
trees.

"Sometimes" is an understatement. It should be possible, even now,
to empathize with the acute sense of frustration experienced by men,
college graduates and qualified teachers among them, who were required to spend their days trimming branches off trees that had fall-
en years before, while at the same time schools were being closed for
lack of teachers. So great a disparity between the truly important
services they could have performed and the patently unimportant
work they were asked to do in the woods of New Hampshire was not
at all conducive to a spirit of high dedication or morale.

Such frustration reinforced the alienation between men in the
camps and the pacifist leadership. Rightly or wrongly, the men held
them responsible for the inadequacies of the work program, just as
they held them responsible for maintaining the illusion that it was
being performed "under civilian direction." This was not altogether
fair. It is true that consistent efforts were made throughout the war
by the NSBRO and the religious sponsoring agencies to open new and
more significant work opportunities. That these efforts were, at best,
only marginally successful was not their fault, even though much of
the resulting criticism would be directed at them. On the other hand,
the pacifist leaders did bear some responsibility for this scandalous
waste of talent and effort. The inadequate work program was itself a
function of their prior failure to insist upon full authority over a program which they had invested in so heavily with financial resources
and, more important still, with the prestige and respect they enjoyed
in the eyes of the men who would be called into service.

From the standpoint of the military men at Selective Service headquarters, the CPS program was more of a success. They began with
their own idea of what CPS should be, and it was this idea that prevailed. Not all would have put it so crudely as did a certain Colonel
McLean when he declared, "There is no obligation to provide an assignee with work for which he has been particularly prepared, wishes
to do, or regards as socially significant."[4] Nevertheless one published
study reveals how firmly this principle was applied: of the 55 percent
of the men in AFSC camps who had professional training before entering CPS, 60 percent were employed as unskilled labor; another 30
percent had had skilled training, but 61 percent of this group, too,
was assigned to unskilled tasks.[5] However gratifying the fact that

more significant detached service opportunities were ultimately approved, it remains true (again, the source is Wittner) that of the approximately twelve thousand men assigned to CPS, those much praised guinea pig projects involved no more than five hundred and the number of men assigned to hospital or training school units was only about two thousand in all. The McLean statement, confirmed by this pattern of actual work assignments, lends unquestionable validity to Dean Farfether's charge that "CPS appears more as an isolated detention camp than as any genuine Selective Service."

For explicit confirmation of that charge we can turn to a more auspicious source—General Hershey himself. In the course of one of his many appearances before a congressional committee, the Director of Selective Service said, ". . . the conscientious objector, by my theory, is best handled if no one hears of him."[6] A camp like Warner, situated well away from population centers, with its men isolated and segregated from community contacts as much as possible, was ideally suited to the Hershey theory. Subsequent locations selected for CPS work projects, including the Trenton camp to which many of the Warner men would be sent before "the duration plus six months" came to its end, remained true to those specifications.

From his standpoint the general's theory was eminently sound. The scandalous waste of valuable talent was a minor liability in the calculations of this military bureaucrat when measured against the risk of poor public relations or against the remote threat to the national war morale that COs in more visible circulation might have presented. Even later in the program when, in response to agitation in the camps coupled with the acute crisis of personnel shortages throughout the nation, detached service and assignments to special hospital units and the like became more frequent, the men selected knew that any activity that would bring them to public notice could mean their speedy return to the camp setting. For them the ever-present threat of reassignment was the rock upon which all discipline rested.

And it worked. As the camps were moved farther away from the populous East and Midwest regions from which so many of the men had come, the limited availability of special service opportunities became an important factor in maintaining camp discipline as well. Troublemakers could be fairly sure these desirable options were closed to them. Thus, the opportunity to perform work of national importance, ostensibly the standard to which the entire CPS program was keyed, became instead the heart of Selective Service's sanction system, a reward for the well-behaved and a privilege to be taken away if one did not conform.

It is almost too much to speak of these as concentration camps in a world and at a time when that term assumed dimensions of special horror. Yet that is what they were. More to the point, that is what the military officers of the Selective Service System intended them to be. No matter how liberal the regulations or how relaxed the discipline, the first priority was to gather these potentially troublesome conscientious objectors into isolated work camps, safely out of sight and mind. If the work project to which they were assigned produced something of lasting value, well and good. If not—and this was certainly the case at Stoddard and Warner—that, too, was well and good. Such men, like Cassius, with their lean and hungry look were considered dangerous to the war-supporting consensus simply because they thought too much.

There were no brutal guards, no barbed wire, no dogs, no gas chambers. The men in CPS had it good compared to those unfortunates elsewhere in the world to whom the same pragmatic principle was being applied by the people in power. Even the absence of stringent work requirements (an easy concession to make since the work was unimportant anyway) served a purpose if only by reinforcing the image of democratic restraint in dealing with a deviant few. True, some of the civilian employees assigned to the work project might occasionally express their displeasure over being obliged to supervise a "bunch of yellow bastards." Stafford cites examples of one superintendent who patrolled the camp area after dark carrying a shotgun and of another threatening a camper with a pistol, and tells of a Forestry Service employee who was overheard saying, "I wish I was superintendent of that camp; I'd line 'em up and uh-uh-uh . . . "—making the sounds of a machine gun.[7] Such sentiments, one suspects, were not unusual among foremen and other government employees and were probably expressed more freely among themselves than their charges realized at the time.

Certainly the government staff at Warner gave no evidence of similar hostility. The project superintendent, a rotund, fatherly type, limited himself to periodic pleas to the camp director for assistance in persuading the men to improve production levels; and one foreman, newly arrived, aggravated some of the men for a time by his insistence on a full day's work on project detail. But neither effort came to much, and things went on as they always had. Whatever uncomplimentary opinions the superintendent and his foreman may have held in private, their relationships with the men of Camp Simon were reserved, even friendly, when compared with the attitudes abroad in the land concerning conscientious objectors.

Perhaps a little overt persecution would have strengthened the morale of the men in the camps. At the very least, it would have lessened the sense of utter futility that haunted their days. Alienated from the social surroundings they had known, buried in the planned obscurity and isolation of the camp setting and, most depressing of all, at odds with their own pacifist leaders, they were denied the satisfaction of knowing that the work they were required to perform would serve as a fitting and lasting witness to their rejection of war. Everything, or so it seemed then, added up to nothing as day followed day in a grey succession with no end in sight. Harsh treatment at the hands of their keepers would have meant that someone thought enough of them and their witness to resent both. This, I admit, is a dubious proposition, especially when offered from the safe perspective of the present day, but it is an intriguing possibility nonetheless.

When the war finally came to its end, Stafford's friend greeted the news with an observation that, once again, would have encountered little or no disagreement on the part of the men of Camp Simon. "In the army," Stafford remembers his saying, "the best men think they should be in the army; but in Civilian Public Service the best men know they should be somewhere else—somewhere doing something more important than Forest Service work, at a time like this. What can we say, when, as in the cartoon, our children say, 'Daddy, what did you do to win the peace?' "[8]

This was not too comforting a thought for men, most of whom could look back on years of sacrifice and witness. For all the good intentions and high purpose with which the alternative service program was conceived, it ended up as a cruel double deception. Instead of the "work of national importance under civilian direction" provided for by men committed to the ideals of religious pacifism, it was allowed to degenerate into a punitive program performing work of little or no real importance, imposed by and conducted under de facto military authority. No doubt some good came out of it, but that good was accomplished in spite of, not because of, a shameful experiment in the management of dissent that must never be repeated.

5   *The Men: A Group Portrait*

It is no small challenge to reach back over more than three decades
and try to remember seventy or more men with whom one shared a
few months of communal existence; yet it is astonishing how easily
most of them come to mind and with what sharp detail. In many
cases, of course, the associations begun at Warner continued in the
other camps and units to which we were assigned after the camp
closed. In a few instances this extended into regular or at least occasional contact once our days in CPS were past. Even where these
special circumstances do not apply, however, and the association was
limited to the Camp Simon experiences, it is not at all difficult to
attach some remembered impression to the names listed on the camp
roster.

I discovered that I was not the only one for whom this was true.
To this point my account of the Camp Simon story has been based
on my personal reflections and reminiscences, supplemented by
whatever records or documentary material I could find. This will be
the basic perspective of this and the following chapters as well, and
the reader is advised to make allowance for the fact that the description and interpretation of events will always be colored by my subjective preferences and personal orientation to the camp situation
and the problems and controversies that developed. But the impressions of the men themselves, singly or as a group, have been supplemented and, to a surprising extent, duplicated by the recollections of
other former campers as well.

It was obvious that any reconstruction of the social history of the

Warner camp would require locating others who could provide a more representative range of supplemental perspectives and recollections. Equally obvious was the difficulty, if not hopelessness, of the attempt to trace so widely scattered an assortment of individuals, not even taking into account the possibility that many might not wish to reawaken the memories of a generally unhappy situation. Over the years I had kept in fairly regular contact with about a half-dozen former Warnerites, and these were to serve as the nucleus of my informant group. With the additional addresses they were able to provide of other former campers with whom they had maintained contact and repeating the process with the men thus located, it was ultimately possible to locate thirty-six of the men ever assigned to the Warner camp.

The next step was to send each the complete roster with the request that he provide his remembered impressions of each individual listed. In addition, four open-ended questions were included at the end of the list requesting information about the post-CPS life of the respondent himself and his retrospective evaluation of the CPS experience. As might be expected, not all of the thirty-six replied, and three who did begged off with explanations of their unwillingness to comply. Two claimed too brief a stay in camp (one had been in camp for only a few days), and the third, preferring not to specify his individual recollections, chose to limit his response to general impressions instead.

Altogether there were twenty-six responses, and this represented about a third of the total Warner roster. Several of the returned questionnaires were not very complete, but a surprising number of the respondents were able to recall the majority of the individuals listed and could often add anecdotes or specific experiences to bring them into sharper focus. Some of the responses were so complete and detailed that any one might well have served as the sole source of these remembered impressions.

Leonard Mattano's description of Henry Fallon, for example, is a model of character perception.

Hard worker always. I came to like him—a practical man in every way. He sure could get a motor going, no matter what ailed it. He was a plain man but had grit. Once he was thumbing his way to a dentist and a man gave him a lift, then was going to kick him out of the car when he found out he was a CO because his son was in the army. When Hank told him his son would never be killed by a German or Japanese who thought like he did, the man drove him to the dentist's office.

George Selmon, our diarist, captures the quintessential Dean Farfether in three quick sentences: "Scholarly, objective, glib and with pronounced qualities of leadership. Yet somewhat socially brittle and remote. In the face of personal crisis I found him paradoxically squeamish." And a final example finds William Grandman, whose recollections were consistently illuminating and delightfully subjective, accomplishing the same for the noisy Bill O'Flaherty: "He came into camp quietly enough, then 'exploded' within a day or two with his strong, colorful opinions of everything: Tojo, Mussolini, Hershey, Kosch, etc., etc. Needling, irreverent, voluble, joshing—he must have been sent from New York State [his home] to avoid war with Canada."

Not all the recollections were suffused with sweetness and light. Lowell Bartlett (in a neat confirmation of Lou Swanson's characterization of *him* as a "sweet, old cormudgeon, crusty and opinionated") dismissed one of the more committed members of Camp Simon's Coughlinite bloc as "an authoritarian person, a polite fascist, a biblical fundamentalist. I couldn't stand him, so my remarks are prejudiced."

Individual thumbnail sketches such as these will form the basis of the next chapter with its concentration on the various interest groups and factions that dominated the Warner scene. It is significant to note at this point, however, that all but four of the seventy-five men listed on the complete Warner roster were remembered by at least fifteen of those who responded to my questionnaire and no less than fifty were remembered by twenty or more of those respondents. Therefore, even though the descriptions and discussion to follow reflect my own recollections, these supplemental responses may be taken as a strong measure of confirmation of their accuracy or, in those cases where agreement is lacking, as a means of modifying or correcting them.

Fifteen of my twenty-six respondents had been at the Warner camp for its entire period of existence; these will constitute something of a core validating group. The other eleven either arrived after the camp opened, left for other assignments (in one instance leaving CPS to join the Navy), or received physical discharges before the camp was closed. Their responses will be used to elaborate upon the recollections of the core informants and to provide particular insights or anecdotes. The high level of agreement in the responses in almost every case should lend the promise of reliability to composite characterizations and descriptions based on them.

A more objective source of data concerning the social backgrounds of the men assigned to Camp Simon is material taken from the NSBRO personnel files on deposit at the Jane Addams Peace Library of Swarthmore College. As noted in the Introduction, these files contain the forms completed by each individual at the time of his registration and induction, and the complete record of his CPS history. Correspondence or other reports relating to special problems or events involving the individual camper and contained in these files provided other valuable information in certain cases.

The Known and the Unknown

There were only four names on the Warner roster that were not remembered by at least ten of the respondents to my questionnaire. One was remembered by no one at all, but this is not too surprising because this individual arrived in camp one day and left the next. In spite of the fact that he had requested reassignment to I-A status before he was to be inducted into CPS, for some reason or other his local draft board decided to keep his IV-E classification in force. As a result, although he was listed on the Warner roster for some time, none of the time between his arrival/departure and his induction into military service four months later was spent in camp.

Essentially the same situation applied for the second unknown, Paul Fitzgerald, but his is a more interesting case in several respects. He, too, had requested reclassification (but to noncombatant I-A-O service) and was ordered to report to Warner instead. He remained in camp for a matter of weeks before returning home to await orders to report for military service. The camp records list him as AWOL for that period, but this was merely a technicality and not, as one might be led to assume, a punitive measure on the part of the camp administration. That Fitzgerald was remembered by five of my respondents is probably due to his background as a former member of the Catholic Worker staff. Of even greater significance, he had been one of the original organizers of the PAX study group out of which ACCO was formed.

His history furnishes a revealing illustration of the problems a

Catholic could encounter in his effort to win the CO classification from a reluctant draft board. Fitzgerald was originally classified IV-F (unavailable for military service because of physical incapacity) because of a bone ailment; he was then given a second examination, consisting entirely of a Wasserman blood test, and reclassified IV-E. At this point he requested the change to I-A-O status, but that was denied and he was ordered to report to Warner. In a letter to General Hershey, a copy of which is in his file, he wrote:

It is my opinion that the hostility stems from one member, the Chairman, who at my hearing as a CO was very much concerned that one of his religious persuasion, Roman Catholic, should hold such views and went to great lengths to question me on theological matters in which I happened to be better versed than he, having been editor of Catholic papers for some time. His confusion so angered him that he elected to so insult me that I was forced to appeal to the other members, knowing that any display of anger on my part would prejudice my case.

The fitting and quite predictable conclusion to the story is that when he finally was called up for induction into the armed forces, he was rejected for reasons of physical disability. This may, in fact, have been what he had in mind when he requested reclassification. It may also have been the reason why his request was denied; the draft board, too, must have known that, although the same standards were supposed to be applied, it was much more unlikely that a man would be rejected on physical grounds for CPS than for any branch of the military service.

Fitzgerald's brief stay in camp was not an easy time for him. In answer to my request for information, he described the strain he was under there. "I had already applied for a change of status before being assigned to Warner. Of course that was no easy decision. I remember I wept for the first time in my life when I finally came to a conclusion. So my few weeks at Warner were a waiting period, and I really didn't enter into the spirit fully, especially as I sometimes felt like a traitor." Presumably he felt traitorous to the men and his own ideals, but not to the nation as so many others, including his draft board, may have thought he should.

The third unknown was characterized only as "quiet" by the two former campers who thought they could vaguely remember him. And quiet he must certainly have been! This man, a twenty-six-year old Catholic from Philadelphia, spent two full months at Warner, moved with the men to the Oakland camp when Warner was closed, and then moved on to the Trenton camp as well. It is remarkable indeed that he was able to spend six months in this company without leaving more of a mark, especially since some of the men who had no recollection of him at all had followed the same route as he.

The last of the four was a man who never should have been sent to camp at all and, once there, had very little contact with the others. One who did remember him characterized him as "he of the constant chill factor. . . . Sad/watery-eyed, with wool blanket wrapped always around his shoulders, waiting, waiting, waiting for his discharge papers." One of the older (thirty-two years) assignees, this man was on the sick list for seventy-three of the seventy-four days between his arrival at Stoddard and the happy day—for his fellow campers almost as much as for himself—when the waiting finally ended and his discharge came through. The six who were able to identify his name had mixed impressions of his condition: one questioned his sincerity as a CO, attributing his presence in camp to the local board's inability to fit him anywhere else under the draft; two others were convinced of his "wretched state of health"; another describes him as "a very maladjusted man," and adds the question, "Was he a true psychotic, or was it all an act?"

At the other extreme of the recognition scale are four campers who were remembered by everyone who returned the questionnaire. Leonard Mattano, already introduced as one of the men who made a particularly strong first impression on me, is clearly the star among these stars. The characterizations, all favorable, include such descriptions as "the most vivid and strongest personality in camp"; "one of the giants on the Warner landscape"; "deservedly one of the best-liked men in camp—what can I add to what you know?" The memory of Leonard's imposing figure and personality leaves one former admirer wondering "if much of his 'old West' manner of style and dress was mostly put-on *or* nostalgia *or* overexposure to Remington paintings *or* reincarnation of an 1850 frontiersman." As the most prominent of the camp artists, Mattano is also remembered as premier storyteller, Civil War buff, and a thoroughly compassionate man. In a touch that says much of both men, Hank Fallon recalls, "I remember one time he insisted on giving me 80¢ to spend when I didn't have any money. And he was the kind of fellow you could accept it from." A practicing Catholic but not too deeply involved in the religious life of the camp, Mattano kept himself aloof from most of the controversies that marked Warner's history. At the same time, he accounted for a goodly number of them himself as one of the principal instigators of the periodic binges that fueled the recurrent demands for more and stronger camp discipline.

A second camper who enjoyed universal recognition was George Selmon, the indefatigable diarist whose insights have already been cited in these pages. He, too, was an artist and had been closely associated with Mattano in their pre-CPS days at college. Selmon earns favorable comment as "hard worker," "good company," "warm, sentimental guy" and as a man able to put people at their ease. He was "our amateur farmer"—not a small matter; as the man in charge of raising (and killing) the chickens, he was responsible for providing the one meal each week worth waiting for. As the only Jew on the roster, he was "the odd one for a Catholic camp" and, to another respondent, "the human litmus test for the anti-Semitism of Pat Rafferty who seemed really confused by George." The observation is cogent. In *his* response to my questionnaire, this devoted disciple of Father Coughlin recalls Selmon as someone he "came to like, " especially after the war when what Pat refers to as "the remnant" gathered in Greenwich Village for drinks and talk. Litmus test or not, Pat would have had to tolerate Selmon to maintain his own close friendship with Mattano. Even so, the fact that he came to like him was significant.

If Mattano is remembered in tones approaching reverence, Louis Swanson joins this select company as something of a fun figure. Once again, the comments have a consistency approaching unanimity: "always fun to be around"; "pleasant, cooperative"; "cheerful"; "good sense of humor"; "good humor and charm"; "he enjoyed smiling"; "easily the most personable of all the people listed—bright, talented, brilliantly humorous." To one of the non-Catholics Swanson was the kind of man who "could sell Catholicism to a confirmed atheist . . . he radiated positivity and good will, was profound in his thinking, could charm the skin off an alligator." This paragon in the eyes of his fellows, a twenty-four-year-old former seminarian, was one of the stalwarts of the chapel group and a steady supporter and defender of the constantly beleaguered camp administration. As a volunteer camp cook he bore a major share of the responsibility for the dietary and culinary deficiencies that sparked some of the more disruptive camp protests, but even this could not diminish his popularity. If anything, the reverse was true. Lou's good nature and popularity may have kept the ever-explosive food crisis within manageable bounds by providing exactly the right touch of humor when disaster threatened or, as was the case in too many of the Warner meals, became an accomplished fact.

The fourth camper remembered by everyone was something of a surprise. Ray Murphy was not as much of a central, or visible, character as the other three, though he was always somewhere on the scene when things were stirring. Possibly because of this, the consistency of attitudes and descriptions relating to him is nowhere nearly as pronounced. Some remember him for his physical appearance: "big," "tall," "handsome," "Rock Hudsonish." The descriptions fit; this impressively built "black Irishman" may well have been the handsomest man in camp. Others were impressed more by a subtle wit which made him, for one respondent at least, "the epitome of Irish humor and hospitality." Still others put their recollections of Ray in a religious context, recalling his orthodox Catholicism and identifying him as a firm supporter of the ACCO administration. Again, both are true but only within limits. He was certainly orthodox, but he was not as rigorist in his views as that term was generally meant to imply. And as far as his attitude toward the camp authorities is concerned,

the pattern was mixed. He took an almost fiendish delight in deflating the pretentiousness of the protests, manifestoes, strike threats, and the like that were always circulating—and that of their initiators as well—and he could be counted on to oppose any action that threatened to undermine the Catholic character of the camp. At the same time, he was sharply critical of the basic injustices of the CPS program and Selective Service's restrictive policies and procedures.

Genuine independence and a scathing tongue combined to make Murphy an unpredictable quantity in any controversy that did not endanger the camp's existence as a corporate witness. This combination probably explains the occasional unfavorable note that enters a few of the recollections, describing him as "proud" or "a member of the crowd." One former camper who apparently had experienced the sharpness of Ray's needle dismisses him as "critical of me, interested in himself." "Another Irishman who was always trying to beat the CPS work game," writes another. The characterization Ray would appreciate most, I suspect, is the one which sees him as "Big, handsome. . . . Quite a character. . . . Would have made a good 'con' man."

Social Backgrounds

The preferred sociological approach for describing so varied a group as this would be to undertake an intensive analysis in terms of social background characteristics measured and weighted to reveal why they, and not others, decided to take their deviant stand in face of the almost complete national consensus in support of the war. This is not, I fear, possible in this instance. It should be obvious, first of all, that the Warner population, everyone included, was too small to yield any promise of significance for whatever statistical measurements or comparisons one might hope to make. Even were this not the case, however, we would still have to question how useful or reliable such findings can be in explaining what had to be essentially a *personal* moral decision unique to each man. The most we can hope for is to uncover some similarities and differences in backgrounds that might highlight possible factors contributing to such decisions or making them more probable, even though this cannot be done with the degree of confidence sociological scholarship would ordinarily demand. There is the very real possibility that such efforts to reduce their social background characteristics to a more precise analysis and explanation might obscure the more meaningful impressions that are to be gained at the level of simple description and recollection alone.

The reader who seeks a closer approximation to such analysis may find it in the breakdown and summary of the data obtained from the Swarthmore files provided in the Appendix. Here we shall satisfy ourselves with a brief, and admittedly superficial, survey of the more outstanding general characteristics of the Camp Simon population.

That population, of course, was exclusively male, the popular uncomplimentary stereotypes challenging the masculinity of the conscientious objector to the contrary notwithstanding. By the time of the move to Warner, that kindly Vermont lady who had served as volunteer cook and nurse at Stoddard was long since gone as was her younger and "buxom" assistant. Except for our one Negro assignee, a thirty-three-year-old hairdresser from Philadelphia (whose future career in CPS would be marked by an extraordinary series of forced transfers, AWOLs, indictments, and the like), we were all Caucasoid by racial classification. This man's minority status presented no special difficulty for him beyond having to endure the patronization at the hands of the liberals who welcomed the opportunity to demonstrate their commitment to interracial justice. (Interestingly enough, despite the constant ferment and turmoil in camp, he gave not the slightest hint of the disruptive potential that would make him something of a CPS legend before he was finished.) Only one of the Warner men was married, and he left camp to volunteer for Air Force service. It was generally, and perhaps too easily, assumed that he fell victim to family pressures and to the structured injustice of a system requiring men to work without pay, allotments, or the other benefits enjoyed by those drafted into the other, armed services.

Except for these, the men on the Warner roster were all white and single. More than two-thirds of them were Easterners; the others came to camp from the midwestern states. This, as noted before, was consistent with Selective Service practice: public relations considerations imposed a ruling under which conscientious objectors had to be sent to camps at least a hundred miles from their homes; the desire to limit government travel costs resulted in the policy of using the Mississippi River as a dividing line.

Later, of course, as the eastern camps were filled or closed, this economic consideration gave way. The ultimate transfer of a bloc of Warner men to North Dakota was one result of that change in policy, a most unwelcome result from the standpoint of the men involved.

As the only Catholic camp, Warner may have drawn from a broader area; indeed, a Catholic inductee's request for assignment there would almost certainly be honored—unless he were on the wrong side of the Mississippi, but possibly even then.

Only five of the men came from rural or small-town backgrounds. The others were not only of urban origin, but most came from cities with populations of one hundred thousand or more. Given the overwhelmingly urban character of the American Catholic population, this is not surprising. The implications of this for the Warner situation should be easy enough to see. This was a group of men totally inexperienced in, and in large part physically and psychologically unsuited for, the kind of work they were expected to perform. Add to this the fact that they were there under the compulsion of conscription, and the likelihood of trouble is multiplied. A great adjustment was required in attitudes and behavior, not only of the men themselves but also for the none too receptive New Hampshire natives in whose midst they had been deposited. It was an adjustment that was never made.

The age distribution was more or less determined by Selective Service induction priorities and schedules. Most fell within the twenty-two to thirty-six year age range, but there were three in the twenty-year-old category and three others (at thirty-seven, thirty-nine, and forty-two respectively) beyond the upper limit of that range. The over-all average age of twenty-seven may have put Warner men somewhat above that of CPS as a whole.

Even allowing for the fact that fifteen of the men had not completed high school (two had not completed the primary grades), this was a surprisingly well-educated group. More than half had attended college; eleven had completed undergraduate studies and six had gone beyond this to the M.A. degree. One had completed work for his Ph.D. at the time he was assigned to camp. The point is developed more fully in the Appendix analysis, but it is clear that the men of Camp Simon ranked well above the national average in their level of educational attainment.

Religious identity and commitment, for obvious reasons, are the crucial factors in this composite description of the Warner population. That the two are not the same would find dramatic demonstration in the few months of the camp's existence. As already noted, the majority (sixty-one of the seventy-five men ever assigned) were identified as Roman Catholic on their individual personnel records, but this figure suggests a level of shared religious interest that was never present. There is no record or other tangible evidence of the religious performance or participation of the individual campers; but it was my impression at the time, and one still shared by Dorothy Day, that no more than thirty-five or forty of the campers were, or considered themselves to be, active or practicing Catholics. Perhaps there were even fewer. And even these more active Catholics varied greatly in the intensity of their expressed commitment and the regularity of their involvement in the camp's religious activities. That the others retained their Catholic identity on the personnel records is most likely explained by the legal requirement that the conscientious objector be one who rejected all war and did so on the basis of his religious training and belief. The likely alternative, rejection of one's application for the IV-E classification and the prospect of being forced into the choice between the military or jail, was a most effective incentive for making at least that much of a verbal religious affirmation.

In spite of this, the Warner roster did include eight men who openly declared no religious affiliation. Whether their presence in camp testified to an unusual degree of open-mindedness on the part of the draft board or, more likely perhaps, laxity or incompetence in applying the law, it must have seemed altogether reasonable to Selective Service to send such unattached and unaffiliated inductees to the always underpopulated camp at Warner. The remaining six campers represented one each of a scattering of religious identifications: Methodist, Unitarian, Friend, Episcopal, Orthodox, and Jew. The Orthodox camper described himself as "inactive" on his Selective Service form; Selmon, our solitary Jew, cited membership in the nonreligious War Resisters' League in lieu of a formal religious identification.

This was the rock on which the Camp Simon experiment was to founder. Not that these religious differences degenerated into open animosity (though they did lead occasionally to suspicion and misinterpretation of motives); instead, the absence of a shared religious commitment, which could have been a unifying force to hold the camp together, spelled its doom. All the other problems, not even excluding the desperate poverty and the inadequate diet and living conditions related to it, might have been accepted and overcome in a spiritual setting keyed to mutual trust and a sharing of sacrifice. It was bad enough that half or more of the men were not actively practicing Catholics, that some would be regarded as apostates with all the strains that would bring to the relationships between them and the others who remained "true to the Faith." Added to this was the crippling division among those who did profess to represent an authentic Catholic witness against the war but differed as to what the nature of that witness should be. As we have seen, there were at least four divergent versions of the correct Catholic position on the morality of war, each of them to a significant degree incompatible with the others.

It is true that these differences contributed much to the exciting atmosphere of intellectual and theological confrontation. In another sense, however, the lack of consensus, sometimes bordering on antagonism, on what should have been the most fundamental bond of unity was the flaw that weakened and ultimately destroyed whatever prospects for an effective corporate witness against the war there may have been at the start.

Cliques and Interest Groups

Lacking unanimity on anything beyond the common rejection of military service, the decision that had brought them to Warner in the first place, the campers were probably fated to split into the often highly contentious factions and cliques that would produce the succession of crises and controversies to be described in a later chapter. To even speak of factions and controversies among men ostensibly committed to the cause of peace may seem at first a contradiction in terms or, to the less charitable, evidence of insincerity. Nevertheless such was the situation at Warner. One former camper, asked to describe his single most dominant impression of those days writes:

Had you asked me this question in the years just afterwards, I would probably have answered you with one word: conflict. *My basic reaction to the Warner-Stoddard experience was surprise that a group of men who took a highly unpopular stand fundamentally for such reasons should behave so badly and cause so much dissension.*

He has since modified that judgment, at least to the extent of attributing his surprise to "ignorance of human nature and naivete." Those second thoughts may be valid, but they do not dispel completely the aura of inconsistency that provoked his original disappointment. One should be able to expect that men united in their opposition to war will be able to live peaceably together; a common commitment to reconciliation as the solution to international tensions and conflict ought to carry over to relatively minor strains and problems of the kind encountered in camp. The failure to come closer to the ideal at Warner deserves a more thorough exploration and analysis than his revised explanation, however wise and generous, provides.

The reader is reminded that the description of the major factions and interest groups that follow, as well as the assignment of specific individuals to each, is based primarily on my own recollections and interpretations. I am confident that my description of the basic divisions would find a considerable measure of agreement among my former colleagues, though it is possible, allowing for overlap in basic categories and the movement of individuals from one clique to another, there would be some difference of opinion as to whom to place where. Suitable allowance must be made for this possibility in what follows below and in the next chapter.

The first and most basic principle of division among the campers has to be the attitude vis-a-vis the camp administration and the ACCO. Applying this principle, at least three major groupings can be identified. The first consists of campers and groups whose posture was essentially supportive. Almost by definition this would include most of the active Catholics if only because they were the ones most interested in establishing and maintaining a corporate Catholic witness against the war. Next in order would be campers whose attitudes are best described as ambivalent; on some issues they were supportive and on others not, with the edge perhaps favoring the latter. And then there were the men who were consistently opposed to the camp administration, the ones considered by the administrators and their supporters to be disrupters.

Another substantial segment of the camp population does not fit into this general pattern because they kept themselves detached from the issues and controversies that so excited the others. Among these were the workers, men who did their assigned work and left the arguments to others; if anything, in their neutrality they were generally supportive of the administration. Next were the loners; they, too, were uninvolved for the most part except when they were forced by circumstances to take sides on some issue or other, at which times they tended to be nonsupportive. Finally, to complete the picture, place must be made for those campers best described as the oddballs, not too charitable a term, perhaps, but one widely used to describe them and their behavior. Though usually not involved in the issues that divided the camp, their noninvolvement was more a recognition of their status in the camp itself than a statement of neutrality.

Within this general outline other, more specific, subdivisions must be acknowledged. One can identify at least three in the supportive category: the chapel group, the Catholic Workers, and the Coughlinites. The first consisted of men who gathered together for regular devotions and who assumed responsibility for decorating and maintaining that part of the school building set apart for religious purposes. It had a core membership of perhaps eight or nine, and an additional fifteen or so peripheral participants joined them with some frequency in the daily Prime and Compline services and other chapel activities.

It should not be surprising that the half-dozen or so men who had been associated with the Catholic Worker movement prior to their assignment to camp should be numbered among the supporters of the ACCO camp administration or that they would hold some of the more responsible positions in camp. Rightly or wrongly, they were often accused of assuming proprietary rights over camp affairs and seeking to impose their particular philosophy and standards upon the rest of the camp.

Though not as easily identified, the Coughlinite faction seemed to be about equal in number to the Catholic Workers. Although one of their most vocal members could be counted among the disrupters on some issues, they were usually to be found among the more ardent supporters of the camp administration. This does not mean that they were in ideological sympathy with the Catholic Worker philosophy and ideals, however. Their principal concern was to affirm and defend the Catholic character of the camp against the threat (as they saw it) posed by the non-Catholics and "heretic" elements in their midst.

The ambivalents in their turn can be divided into what were usually described as the intellectual set (or "college boys") and the artists, a designation broad enough to include the would-be writers and poets as well. Bohemians is another term frequently employed for the latter group. The intellectuals—a term usually carrying overtones of friendly derision when used in camp—numbered about ten with a somewhat smaller contingent of fringe participants. Included in that core were at least two of the Catholic liberals and two men holding administrative posts essential to camp operations. This was the faction which produced the most consistent ideological criticism of the CPS program and accounted for most of the political ferment. But despite all the protests they originated and the petitions they circulated, they were not intentionally destructive of camp morale. On issues involving a more equitable sharing of burdens and responsibilities or upholding regulations designed to protect the rights of campers against selfish abuse of privileges by a few, they usually could be counted on to give principled support to Director Larrowe and the ACCO. On balance, however, because of their consistent and outspoken opposition to what they defined as the inherent injustices of the system and, even more, because of their increasingly insistent calls for government-operated camps to replace the CPS compromise, they were generally regarded as nonsupportive.

The artists were far less likely to involve themselves in political agitation, though they did lend moral support and encouragement to the intellectuals' many causes. A more limited interest group, they shunned excessive entanglements in camp affairs unless their special interests were likely to be affected by some pending issue or proposed action. The incident described earlier was such a case: the threat of a decision which might infringe upon their claim to space already commandeered for their studio brought them out in force to a meeting they otherwise might not have bothered to attend. Apart from this intense commitment to their own interests, the artists and their bohemian hangers-on are not easy to place in the context of general camp rivalries and loyalties. Roger Tennitt, for instance, was one of the storm centers of protest; others, in contrast, adopted a stance of total disinterest, letting nothing interfere with their creative activities. Two without doubt, and possibly a third, were leading figures in the disrupter group to be discussed below. In sum it is fair to say that the artists' posture was generally nonsupportive of the camp administration.

With dissension and controversy the normal state of affairs, it may seem redundant to single out any individuals or groups as especially disruptive. Still there were a few men so dedicated in their rejection of camp authority and so openly contemptuous of work assignments, whether out on project or in camp, that they deserve special distinction on this score. Commonly referred to as "the New York crowd," the five or so men who gravitated around the two dominant figures in this category were regarded, certainly by the administration supporters and even by many of its ideological opponents, as unprincipled troublemakers and malingerers. This is not to say, however, that they were unpopular. Even when their behavior violated the limits of good taste, their fellow campers found it possible to excuse—or, if not that, forgive—their excesses and, on occasion, even admire them for the daring of their nonconformity. It is easy enough to identify individuals who fit this designation but much more difficult to treat them as a coherent group. Instead they served more as a personification, if you will, of a malignant force, a festering center of chronic malcontent. Though they may not always have been the ones to initiate the problem, they often managed to intensify and polarize opinion on issues that might have passed over as transitory inconveniences or petty complaints.

The workers and loners were similar enough in their remoteness from camp affairs to be regarded as a single category. The detachment they cherished, however, differed both in quality and source. The workers numbered about a dozen or so and included several of the older campers. For the most part they were satisfied to do their jobs and go their own way, watching from the sidelines as their more engaged fellow campers squandered time and energy in what turned out to be an endless succession of futile wrangles. The loners, about the same in number, also made it their business to stand apart from most of the sound and fury; in their case, however, it was a conscious expression of independence and unwillingness to risk even a partial or temporary surrender of their prized autonomy. Unlike the workers, they did take a philosophical interest in whatever issue might be in controversy and would usually take part in the informal bull sessions preceding or following the camp meeting called to resolve it; but only in the rarest of instances, and then usually when they felt their precious circle of privacy and autonomy might be threatened, were they likely to play a direct or active part in the meeting itself.

Indeed, a few of the loners made such a fetish of keeping themselves apart that they might have qualified for that last remaining category, the so-called oddballs. "Oddness" in this context ranged from the eccentricity of individuals like Jimmy O'Toole and Dave Komiker, already introduced in chapter 1, to more serious indications of neurosis and psychosis. Joe Moroni, for example, arrived in camp early in November and immediately demanded exemption from any work assignment on grounds of an impressive assortment of disqualifying ailments. His hypochondria became something of a camp joke at first but soon escalated into a camp burden until, one snowy sub-zero evening, it provoked his bunkhouse neighbors to direct retaliatory action. Thoroughly fed up with his moaned protests that their conversation was keeping him awake (his fragile health requiring that he retire well before the scheduled "lights out"), they simply picked him up, bunk and all, and transported him to the camp infirmary some distance away. It made for quite a scene, Joe protesting every step of the way and threatening all manner of official reprisals against the malefactors.*

Somewhere between the eccentrics and the mental cases were "the walking dead," men who for reasons of physical disability, real or fancied (or, one sometimes suspected, feigned), were permanently on sick status and relieved of all work responsibilities on project or in camp. Most, like Mark Roselli, spent their days "waiting, waiting, waiting" for their discharge papers; others, though they must have been aware of their oddball standing in the eyes of their fellow campers, did not seem to consider themselves in any way disqualified for Civilian Public Service. Some gave the impression of being fully resigned to, and possibly even enjoying, the experience of being in camp. Taken together, about a dozen men clearly fit into this category with four others marginally qualified for the dubious honor of inclusion.

These, then, are the major divisions among the Warner campers, as I remember them. To leave it at the level of general description, however, would be to miss the peculiarly human dimension of the Camp Simon experience. The next chapter, therefore, will focus more on individuals, using the material here as a framework within which the individuals are introduced into the narrative. Readers of pacifist persuasion might be more comfortable with a portrait of the CPS man of World War II presenting him as the shining hero of conscience, a man consumed by a spirit of self-sacrifice and free of the ordinary character and behavioral flaws that beset the men of Camp Simon. But the

*Confirmatory evidence is not available, but it appears Moroni did send letters of indignant protest to General Hershey, Paul Comly French, and other officials. Hypochondria was not his only problem in camp. He also acted as self-appointed overseer of the campers' morals which, on several counts (loose and vulgar talk, by his highly puritanical definition, being only one) he felt were sadly lacking. He claimed to have written letters to the local ecclesiastical authorities appealing to them to do something about the "sinful" behavior rampant at Warner. Here, too, evidence is not at hand to prove or disprove that claim.

truth, I fear, was otherwise; and once this simple fact is recognized, some of the misunderstandings and uncomplimentary stereotypes that still persist may disappear. Conscientious objectors called into alternative service were really not too different from their brothers drafted into the other services except in that all-important matter of commitment to what they interpreted as a moral and religious obligation. All they could ask—and this they deserved—was a measure of respect equal to that given those whose moral convictions permitted or impelled them to go to war.

To be a CO is to be a deviant—for whatever purpose. Obviously many categories of CO's were involved: religious, political, egotistical, etc. I know of no test of sincerity. Some were neurotic and psychotic, but this results from any attempt to assess contemporary events. There were many isolates at Warner, and I think of myself as one. I didn't get very close to anybody and belonged to none of the sub-communities or cliques . . . chapel, "Canory Express," art colonies, CW in-group, etc. Many of the men came from the upper middle class, with college background and a level of sophistication not easily to be identified with by a person from the milk-shed of New York State—and a factory worker at that. No doubt an implicit stratification system was in existence based on one's social background. Warner was such a brief period. The men we remember best went on to Oakland and then to Rosewood. One of my best remembrances at Warner is the attempt to stay warm on a cold mountain. Much of our project work was geared only to obtaining the wood necessary for the task. In my bunkhouse I was surrounded by the Luzons and Canory, not the most stimulating milieu. . . .

That opening line tells it all: to be a CO is to be a deviant. The former camper whose response provided this epigraph uses the term in its technical sense. The conscientious objector is a social deviant, first, because the course of behavior he has chosen to adopt is a departure from the statistical norms. The great majority of men called up for military service in time of war obey and serve. In another more important sense he is a deviant from the moral norms. As most of his fellow citizens see it, he is deliberately refusing to meet his obligations to the welfare of the society of which he is a part. This general assumption finds additional reinforcement in traditional Catholic thought, in that failure to obey the commands of legitimate authority is viewed as a serious fault in a religious sense as well.

The religiously motivated conscientious objector is prepared to accept the deviant classification in its civil connotation but not in the second; statistically he may have been deviant there, too, but even though he may have been the proverbial minority of one (which each was in a sense), it was the majority that, in his eyes at least, had deviated from the moral norms. Even those who were encouraged to take that stand by the doctrinal teachings of peace-oriented churches or who enjoyed the support of other pacifist affiliations had to recognize the fact that in every objector's case it was a matter of the individual making a personal witness against war, alone. Since by his own definition he was expressing the true moral norms, rightly understood, he could satisfy himself that he was upholding the standards of the good citizen by refusing to contribute to the immorality of war. As far as the men of Camp Simon were concerned (at least those who held to their religious practices and beliefs), what others may have regarded as deviance was a simple act of obedience to God and a fulfillment of their Christian obligation to Church and State.

To move from the group dimensions described in the previous chapter to the more individual focus would seem to call for a separate case study devoted to each man on the Warner roster. The sketches offered here, composed from the remembered impressions they made upon their fellow campers, fall short of this ideal but should be enough to provide the reader with some faint sense of the atmosphere and relationships experienced in those few and generally unhappy months.

Partly for the sake of convenience, but more important because of their critical relevance to the people and events to be dealt with here and in succeeding chapters, the individual thumbnail sketches will follow the divisions set forth in chapter 5. First attention will be given to the supporters of the Camp Simon administration, and these, as we have seen, can be subdivided into the chapel group, the Catholic Workers, and the Coughlinites.

The Chapel Group

One of the four men remembered by all the respondents to my questionnaire was Louis Swanson, one of the leaders of the group that assumed responsibility for an active religious program, first at Stoddard and later at Warner as well. There is no need to repeat what has already been said about his personality and general popularity. The moving force behind the chapel group, however, was "Mother Pat" Meany. The nickname derives from a hilarious incident that, I am sorry to say, I missed and had to enjoy secondhand. Meany, a man of roly-poly build and possessed of great improvisational gifts, dressed himself up in makeshift nun's garb and arranged to be squired about camp as a visiting mother superior who, so the story went, was inspecting the premises as a preliminary to approving a new detached service unit being considered by her order. By all reports the masquerade was a smashing success,[1] and the "Mother Pat" image would stay with him for the remainder of his CPS career. One of his collaborators in that performance describes him as "our resident medieval monk-artist and man-about-town. Joyous, raucous, creative, unpredictable. Nostalgic about Yale and the Middle Ages." That latter reference relates to his background as an accomplished liturgical artist and the training he had received at his much revered alma mater. It was Meany who assumed major responsibility for converting the drab schoolhouse space into a tasteful chapel and organizing the liturgical services and other chapel activities. Swanson and Meany combined to provide the spirit and dedication needed to keep the chapel group going in the face of sporadic support and participation on the part of the other Catholics in camp. The two also shared the tasks of cook and baker and kept the kitchen going as well. What they lacked in culinary talent was more than compensated for by their bubbling personalities, which on more than one occasion saved the camp from the utter chaos and rebellion that might have been provoked by a particularly skimpy or unpalatable meal.

Chuck Sterner earned his place among the chapel group leaders by virtue of his argumentative and athletic endeavors. Like Swanson a former seminarian, Sterner's voice was one of the strongest (in volume as well as in strength of argument) raised in defense of orthodoxy as represented in the just-war teachings of Thomas Aquinas and the Neo-Scholastic theologians. Faced with the more fundamental pacifism of some of the non-Catholic campers, and even more dismayed by the assaults mounted against those traditional teachings by the Catholic liberals, Chuck was a pivotal figure in the seemingly endless philosophical and theological debates that monopolized so much of the campers' free time. Athletic in build, background, and interests, he assumed the role of camp jock, and was the enthusiastic leader of whatever spontaneous sports and games he could organize. At best these efforts met with middling success, but at that it was more than can be claimed for his equally enthusiastic efforts to round up volunteer camp groups for work to be done around the camp.

Robert Langner deserves a prominent place here, too, even though he was one of the few active Protestants on the scene. He might just as easily be classified among the college-educated liberals in recognition of the leading part he played in composing and circulating their ideological critiques of CPS. (Later in his CPS career he would be one of the rare rebels to turn to more activist protest, leaving the program and risking imprisonment as a violator of the conscription law.) The chapel group identification seems more appropriate, however, not only because, without weakening his opposition to the over-all system, he was generally supportive of the camp administration, but because he was more regular and active in the religious life of the Warner community than were most of the Catholic campers. Extremely boyish in appearance—the description "choir boy" is repeatedly encountered—he was a model advocate of ecumenism long before that became the approved objective among the principal Christian communions. His "high Anglican *Ah*-men," as one describes it, may have disconcerted some participants in the religious services at camp, but few could deny him recognition as an active regular of the chapel group.

Two Pennsylvanians, both products of a Catholic college education, complete the inner chapel circle as I remember it. Like Sterner and the others in this group, both were ardent defenders of Thomism and the just-war teachings, but they approached that task in almost diametrically opposite ways. William Grandman, described by Sterner in his response as "the only other person than myself who could present St. Thomas's teachings on the just war," proceeded in a quiet and scholarly manner, favoring a style of persuasion that allowed respect for the intellectual and moral arguments of those with whom he engaged in friendly debate. George Andrews, in contrast, was frankly inquisitorial in his insistence upon the most narrow and rigid definition of the Catholic character of the camp. As one of the more liberally inclined Catholic pacifists, I must confess that I did not get on too well with him and found his ultradogmatic manner insufferable; though he was one of the campers I was not able to track down, I suspect he would have found my point of view on matters theological and social verging on heresy and equally insufferable. Conscious of the possibility of a distortion caused by this obvious bias, I found it most gratifying to note that whereas Grandman is remembered with favor by my respondents, my own negative recollections of Andrews find their echo in descriptions that see him as "a cross between an evangelist and a lawyer," "a great polemicist in the Jesuit tradition," and "the most right-wing member of the chapel crowd." Even within the more limited circle of his chapel group associates, one admits to a "love/hate relationship" with him because "no other person in camp had ideas so antithetical to my own." He was, in Grandman's recollection, an individual who combined "some of the best and worst aspects of Jesuit training," a man bright but "verbally cruel" in debate ". . . sardonic, supercilious, he could have been torchman for Torquemada."

Swanson, Meany, Sterner, Grandman, and even the Protestant Langner were committed and effective supporters of the camp administration, and their effectiveness was due in large part to their personalities and their ability to maintain friendly contact with the less supportive and more disruptive elements. Andrews, combining as he did the inflexibility of his views with an almost calculated abrasiveness of style, was the kind of friend the hapless administration really did not need in a situation marked by serious divisions of every kind.

The Catholic Workers

The campers with the largest stake in the success of the Stoddard-Warner venture were the men who had been active in the Catholic Worker movement prior to their induction. The ACCO, after all, was their enterprise, a spin-off of the movement itself and still so closely tied to it that it was completely dependent upon it for financial support. It comes as something of a surprise, then, that not all of the draft eligible Workers sought the IV-E classification and that, considering all the effort the paper had put into persuading Catholics to refuse military service, the number who actually entered CPS* was small. This is not to say, however, that their influence was equally limited. On the contrary, they constituted the most influential element in both policy-making and operational spheres of camp affairs.

*Even more surprising is the fact that those who did come to camp would ultimately leave CPS for military service of one kind or another. But this is something to be developed at a later point.

Director Dwight Larrowe, though himself not an assignee, had the most profound impact, and this not only because of his position of authority. Even today he remains for some the epitome of the saintly Catholic scholar-mystic; for others, though the resentment has died down, he remains the compulsive taskmaster, the "Dwight Lagree" of much camp humor. A more extended discussion of the camp director and his changing perception of his role is reserved for later, but what is important here is the fact that for the first couple of months of Warner's operations he was absent from the scene, having returned for some reason to his former work at the Catholic Worker's Mott Street headquarters in New York City. The Warner story may have been much different had he been in charge during that crucial period of adjustment to the new location and project.

Instead his stand-in as acting director was Tony Saunders, a most unhappy choice for an ungrateful task. Not only was he an assignee, he was the personification of the Catholic Worker virtues of humility, sacrifice, and almost monastic piety. One who worked with him in the camp office mentioned that he had "a mighty temper," but this is a characteristic few would have associated with Saunders. The virtually inescapable impression he left was of the much despised "200-percenter" and "second-miler." There is reason to doubt that this image was entirely fair to him. After all, it was Saunders who provided that dramatic display of commitment at Stoddard by leaving camp in protest against conscription as "fundamentally wrong and an evil I can no longer cooperate with or submit to." After a couple of weeks of reflection and meditation, during which time he was recorded as AWOL on the camp roster, he returned; but this might be more a reflection of his prayerful humility than a reversal of views. To the critic it was evidence of the chronic indecisiveness with which he was, and still is, charged. Friend and critic alike, however, would probably agree that he was not the man to be given responsibility for a camp filled with headstrong, articulate, and increasingly resentful individualists.

Remembered impressions of Tony Saunders, predictably enough, range from the laudatory to the unkind. "One of the pillars of the Catholic group, an honest and admirable man," writes one former camper; "a typical CW-guy—always a towel in his back pocket to give the impression of being busy," recalls another. None questioned his sincerity, his conscientious concern for the welfare of the camp, or his good character. His principal failings, as they emerge from the responses to the questionnaire, were an inability to deal with a wide variety of people and the equally disastrous, but possibly understandable, inability to make decisions; to one of those formerly in his charge he was "as indecisive a person as I have ever met." Personal idiosyncracies loom large in the responses, and again the tone varies. There are references to his high-pitched and rather nervous giggle ("weird laugh" as one preferred to describe it). His refusal to see leftovers go to waste—was he perhaps setting an example for others by eating the food they rejected?—earned him one characterization as "the human garbage can." Somewhat less in character is a remembered incident in which Saunders reportedly knocked a kitten off a bench for making noise while prayers were in progress. "I guess he thought it should have been meowing a 'Hail Mary,' " this informant writes. "I was mad about it then, but time mellows most things and it seems more funny now—but not for the kitten."

Whether one regards them as administrative shortcomings or not, there is little question but that the reticence, humility, and indecisiveness of the Saunders regime stood in the sharpest conceivable contrast to the "functional authoritarianism" Director Larrowe would bring with him upon his return to the active exercise of his office. It would be too much to attribute the rapid decline in morale that marked the final weeks of Camp Simon to this change; but one can say with some confidence that neither the one nor the other—and certainly not the sudden shift from the former to the latter—contributed much to camp stability or inspired a more supportive attitude toward the ACCO and its policies.

A few other Catholic Workers deserve mention. Walter North, one of the older campers, had come to Camp Simon from one of the CW farm experiments. Once there, he fit more into the detached workers group than with his more ideological Catholic Worker counterparts. Late in Warner's rocky history he assumed the responsibilities of camp purchasing officer and at one point shocked Director Larrowe by his rebellious insistence upon providing the men with a more adequate diet. He is remembered most often for his small size and his quick and explosive temper. "A bantam rooster—fighting pacifist—dedicated CW" is one characterization; "Feisty, lovable character with strong set of ideals and one of the few able to translate them into action" is another. North himself provides confirmation of these general impressions in a self-characterization as "strictly a CO on a

Thomistic basis who probably had the most non-pacifist personality and nature in the entire camp."

There were others: Joe Burt, a relatively late arrival, is remembered as a "real CW-type with a vengeance. Gothic character." Dave Komiker, my strange companion in the potato bins, was a dedicated Catholic Worker and utterly subservient to the policies and goals set by the camp administration. Komiker clearly belongs in the oddball category, however, as does Alan Survich, a tall, black-haired, dour-visaged, religion-obsessed individual who was remembered by one of his fellow CWs as "a mixed-up kid who didn't know which way to turn." Even more telling is the brief, but incisive, note appended by another former camper: "I believe he was invented by Dostoievsky."

The Coughlinites

The point has been made several times that, even though Warner was a Catholic camp with Catholicism the dominant religious affiliation, there were profound differences among the members as to their reasons for rejecting military service. The chapel group, with only one or two exceptions, were Thomists; applying the just-war criteria to World War II, they had come to the conclusion that it did not pass the test and, therefore, was to be opposed. The Catholic Worker ideology was more perfectionist—though in some cases, as North's comment indicates, the Thomist approach applied to some of them as well. In the main, however, the Catholic Workers rejected war and violence as a reversal of the sacrificial love ethic to which they believed the Christian is called. There were others, like me, who openly professed an intellectualized or sentimentalized form of pacifism, a position most of the others regarded as theologically suspect, certainly not orthodox. And then we have the Coughlinites whose opposition to war was essentially political in emphasis and direction. They were conscientious objectors because they believed service in the Allied forces would violate their moral obligations as Catholics and Christians (and this would be a redundancy in their eyes since only the Catholic could be a true Christian). Their opposition was in no sense pacifist; as already mentioned, Pat Rafferty argued that, were the nation on the other side of the conflict, i.e., fighting against rather than allied with the Soviet Union, every Catholic would be morally bound to fight. Their conviction that the war had been arranged by an international Jewish conspiracy to advance the diabolical forces of Bolshevism could probably be seen as related to the violation of one or another of the conditions of the just war, but few if any of the Thomists in camp would have welcomed them as their ideological brothers.

When one considers how hard it was for Catholics to win recognition as conscientious objectors from their reluctant draft boards, it is something of a mystery that a position that so obviously did not reject *all* war and that was so clearly political in nature won the coveted classification for men of this group. The suggestion has already been offered that the favorable decision reflected a faulty understanding of the law and its strict requirements on this score. It is also possible that the arguments they presented found a receptive hearing, a plausible hypothesis certainly when applied to draft boards operating in the Christian Front strongholds of Brooklyn and Chicago from which several of Warner's Coughlinites had come. And even draft boards not inclined to be sympathetic could be impressed, if not overwhelmed , by the sheer weight of the case they could present. Objectors of the Coughlinite variety could draw upon a great wealth of explicit papal denunciations and directives in support of their refusal to "fight for Communism," not to mention the commentaries of Father Coughlin himself and the writings and speeches of many other clergymen of some prominence. Finally, and this may be the most suitable explanation of all, the local boards confronted by these highly articulate and almost obsessively committed men might well have deemed it the better part of prudence to give them the classification they sought if only to rid their communities of whatever threat they may have posed to wartime morale.

However we explain their presence in Camp Simon, these men presented a very real challenge to their fellow campers. Their anti-Semitism would have been offensive to most even if there had not been a Jew on the camp roster. Their admiration, spoken or unspoken, for Hitler and the fascist way of life was certainly not shared by the others. It was particularly disturbing to the socialists and humanists among us who already had trouble reconciling our own refusal to join in a war fought against these evils with our political and philosophical ideals.[2] To have before us this insistent reminder that, for some at least, conscientious objection was indeed linked to support for the detested fascism was a burden not easily borne.

As far as camp affairs were concerned, the Coughlinites presented

a problem of quite another order. Religious rigorists to the point of
being puritanical, they occasionally tried to impose their triumphal-
ist view of Catholic beliefs and practices upon this collection of men
with diverse and contradictory perspectives on religion and morality.
On at least two occasions, as we shall see, individual Coughlinites
took it upon themselves to preserve the moral tone of the camp
by means of ill-advised acts of censorship. A more basic source of
tension was the antiintellectual bias which made them suspicious
of the political and religious liberalism that had brought the majority
of their fellow campers to Warner in the first place. Their suspicions
made them aggressively defensive against actions or statements they
regarded as unduly critical or antagonistic to Catholicism as "the One
True Faith." Predictably enough, they found threats enough to keep
them ever on the alert. As they defined the situation, the non-Catholics, and the nonpracticing Catholics as well, were there at the suffer-
ance of more orthodox elements like themselves and, on any issue
that bore upon the Catholic character of the camp, were not entitled
to a full share of responsibility for whatever decisions were proposed
or made.

   Not all the Coughlinites were as blatantly anti-Semitic as Pat Rafferty perhaps, but the belief in a Jewish world conspiracy of which
World War II was but one sinister manifestation, took several bizarre
forms. Pat, for instance, was always ready to prove his case by carefully enumerating the *real* (i.e., Jewish) names of Roosevelt and other national and allied political or military leaders. Dave Connolly's
evidence was so fantastic that it, too, became something of a standing joke: he insisted the key to the whole plot lay in Scriptural references identifying the Anti-Christ with the number 666, which just
happened to match some number associated with the archvillain,
FDR (memory fades—I can no longer recall whether it was his license
number, his Social Security number, or even, perhaps, his telephone
number); of course, FDR's number was 999, but Satanic duplicity
being what it is, this inversion was merely further evidence of an effort to spread diabolical confusion. In no time at all, Dave, older and
of short and portly build, was nicknamed "Mr. 666" and "set to
music" with appropriate lyrics to the popular song, "Mr. Five-by-
Five." All in good fun, of course, but the serious implications behind
his outlandish theory were not overlooked.

   By no stretch of the imagination could James O'Donnell be viewed
as a figure of fun. Like Connolly, he was one of the older campers, a

hard and serious worker, one of the more reliable supporters of the camp administration. Though in most respects he was a steadying influence, his puritanical outlook would be a source of serious controversy on occasion. Unlike Rafferty with his readiness to make his case to all and sundry, O'Donnell did not go out of his way to impose his political or religious beliefs on an unsolicited or unreceptive audience. On the other hand, anyone careless enough to give him even the slightest opening would be deluged by the flood of pamphlets and other materials Jim had in his possession, ready to prove or disprove any point he wished to make. Responses to my questionnaire (and only one of the former campers was unable to identify his name) repeatedly struck the same note. "Zealous for causes," notes one; "one of the few zealots I have ever known," echoes another. The "inveterate pamphleteer" recalled by yet another matches the reference to the man who "had a pamphlet for all occasions" advanced by a fourth. One particularly revealing, and perhaps amusing, insight is provided by two former campers who remember the assortment of candy bars O'Donnell kept in his footlocker—not, as one might think, hoarded for personal enjoyment but, rather, as a handy empirical demonstration of their progressive diminution in size (presumably one more proof of the insidious exploitation of the American public by the "masters" of the economy).

Most respondents describe this elder statesman of the Coughlinite group as an agreeable man, able to get along with everyone, "a very solid and attractive person in spite of himself and his prejudices," reliable, responsible, a good worker. There were less complimentary responses too. One non-Catholic, most of whose recollections of his former colleagues were favorable in thrust, departs from that pattern by describing O'Donnell as "prudish and narrow in his thinking—intensely religionistic—he had a wall between him and those not of his faith." One of the Catholic liberals dismisses him in even stronger terms as "an authoritarian person; a polite fascist; a biblical fundamentalist," confessing in an addendum that he couldn't stand the man and his remarks were prejudiced by that fact.

It is probably well to note in this connection that this same respondent expressed a warm regard for the more outspoken Rafferty precisely because "he admitted what he was and didn't try to smooth it over like O'Donnell. . . ." He regarded Pat as "a great drinking companion (unless you got on the subject of liberals, Jews, etc.)." This evaluation of that most argumentative member of the Coughlinite faction was widely shared. Even the Jewish camper speaks well of him. "In spite of his racism, he was a good schnook, and he was a funny man. And an honest one." To one of his fellow Brooklynites Pat was an "unreconstructed Coughlin-type . . . had a certain Brooklyn-type charm, somewhat akin to Runyan's boys from across the river." Though, as noted earlier, Rafferty was a merciless needler of any and all who gave him the opportunity, most of his victims took his needling in stride, only one admitting that he disliked him because of his cutting criticism. Unlikely though it might seem, this crusader for a generally unpopular cause was himself one of the most popular men in camp. Lou Swanson, one of the very few who outranked him in popularity, summed it up nicely in his description of Rafferty as "a born fighter and leader; good strong Irish type who made no bones about where he stood. Although I almost never agreed with him, I liked him very much and respected him even more."

College Boys and Intellectuals

Both terms, in the camp usage, were often employed as taunts or even sneers rather than as terms of praise or admiration, but this should not be taken to imply a lack of popularity for the individuals included in this category. These men, perhaps even more than the hard-core supporters of the ACCO, were committed to what might best be described as an ideological peace witness and, even though the majority of them were not active members of the Church, they recognized and defended the importance of maintaining a specifically Catholic presence in the CPS program. It has been noted that some of these men made it possible for Camp Simon to get under way by voluntarily transferring from other camps to Stoddard in order to provide the necessary number of assignees to justify its existence. However much they may have differed with the policies of the camp administration—and this category includes several of its most vocal and consistent critics—these men could usually be relied on as a source of strength and support in moments of crisis. It is in this sense that they can be described as representing an ambivalent position, at once a continuing center of resistance and criticism but seldom a disruptive one.

Except for one or two of the Catholics included in their number, they were pacifists in the fullest sense of the word, some professing what is often described as the absolutist pacifist position. Their presence in camp meant that they had cooperated to the extent of registering for the draft and accepting assignment to alternative service (and none would carry his opposition to the point of leaving camp and risking a prison sentence), but this gap between theory and practice should not be interpreted as a lack of sincerity. These were the men who kept Camp Simon in touch with the resistance actions centered in other CPS camps. They led the agitation for pay and the establishment of government camps as an option for those who were dissatisfied with the NSBRO and its policies. Though most of their concern and protest focused upon the higher level system-wide issues, they played a most significant role in organizing protests against the inadequate diet, the lack of suitable medical facilities, Director Larrowe's allegedly arbitrary and undemocratic decision-making procedures, and the other local camp issues as well.

Most of these men were what the categorical heading suggests, college students and graduates with a few would-be writers, poets, and the like thrown in. They were intellectual in the sense that their interests tended to favor literary or philosophical subjects and heavy theoretical political discussions. A small group met regularly for a time to read aloud to each other. They were open-minded about religion with some professing agnostic or even atheist preferences for themselves without letting that interfere with their forming close friendships with the Catholics sharing their intellectual and political interests. There was a wider gulf between them and the rougher elements of the disrupter group, even though the two factions were allied more often than not in protesting camp conditions. The intellectuals frowned upon what seemed to them an overly selfish and negativistic attitude; the disrupters, in their turn, scorned their more abstract and namby-pamby approach.

Two men in particular, Dean Farfether and Ronald Baxter, could serve as models for the group. Neither was Catholic, and both had been among the original volunteers from Quaker camps. Farfether, already introduced as one of the men who met me at the bus stop, was regarded as the more radical thinker, though in behavior and appearance he was the epitome of the detached, even remote, scholar. Most of the remembered impressions of him stress both aspects. Pat Rafferty, fixed at the opposite pole from Farfether's Marxism, reveals an edge of praise for this "rare intellectual leftist; the rarest of the rare—one who would listen. Open to both sides." The same quality, given a more negative cast, is remembered by another camper's description of Dean as "a man of fierce intelligence and high ideals. In Dean's case these admirable qualities tended to separate him from, rather than bind him to, his fellow men." Terms like "socially brittle and remote" used by others suggest the same mix of approval and criticism.

Baxter, the camp clerk, was a more consistent supporter of the ACCO administration, but in other respects he and Farfether were a close match. He, too, had come to CPS with a background of extensive associations with the traditional peace movement; but just as Dean had moved from Quakerism to agnosticism and intellectual Marxism, Baxter had gravitated toward the more intellectualized forms of Catholicism. He and Bob Langner were Protestants who attached themselves to the chapel group and participated regularly in the camp's liturgical activites. Though no more than a handful of the campers could be said to be suited to a forestry camp environment, it was Baxter, the shy, reserved, almost patrician scholar, who seemed most definitely out of place. All the remembered impressions of him make some reference to that shy restraint, to his cultural bearing as a Harvard man (complete with accent, as several took pains to note), to his obvious gentility. His good manners were mentioned with some regularity and occasionally supplemented with specific examples to illustrate his consideration for the feelings of others or, again, those qualities of shyness and reserve. Some referred to him as "distant," testimony perhaps to his official status as camp clerk, but even more to the difficulty he seemed to have in breaking out of his shell of privacy and reserve. An almost perfect capsule description of Baxter in the Warner setting reads, "Like some rich, spoiled, remote son in a Marquand novel, Ron stood out in any CPS settting. His Harvardian accent intimidated some, angered some. Quiet, mystical quality. Tended to stare distantly, vacantly as he thought."

In a way it is extremely difficult to think of these men as a category; all were such different and obviously gifted individuals. Alvin Manton left a particularly strong impression on me in the brief two or three weeks of our time shared in camp, although our association came to a dramatic and nearly tragic end in his efforts to teach me the finer points of woodsmanship. He had been one of the leading figures on the Stoddard scene, but that accident on the first day on project and his subsequent hospitalization and transfer reduced his influence at Warner to a minimum. Carl Terry was another much ad-

mired Ivy Leaguer. A large and soft-spoken man, he was treated with
a certain measure of respect and caution because of his surprisingly
short temper and ready fists when it was aroused. These qualities,
plus his status as a nominal Catholic, earned him a kind of leadership
role among the camp's more dissident elements. At one point he was
put forth as "the people's choice" for the post of assistant director,
an act of defiance that was promptly and predictably overruled by
the ACCO officials in New York.

There were a few active Catholics who deserve to be included under this heading, usually referred to in camp as the Catholic liberals.
Whatever complimentary overtones that term may have had for their
college boy-intellectual peers, it carried quite different connotations
for many of their fellow Catholics. Their *political* liberalism as reflected in their opposition to race prejudice, their support for the
rights of labor, and the socialist tendencies which favored the use of
public authority to provide for the poor and otherwise disadvantaged
was shared, with some modifications in scope and intensity of commitment, by most of the other Catholics in camp. There was more of
a problem, however, with respect to their willingness to defend and
respect the rights of other religions and their adherents. In the eyes
of some this came dangerously close to religious indifference if not
outright apostasy. It would be going too far to equate the open-
mindness of these Catholic liberals with today's more ecumenical
spirit. At best it represented a kind of ecclesiastical condescension,
affirming Roman Catholicism as the "one true Church" even as they
spoke for tolerance and recognition of the good faith of those who
had not yet found their way to the fullness of the Catholic truth.
Even so modest a concession was enough to provoke sometimes
heated controversy with the more rigorist Catholics like George Andrews who felt called upon to provide "fraternal correction" to his
misguided liberal brethren who, in their laxity, were slipping down
the road to heresy.*

George's most consistent and most effective adversary in these occasionally bitter exchanges was Lowell Bartlett. Both were graduates
of Catholic colleges, but it was Lowell who clearly held the intellec-

*On one occasion, it is reported, Andrews objected to saying "amen" to the
Kaddish prayer offered in chapel by George Selmon for the deceased relative
of one of the Catholic campers. By merely giving that response, he argued, he
would be participating in a non-Catholic religious service and committing what
was then considered a mortal sin.

tual advantage. In appearance, and most of the time in his actions, he struck one as a rather mousy background figure, slight in stature, with a shock of dark hair and glasses, quiet to the point of seeming withdrawn. Unmistakably the scholar, he was given to expressing himself in impatiently dogmatic terms and in a manner seemingly calculated to give offense. One member of the Coughlinite faction remembers him as "brilliant, though unsteady; perhaps too sure of his judgments." Such, at least, was the normal Bartlett persona; but a glass or two of beer could suddenly transform this paragon of academic rectitude into a wildly extravagant polemicist (to continue the description offered by our Coughlinite colleague, "a delayed time-bomb . . . called everyone a 'piss-pot' . . . Carl Terry avowed he was too little to drink").

Virtually all of the questionnaire responses pair the two Bartletts. "Wild swings of mood from extreme introversion to noisy alcoholic camaraderie" or, again, "He was pleasant and had a picturesque, acid tongue when slightly drunk, but that gave him his individuality." Not only that, it assured this otherwise remote intellectual a firm place among the more unforgettable characters at Warner. This "sweet, old curmudgeon, crusty and opinionated" may have stirred mixed responses at the time, but he seems to have left his mark as "possibly the finest mind of all the campers" and, when properly inspirited, the "life of the party." One of the comic high points of camp history found Lowell, very drunk, conducting a hilarious mock excommunication of Grand Inquisitor Andrews, complete with a most impressive Latin chant and the ceremonial sprinkling of the victim's head with ashes from the kitchen stove.

Shelden Dennison's claim to membership in the intellectual set had no comparable basis in academic qualifications, and his Catholic liberal inclinations probably reflected an unfamiliarity with church history and theological tradition more than any maturely reasoned interpretation of his Catholic faith. A product of public school education, he had gone to work in an office immediately after graduation from high school. But he had kept his literary interests and writing aspirations alive through voracious reading and immersion in a fairly wide range of cultural pursuits. The latter were also the principal source of his radically pacifist interpretation of New Testament teachings, interpretations that caused his more traditionally educated fellow Catholics considerable consternation at times. He was, however, an active Catholic in good standing, regular in Mass attendance and an occasional participant in the evening chapel devotions. The close association he was able to establish with the intellectual, especially the literary, types came about more at his initiation than theirs, but he had little difficulty in gaining acceptance in their ranks. He is remembered, with some justice, as having "a genius for finding ways to stay out of the hard, physical labor," but this seemingly negative judgment is balanced by the same respondent's approving observation that Dennison found compensation in "his poison pen—for what the body was reluctant to do, the head more than made up for it." The "poison pen" reference is a mock-critical acknowledgment of Dennison's penchant for dashing off petitions and pronouncements, sometimes satirical but often deadly serious, whenever the occasion seemed to arise. And the occasions were never lacking at Warner.

In the context of camp politics, Dennison illustrates the tenuous relationship between the college boy-intellectual faction and the camp administration and its supporters. As a Catholic there was never any question of his support for the ACCO and his commitment to the objective of preserving Camp Simon as a corporate Catholic witness against the war; yet on most of the issues and controversies that raged throughout the six months of Warner's history, he was almost always allied with the critics and protesters. Unable to match Bartlett in intellectual brilliance or theological competence, he nonetheless teamed with him to form a loyal Catholic opposition so that, if nothing else, the combination of Bartlett's erudition and Dennison's poison pen helped prevent what might otherwise have developed into a split along strictly religious lines between the opponents and supporters of the camp administration.

The Artists

Leonard Mattano and, to a lesser extent, George Selmon were the dominant figures of this important and influential special interest clique, a fact which probably explains their being two of the four men remembered by all respondents to my questionnaire. But their studio domain was shared by some other extremely individualistic and independent spirits. One of the most memorable was Roger Tennitt, impassioned rebel against all authority, religious or other, bitterly scornful of anything and everything that smacked of bourgeois convention and that, to Tennitt, encompassed almost anything and everything. He was at one and the same time a living personification of the stereotyped garret-dwelling, starvation-haunted bohemian ("I always felt he was dying of consumption," writes one former camper), and a precursor of philosophies and life styles that would follow a generation later ("As prophet of the perverse, he was surely entitled to say, 'Before any beat or hip or hippie or yippee *was*, I *AM*' "). Several replies drew a connection between Tennitt's personal disorganization and iconoclastic fervor and his wildly avant-garde artistic creations. And, in truth, had he intentionally set out to costume himself and rehearse the role, he could not have done a better job of fitting the artist-revolutionary mold of old, romantic novels. His language was generously laced with what passed for obscenities in those innocent days; his bunk area was a veritable rat's nest, a public statement of principled rejection of the bourgeois values of neatness and cleanliness. It is the characterization offered by one of his fellow artists that best captures this hippie-before-his-time: ". . . surrounded perpetually by a cloud of cigarette smoke . . . took aspirins by the handful. Unkempt—good humor—intelligent. Gentle and a very creative person. Bellicose laughter exposed tobacco-stained teeth."

No two members of the Warner community were more different in outlook and commitment than Tennitt and Tony Saunders, the consummate Catholic Worker. During the latter's unhappy reign at Warner, the always disgruntled Roger was one of the more aggressive agitators behind the protests and hassles that made life so miserable for him. It is a neat irony, then, that they shared the distinction of being the only ones to carry protest to the point of actual rebellion—Saunders in his short-lived walk-out at Stoddard; Tennitt, always the more imaginative, in a formally declared strike. In a statement addressed to the NSBRO he declared his art to be "work of national importance" and spelled out the conditions of the service he would henceforth perform: the forty-four-hour regulation work week would be devoted to his painting during which time he would undertake to produce one painting of specified dimensions (not less than 24" x 30", frame not included) every two months; these he would donate "to any public or private institution so designated by proper authority." Materials, their cost calculated by Tennitt, were to be furnished him, presumably by the government or the benefitting institution. Like Saunders before him, Tennitt ended his protest before the camp authorities were forced to apply the penalty specified in Selective Service regulations; but even this decision was announced formally as a suspension of the strike and not capitulation. To the very end, Tennitt remained "the wild man of camp: roaring anger; stammering rage; undisciplined screaming from time to time," openly disliked by many but tolerated and even, if the truth be known, enjoyed and respected by most.

The remaining members of the artists' colony kept to themselves in their studio enclave, taking active part in camp affairs only when some issue of immediate concern to them was under discussion. LeRoy Torto and the Luzon brothers gravitated more toward the disrupter group to be discussed below, the elder Luzon having gained recognition as one of the two or three ringleaders in the Stoddard period. An exception to the rule in the other direction was Pat Meany, perhaps more entitled to the artist designation than many of the other studio habitues, but, as already noted, better included as one of the leaders of the chapel group and a staunch defender of the camp administration and its policies.

Melvin Korlutsch was another artist who did not seem to fit too well into the bohemian atmosphere of the studio. He was too gregarious for that, an open and congenial would-be friend to all. For some reason his ingratiating manner made him the victim of many camp jokes, the most notable being a "Hate Korlutsch Movement" initiated by Dennison, one of his more frequent companions. This became a long-running gag in which other campers soon joined, possibly as a backhanded testimony to the man's irrepressible good nature. As one of the camp's night watchmen, it was Mel's practice to wake the men with a rousing "Rise and Shine!" greeting in a cheery singsong voice guaranteed to stir a chorus of ungrateful responses. Unlike most of the other artists who were not at all reticent about discussing their work and their personal theories of art, Korlutsch seemed reluctant to put his on display. This may have been because he, a serious and accomplished craftsman, felt somewhat out of place in the company of the more self-consciously experimental and avant-garde types who dominated the discussions.

The good fellow image characterizes most of the remembered impressions of Korlutsch, but there were occasionally discordant notes. This man who was considered a "very private person" by one is viewed as "slightly neurotic" by another. The most surprising response of all (could this respondent have been taken in by the "Hate Korlutsch" campaign?) describes him as "a sad, introverted chap who had few friends." A fellow artist remembers him more accurately as "a young fellow, harmless, well-intentioned who had a tremendous sense of comedy that was layered with a frosting of corn. Good for many a laugh." That "layer of corn" description is important; so, too, is another remembered observation to the effect that he "appeared to spend about three hours a day cleaning his teeth with dental floss." This practice, which I had forgotten, was the cause of many another jibe at his expense. This respondent continued to make a summary judgment that perhaps most of the campers would have shared: "Mr. Malaprop. Good Fellow. Laughed a lot."

The Disrupters

To recapitulate for a moment, the chapel group, the Catholic Workers, and the Coughlinites, supported most of the time by the other Catholics as well, tended to back the ACCO administration to the extent necessary to assure continuity for Camp Simon as a corporate Catholic witness against World War II. The workers and some of the loners, both groups still to be described, were indirectly supportive of the administration in their neutrality and detachment from the debates and agitation over camp policies or practices and, in a more positive sense, by virtue of the essential services they, or at least the workers, performed. The artists for the most part were negative in their attitudes toward the camp administration and indifferent toward the elected camp government, but they were not much of a problem if they were left alone. The intellectuals directed a steady drumfire of criticism against the camp administration, the ACCO, the NSBRO, the CPS program, and the Selective Service System as the font of all injustice. These critiques, however, were mainly ideological in character and, however much these efforts may have undermined camp authority, they were a principled resistance that was studiously considerate of the rights of others.

The disrupters presented a resistance of quite another kind. The behavior characteristic of these men seemed to be disruptive for the sake of being disruptive or to serve purely selfish ends. Their blatantly uncooperative attitude expressed a frankly contemptuous rejection of camp authority along with a scornful disdain for those who were ready to assume any share of extra responsibility for the camp or its future. The disrupters' ostentatious malingering on work project and in the camp setting as well went far beyond the normal gold-bricking pattern which, as I have suggested, was a more principled demonstration of unwillingness to perform "slave labor." If there were echoes of this principled protest in their dedicated avoidance of work, it was carried to a greater level of intensity by their challenging "and-what-are-you-going-to-do-about-it" attitude and by their complete lack of concern over the fact that the more essential tasks could not be left undone. More annoying still was their response to those who did come forward to assume that extra share of the burden; as far as they were concerned, such volunteers were objects of scorn and ridicule as "second-milers" and "200-percenters."

Harsh though this uncomplimentary description may seem, it is not unfair. What might be unfair is the assignment of particular campers to the disrupter category, especially since all so designated here could just as easily have been included in one or another of the various categories. Thus the Luzons, signpainters by occupation in pre-CPS days, preferred to think of themselves as commercial artists and had as legitimate a claim to the artist designation as some of the late-blooming amateurs accepted as members of the studio community. John Canory, were it not for his close (and partly commercial) association with the "New York crowd" that utilized his Canory Express, could just as easily have fit into the loner category.

It would be best, then, to regard this disrupter designation as referring more to a mode of behavior than to a defined group of individuals. Those identified for the dubious honor of being discussed under this classification are there simply because they were consistent enough in this mode of behavior to earn the disapproval of others. It should be noted, however, that the disruption attributed to this faction is not to be confused with the periodic binges to be discussed later. The binges were disturbances all right, and some of these men were usually involved; but the disruption caused by the sprees was altogether different in quality and involved a more broadly representative selection of the camp membership.

In his study of the Stoddard phase, Winchester described what he called the Canory-Luzon "crowd" as being distinguished by several characteristics: an overt hostility toward the ACCO and the other religious agencies; an unwillingness to do even a minimally respectable day's work on project; a refusal to volunteer to help out with camp projects or needs; and a pattern of insistent complaints about the camp's shortcomings.

By the time of the move to Warner, Winchester's crowd had been reduced to the men he identified as its leaders, John Canory and

John Luzon. Others had sought and received transfers to the Alexian unit. One of the transferees, a fiery Joycean Irishman named Monaghan, would return to the Warner roster in late November but only to stay a week or so before departing again, this time to await induction to noncombatant military service. At Warner, possibly because the old gang had broken up, the Canory-Luzon influence in camp affairs seemed greatly diminished. Perhaps this was more a function of the fact that the over-all morale declined so rapidly and so drastically that whatever disruption the Canory-Luzon remnant once caused was then overshadowed by the universally prevailing mood of resistance and frustration.

But this does not mean the remnants failed to make their presence known. John Luzon remained a force to be reckoned with, one which is still variously assessed by the men who served with him. Ostentatiously macho and ruggedly handsome, he made much of his amorous successes with women—including, by his report, a number of willing maids met at dances in the Warner vicinity—and he was not at all shy about describing his conquests. He was equally explicit in expressing his attitude toward work: it was an annoyance and an affront, something to be avoided at all costs and by any means. Nominally Catholic, he was openly contemptuous of religion and not above ridiculing those who put a spiritual connotation upon their presence in CPS and their camp activities. It is possible that he exaggerated the crudity of his language and the details of his sexual exploits to shock the goody-goody boys he felt surrounded him. There was certainly nothing in his camp behavior to support his strong affirmation of his Catholic faith in a note he had sent to his draft board before assignment to Stoddard; and his performance on project did not match his assurance in that same communication that he would prefer "vigorous, healthy, outdoor work" in his alternative service.

He was extremely self-oriented, and intellectual discussions of war and pacifism did not interest him at all, but he was always outspoken on matters relating to personal comfort and convenience. His loud and insistent demands that the windows in the cold bunkhouse be opened in sub-zero weather almost led to blows one desperately cold night; yet when the camp broke up it was discovered that he had somehow appropriated several extra government-issue blankets for his bunk. Surprisingly enough, for all of this he was not unpopular. Even those who regarded him as a self-centered troublemaker and who, on that count alone, questioned the sincerity of his conscien-tious objection still credit him with a measure of charm and a person-ally friendly manner. For one, his "oversize sense of humor with an undertone of promiscuousness" made him an asset if only in that he "helped to break the monotony" of camp life. He was, recalls anoth-er, "the 'big' Luzon—slow moving, slow walking, slow breathing, moderately active big John (rhymes with big con). Unabashedly said he was in camp only to get out of it."

The reference to "big" John refers to the presence in camp of his younger brother, Kenneth, who is universally remembered only in the context of the elder. This is no doubt due to the fact that Ken-neth arrived at Warner in November and quite naturally took much of his identity from the record John had already established at Stod-dard. But there was more to it than that. There was every indication that Ken was so completely dominated by his older brother (one former camper goes so far as to describe him as John's "creature") that he consciously modeled his behavior accordingly. He, too, boasted of his successes with the ladies and was most forthcoming in making his claims; instead of John's rugged "he-man" features, Ken's was more the "pretty boy" kind of handsomeness, but there was no reason to doubt that both were probably quite attractive to women. Again like John, he made much of his total disinterest in things intellectual or idealistic, though he could be lured into some of the deeper discussions his brother was inclined to shun. Neither gave the slightest hint of an ideological commitment to pacifism, religious or otherwise, nor did they try to dispel the widely held view that their presence in camp was simply their way of avoiding the risks and inconveniences of military service. Not everyone made so ungenerous an assessment, however. One former camper, reflecting upon the absence of any ideological basis for their stand, went on to credit both with a sincere aversion to killing, which was a sound enough reason for their being in CPS.

That respondent, who was at least willing to regard John as an as-set, took a less generous view of the brother. Describing Kenneth as "a little less forceful" than the elder Luzon, he adds, "Somehow the concept of peace was remote to them. Should never have been in camp. Goes for John too—but he was basically a good fellow, well-intentioned."

A third principal in the disrupter group was the other of Winches-ter's Stoddard ringleaders, John Canory. My own recollection of him is vague; he remains one of the background figures at Warner, tall and rangy in build and secretive in manner, quite possibly the sharp operator deserving of his nickname, "Cagey." For what it is worth, he seems to have left a generally unfavorable impression upon his fellow campers. Even one of his erstwhile friends and regular companions on the Canory Express described him as "a bit on the weird side." He is remembered for dismissing the artists as "phonies" and mocking them in their search for "the right *poi*ple in a sunset." Another remembers him as totally unreceptive to any kind of ideas, an attitude that made him stand out in a group of men whose very presence in camp was testimony to some idea or ideals. Not one of the questionnaire responses credited him with being sincere in his stand. Even the friendliest recollection went no further than to describe Canory as "outrageous—gawky—funny. A buffoon who somehow didn't fit into the peace movement. But neither did he fit into the war movement." Others described him as "an enigma . . . cunning in a slow-witted way, looking for an angle" and, the harshest judgment of all, "greedy, uncooperative, and lazy—or so he struck me. No group feeling at all. Loafed a good deal on work project."

That "no group feeling at all," of course, is the characteristic that sets the men of the disrupter category apart from the more principled troublemakers like Farfether of the intellectual set and Tennitt of the artists. As far as the disrupters were concerned, there was nothing beyond their own narrow and selfish interests to motivate their constant complaints and criticisms. At times, indeed, they seemed to set themselves against the rest of the men, though this did not preclude establishing some individual friendly relationships. In his comment on John Luzon, the author of that most severe judgment on Canory linked the two: "I associate him with Canory. To me they were 'Luzon and Canory' sensualists out for themselves, without any real concern for the meaning of the camp."

Few, certainly not I, would challenge that judgment; but in all fairness there is something more to be said. It is possible that their recalcitrance was not entirely what it appeared to be on the surface. Instead it may have testified to a sense of inferiority arising from the very things they made so public a show of rejecting. If we take these three as the principal and most representative members of the disrupter group, ignoring for the moment the others that gravitated to their leadership from time to time, it can be said that they were sadly out of place in several respects. High school graduates in a setting dominated by articulate intellectual types; fallen away Catholics in the midst of highly motivated believers intent upon stressing the camp's Catholic identity and character; and, in the case of the Luzons, signpainters sharing a studio with academy-trained artists and way-out theorists of experimental styles—on all of these grounds they were outsiders and must have been conscious of the fact.

Of course, everyone in camp was an outsider to some extent, yet others did not react as negatively or with such destructive impact upon camp morale. Here the quality of their commitment becomes relevant. If, as so many were convinced, they were not completely sincere in the stand they had taken, it is possible that they could not really understand those who were, that they may even have shared the popularly held unfavorable stereotypes of the pacifist and conscientious objector. If so, the sensualist image they projected in the roughness of their language and the boasts of sexual prowess may have been a defensive assertion of a masculinity they felt was threatened by association with a group of men whose masculinity was challenged, if not denied altogether, in the public's mind. If there is merit to this hypothesis, they were more to be pitied than censured. All things considered, this active disrupter minority may have had a far harder time bearing with CPS and its shortcomings than did their fellow campers. The latter could take comfort in believing that the experiences and the sacrifices still had some meaning in the context of a commitment to pacifist values and the virtue of individual witness for a cause. The Canory-Luzon crowd, lacking such a commitment and concerned almost exclusively with their own interests and well-being, would have no similar rationale to fall back on.

The Workers

If it were not for the men grouped under this heading, men who were given or voluntarily assumed responsibility for keeping the camp going, Warner's brief existence would have been briefer, its chaos more chaotic. Most of them were assigned to tasks related to the care of the government's project equipment (trucks, axes and saws, and other work instruments), but their technical know-how and background in practical manual labor were invaluable assets whenever functional crises developed in any area of daily operations. In many respects the men who formed the workshop and toolroom enclave were a more tightly knit group than the bohemians who populated the artists'

studio. Most of them had been engaged in factory, crafts, or other manual labor before their assignment to camp; this work experience set them apart from the bulk of their fellow campers and, at the same time, brought them closer in their interests and thinking (with the obvious exception, of course, of differing attitudes toward the war) to the government employees charged with responsibility for directing the "work of national importance."

Two or three of the men became cronies of the project superintendent, a rotund, middle-aged Forestry Service employee who must have found his job of riding herd on Warner's assortment of incompetent and unwilling woodsmen exasperating at times. To his credit, as already noted, he maintained a remarkably low profile with respect to exerting the authority over the conscript labor vested in him under Selective Service regulations. Camper Robert Dunfey, the only professional woodsman on the roster (word had it he had been a woodchopper champion in Maine), must have been a source of special solace to this burdened man, and the two became almost inseparable companions. As one former camper put it, "Like God, if he did not exist, he would have had to be invented to keep Wilson company and sane." It probably worked both ways. Possibly to protect *his* sanity, Dunfey was rarely assigned to the forestry crew, and was thus spared the trauma of watching his fellow campers as they used and misused the tools he took such expert care to maintain. As a result, Dunfey had little contact with most of the men either during working hours or in the free time. The only contribution he is remembered as making to camp issues and food protests was his frequent and loud complaint about the "pig bread" produced by the amateur bakers.

The workers were also set apart from the general camp population by age and educational background. Though the record shows a 22–42 year age range for the men included in this group, this is deceptive in that all but two were more than 25 years old. The median age was 31.7 years, compared with the 27.3 years for the entire camp roster. The disparity in educational level is even more impressive. An average of 11.4 years of schooling was recorded for these workers, a full two years less than the average for the total camp population. Only four of the nine included under this heading had completed high school and only one had continued beyond that level to complete art school. The remaining four had never gone to high school; one had terminated his education at the sixth grade.

Eduard Amata at forty-two was the oldest man in camp, a carpenter and cabinet assembler by occupation who had been born in Italy. Though the personnel file records his religious affiliation as "none," and he is treated accordingly as one of the non-Catholic minority, it is probably safe to assume that he had been Catholic in his earlier life. He is remembered kindly as "a genuine mystic," a man of great dignity," a "peacemaker." One of the artists draws Amata in sharper detail: " 'Everyt'ing be all right' in Italian accent was what this gentle soul would say repeatedly in benign acceptance. Battered hat, cigarette stub in mouth; a slight smile; an instrument of hard work and optimism." Life with his younger and better educated campmates must have been a trial at times, but whenever attempts were made to draw him into some argument or other that might be swirling about his bunk, his usual response would be a shrug of the shoulders, a friendly smile, and the gentle advice, "Let's talk about the weather." John Luzon and Pat Rafferty would occasionally team to tease him about his love life as a younger man, but his response would be the same. So standard was that line, in fact, that it was soon taken over by others as a humorous device for changing any subject under discussion.

Henry Fallon was anything but quiet and retiring. Of all the workers, he was the most gregarious, and he insisted upon taking active part in chapel activities and camp affairs. At thirty-seven he apparently viewed himself as the knowledgeable elder brother, and he played the role with a vengeance quite undeterred by the fact that many of the others treated him as a comic irrelevancy. His greatest contribution lay in his genius for keeping the camp's panel truck in minimal running condition, and it is for this that he is most remembered with fondness and respect.* A talkative, even garrulous man, he had a virtually inexhaustible stock of seemingly endless narratives, all leading to a moral or application appropriate to a given situation. Unfortunately, the point he intended to make might be lost in the telling because of his habit of smothering the tale in a multitude of tangential or unconnected asides. But if the listener had sufficient patience to endure the nasal drone of his voice and learned to watch for the often obscure links between disjointed segments of the story, the experience usually proved well worth the effort. That anecdote cited by Mattano about Fallon's ride to the dentist's office is typical of his style of exposition. Taking Fallon's discursive style into consideration, I suspect his point was not made clear much before they actually arrived at his destination.

The workers, in summary, were the quiet ones, the steady ones, the reliable backbone of Camp Simon. A group apart, they were usually accessible enough as individuals, friendly and helpful when approached for assistance or advice. Except for Fallon, who did it all the time, I can not recall any of them entering into a discussion of the war and the various rationales for opposing it. It was almost as if they were sitting it out on the sidelines, bemused observers from a distance of the ideological debates and political controversies that occupied most of the others.

---

*This was a most important contribution. Government regulations prohibited the use of project trucks for private or camp purposes. This meant that, had the "White Ghost" expired as it was always on the point of doing, there would have been no way to get to Concord for provisions and occasional release or to transport the churchgoers to weekly Mass in Contoocook. In the divine economy, that latter service may have earned Hank a greater measure of spiritual grace than all the high level theological and liturgical disputations engaged in by his more enlightened fellow campers.

The Loners

The two remaining categories, the loners and the oddballs, defy
generalization almost by definition. In a population consisting of
individualists who had gone against the stream by refusing military
service in a war supported by a united nation, these men represent
individualism in its purest distillation. Some were serious workers,
holding it a matter of principle to fulfill their part of the CPS bargain.
Others, also on principle, resisted the notion of imposed obligation,
a few going so far as to deny that any man or group of men could
legitimately exercise authority over others no matter what the situation. Unlike some of the oddballs who seemed to exist in a world
of their own definition, the loners did not isolate themselves completely, though they did remain detached from most camp issues and
events. For some it was a matter of simply not wanting to be bothered, of living out each day until "the duration plus six months" had
passed. For others, and these attitudes were not always mutually ex-
clusive, the unwillingness to become involved reflected a desire not
to intrude upon the autonomy of others as much as a means of
claiming and preserving their own.

William O'Flaherty, author of the statement quoted at the beginning of this chapter, confirms the classification he had no way of
knowing would be applied to him. His self-characterization matches
the assessment made of him by his former colleagues. It would be a
mistake to conclude, however, that his loner status and disposition
should be equated with unsociability. The opposite would be closer
to the truth. O'Flaherty is remembered affectionately as one of the
most outgoing, gregarious, and loudest of the men at Warner. It is
probably the loudness that is mentioned most often; almost every
respondent has something to say about that. Other characteristics
mentioned were his intense religiosity ("morning prayers on knees"
is fixed in one former camper's memory), his helpfulness, his outspoken and usually immoderate opinions tempered with the saving
grace of good humor. "Wore buttons declaring 'Free India Now,' "
writes one; "also had problems with 'dizzy shits,' but he said it with
his great big smile."

Similar in many respects but very different in others was Ernest
Rider, one of the freest spirits on the scene. His ethnic origins, his
gloomy humor, his swarthy countenance and straggly mustache all
combined to earn him the nickname, "the Gypsy King." But the

quality people remember most of him was his argumentativeness. This was not a belligerent argumentativeness, however. The remarkable thing about Rider was his eagerness to take almost any side of any discussion for the sheer joy he found in taking sides; and the more abstract and philosophical, the better. Like O'Flaherty, he scorned the pretentiously intellectual ("agents of confusion," he called them), but he was always there when the discussions turned to subjects like the relativism of truth, the virtues of anarchism or nihilism, anything at all. One description pictures the "tall, jaunty, homespun humorist with the unexpected retorts—individualist—eager to argue about anything. I believe he originated the remarks, 'a suggestion is a mild form of command' and 'an intellectual is a person educated beyond his capacity.' " An occasional respondent recalled specific philosophical arguments that engaged Rider's interest: "He held nothing is real or exists. Someone wanted him to prove the stove existed and was hot by placing his hand on it. He refused." Another in the same vein: "He gave the answer to the little problem about how fast the stream was running."

Men like Rider and O'Flaherty were loners in the sense that they were not affiliated with any of the cliques or special interest factions that tended to divide the camp. Others were loners in the sense that they kept so much to themselves that they seemed to avoid contact with their fellows intentionally. "Silent Larry" Kenniston, as the name suggests, was remembered mainly for his quiet and withdrawn nature. It was a surprise bordering on shock when, on some rare occasion, he would loosen up enough to speak a few words. Raymond Lafferty was quiet and reserved too, but in his case these qualities were attributed to innate shrewdness, even secretiveness. Already a lawyer and the favored son of an apparently well-established family, he was regarded by some as snobbish, cool, and altogether too calculating in his manner. It was his rare distinction to have gained release from military service to enter CPS, but few ever knew the precise basis for his conscientious objection. He participated in the chapel group activities and might well have been included under that classification except for the fact that he did not throw himself into those activities with the same degree of dedication of the others.

Shrewdness of an altogether different kind was represented by "Good Food Walt" Berryman, perhaps the most selfish man I have ever met. So flatly unfavorable a judgment would be out of the place here were it not for the fact that this impression was shared by the

former campers who replied to my questionnaire. Berryman served
for a time as cook for a small side camp associated with the Stoddard-
Warner project, and the reports of the generous quantity and superior quality of the food available there tormented the rest of us who
existed on the meagre and unsatisfactory rations of the home camp.
Shortly after the side camp closed, he joined the kitchen staff at
Warner, where he soon gained a reputation for sneaking special deli-
cacies for his private consumption. On more than one occasion he
squandered the scarce supply of sugar to make some pies, one of
which he secreted for his private consumption. It is perhaps significant that even those who enjoyed the reputed largess of the side
camp have less than complimentary recollected impressions to offer.
One questioned his intellectual capacity, noting that "at Mt. Cardigan he lit the stove with kerosene and nearly burned us out." To
another he was "perhaps our 'most unlikely CO.' I have met few apparently self-interested *in toto* people. Walt qualified. Since he lived
in our small group at Mt. Cardigan over several weeks, I found him to
be virtually unthinking and uncaring about anyone else." Terms like
"a fox" and "a real operator" are used to describe him; even the respondent who seldom had anything but favorable things to say about
the men of Camp Simon was forced to confess that "Good Food
Walt" was "not too much of what I thought a CO ought to be."

The Oddballs

The term is uncharitable; the most suitable alternative, "misfit,"
would be scarcely less so. Of course, as far as the general public was
concerned, both terms would apply to the entire Warner roster and
not just the dozen or so to whom they were applied by their fellow
campers. Some have already been introduced. Jimmy O'Toole, "the
Pepsi Kid," is remembered by many for his childish ways ("arrested
development," as one puts it) and his gluttony. Several responses refer to the constant bickering that went on between him and Pat Rafferty, at once Jimmy's chief tormenter and the principal target of his
incessant, nagging, and usually trivial questions. It is Bill Grandman
who, once again, captures both the character and the relationship in
his response to the questionnaire. To him, Jimmy was "strange—
strange—strange. Smiling to himself on the truck rides to and from
work; childishly, weakly trying to chop wood; in his curiously re-
spectful, quasi-British accent, both reproving Rafferty and avoiding

Pat's antagonism. 'You are a card, you know, Pat, saying those terrible things about the Jews. You don't really admire Hitler, to you?' "

Dave Komiker, my companion of those first days at the stinking potato heap, is also remembered for his immaturity; but in his case this was related to his clownishness and simplicity, both of which combined into an impression of near sanctity. "A jovial little figure with a kindly face and a homely figure," remembers one, and he immediately asks the thoroughly reasonable question, "How did he get there?" To another Dave was "a spectacularly different little guy; he could have been any of the Seven Dwarfs. . . . Active, talkative in a stuttering, disconnected kind of way." Komiker, again, was one of those whose objection to war and military service was purely idiosyncratic, the claimed result of a personal visitation or vision. And for all one could tell, this was not impossible. If anyone were to receive direct spiritual instruction from on high, it would almost certainly have been this simple and humble fellow.

Mark Roselli has already been discussed as one of the four forgotten men of the Warner camp as has Joe Moroni, he of the abrupt and involuntary transfer, bunk and all, to the infirmary in the night cold of New Hampshire. Henry Blasek, the "Submarine Captain," earned that designation as much for his costume (knitted black cap, black pea jacket, black knickers, black stockings, and black shoes) as for his manner of communicating in monosyllabic grunts. Most of the time he stood apart from the others in some corner or other, never shaking hands or, for that matter, touching doorknobs or any other potentially germ-laden surfaces. It was Blasek whose ultimate deterioration at the North Dakota camp to which he was ultimately transferred has already been described in the discussion of Selective Service's cavalier attitude toward the mental or physical condition of men inducted into Civilian Public Service.

Perhaps the most striking of "the walking dead," the unsympathetic term applied to men on permanent sick status, was Marlon French, better known as "Utopia." This hulking, full-bearded giant was a most imposing figure, anticipating in manner and appearance more contemporary devotees of Eastern mysticism and other esoteric cults. He was the innovator in another sense as well, the first of the Stoddard-Warner campers to fall victim to the clinically unverifiable, and thus not easily refutable, sacroiliac affliction that came to be regarded with varying degrees of serious contemplation as a possible passport out of CPS. The grievous affliction struck him down after only two or three days of project work at Stoddard and rendered him unavailable for work assignments of any kind from that time until his final discharge.

This former hotel bellman established his claim to the oddball category at Stoddard; at Warner he was little more than a strange, shadowy figure inhabiting the infirmary. Campers remember him as "a weird character," even as "the first of the 'weirdos' before the word was invented." Several commented upon his penchant at Stoddard for sun-bathing and his devotion to other physical culture fetishes. Both recollections insinuate a note of doubt as to the validity of the incapacity he exploited so successfully. One of the artists who had known him at both Stoddard and Warner sums it all up: "The originator in camp of the sacroiliac as a way to fly the coop. Big rolling eyes; story-teller; gentle person with the physique of an Atlas; sun-worshipper and vegetarian; had his own way of interpreting the peace. Hoarse, jerky voice. Came to camp without a beard—grew one—left camp without a beard." And that paragon of Camp Simon, Leonard Mattano, adds a characteristically sentimental touch by describing Utopia's departure from camp when the physical discharge finally was approved. As he remembers it, the big man broke down and left with the sobbing farewell, "I won't write, but I'll never forget you guys." It was, to say the least, an interesting finale for one who had kept himself so much apart and who must have sensed the sometimes resentful, possibly envious, suspicions with which he and his ailment were regarded by so many of those guys.

One thought that has often troubled me in the intervening years was given expression by one of the respondents to my questionnaire: *Why weren't we more kind?* The questioner did not have Utopia in mind—in fact, he had characterized the man as "one of our more curious comrades" and asked, "was he sincere in his convictions or just an odd-ball?" But the question itself applies to him and to all the others in this category. The sad truth is that relatively few of us distinguished ourselves by the practice of charity or, for that matter, even friendly concern when it came to dealing with these "curious comrades." Eccentric, neurotic or even psychotic, they were often treated as objects of derision behind their backs and, at times, to their faces as well. It seldom reached the point of physically expelling someone into the sub-zero night or teasing him into self-imposed isolation, but that such things could happen even rarely is not fully consistent with the commitment to religious and humanitarian ideals that presumably accounted for our being gathered together at that particular time and place.

Some of the campers may have offended more than others, but even those who did not join in the game of teasing or ridiculing these unfortunates bear some share of the guilt for failing to provide compensatory friendship and moral support. Most of the men in this category clearly should never have been drafted to *any* kind of service. It compounded the injustice already suffered at the hands of the local draft boards and Selective Service that once they were consigned to those remote and forbidding surroundings, they still found themselves among men all too often lacking in the sensibility that could have eased their adjustment to an alien and thoroughly inappropriate life situation. Taking the camp population as a whole, and pleading myself as guilty of the charge as anyone, the fault was not that we were consciously unkind but, rather, that we failed to be as kind as we could and should have been to these more unfortunate among us.[3]

All this means, of course, is that the men of Camp Simon were not the saints they had the opportunity to be, a fairly general mark of the human condition. If one seeks an explanation for this failure beyond that obvious and not particularly startling discovery, it can probably be found in the personal frustrations and problems arising from the special strains and hardships of the Warner situation, and in the extent to which these came to dominate each individual's concerns and behavior. Fully aware that, to most of our fellow citizens, conscience had made "cowards" of us all, we may have succumbed too easily to the temptation to celebrate our alienation, becoming ever more fixated upon our own violated rights and endangered well-being and sacrificing in the process much of the impact our witness might otherwise have had.

This is a possibility deserving the most careful reflection, but it should not be permitted to obscure an equally important truth. Even granting, in retrospect, that many of the issues and controversies that dominated life at Warner were trivial, others were matters of real and serious substance and all, even the most trivial, were magnified by the realities of the camp situation itself. It is to the description and discussion of both, and to the part played in them by some of the men introduced in this chapter, that we must now turn.

PART THREE

WARNER WORK SONG

Here we go
> *taking the high road yonder;*
Here we go
> *into the wood.*
Through the snow,
> *thrilling to Nature's wonder,*
Gay are we
> *everything's good.*

Trusty axe
> *sling we across our shoulders*
Comrades all
> *marching along.*
Though we get no pay
We work all day
> *Simply because . . .*
>> [thoughtful pause]
> *yes, simply because . . .*
>> [quiet, reflective pause]
> *well, simply because . . .*
>> [finally, with exasperation]
> *well, BECAUSE.*

To be sung to the tune of the Army Air Corps March.

To begin we must return to the most fundamental division among the campers, the difference in religious perspectives. Camp Simon, though officially a Catholic camp operated under Catholic auspices, was in fact dominated, numerically at least, by men who did not support or accept the religious outlook of its administration. Almost one-quarter of the assignees were of non-Catholic religious persuasion or of no religion at all. Of those who were classified as Catholics, a large number no longer practiced their faith and some were openly antagonistic to Catholicism, its teachings, and its behavioral expectations. The active Catholics, then, represented no more than half of the Warner population and, more likely, a minority.

Though camps administered by the other religious agencies (except, perhaps, for the Mennonites) seldom contained religiously homogeneous populations, few had to deal with the problems encountered at Warner because of these different, often conflicting, religious points of view. The dissidents of the Farfether type, quiet, almost contemplative in their agnostic intellectualism, were a far cry from the strident atheism of a Roger Tennitt or the loud and scornful ridicule of the nominally Catholic Luzon brothers. A further complication lay in the small size of the camp's population: actions and attitudes that could be more easily absorbed in a larger body were magnified and made more crucial in a group which at its peak strength never reached a total of more than fifty or sixty men. Finally, given the image of the Roman Catholic Church as the epitome of political and ecclesiastical conservatism, an image more justified then than it might be today, one could understand why the dissident ele-

ments in a Catholic camp tended to be more dedicated in their opposition to camp authorities than their counterparts in a Quaker camp,
for instance, might feel the need to be.

The dissidents felt they had reason to suspect that, though all were
equal in shared misfortune at Camp Simon, they were perhaps a little
less equal than others, and they could find support for that suspicion
in the behavior and opinions of the more ardent defenders of the
ACCO administration. The only Warner issue of the camp paper, itself the occasion of one of the sharpest of the controversies to be
discussed in this chapter, contained an ultra-triumphalist challenge
written by George Andrews, that most uncompromising of the
camp's Catholic rigorists. It is short and deserves to be given here in
its entirety as an example of precisely the kind of thinking that
helped to keep tension levels high:

THE FACT

*The whole discussion of the Catholic Church and its doctrines can be reduced to
one sentence. Admit this sentence and you admit all; deny it, and you deny all.
The point on which the Catholic Church rests is this:*

GOD CAME ON EARTH AND LEFT A DIVINELY GUIDED CHURCH

*This sentence is a statement of fact . . . a fact that thousands have died to attest,
a fact that hordes have striven to deny—but still, in spite of all, a fact. As such it
is ascertainable with complete certainty.*

Obviously keyed to the on-going debates in camp, such sentiments
could only serve to widen the gap between the administration's supporters and the non-Catholic and nonpracticing Catholic elements. In
these post-Conciliar days it is easy enough to dismiss the Andrews
position as a theologically unsound extravagance; at that time, however, it enjoyed widespread acceptance in the Church as the most
correct, or orthodox, position. Few of the active Catholics at Warner
would have been as blatantly insensitive in proclaiming that "fact,"
but the majority would have found it more acceptable than the contrary position argued by the Catholic liberals in their midst which
held that every church, even those that recognized only part of the
"truth," was deserving of respect.

This brings us to the second and, in a sense, more serious set of
religious divisions outlined earlier and the special contribution it
made toward creating the controversy-prone situation at Warner. The
half of the camp population that was Catholic in behavior as well as

in identification, was itself ideologically fragmented with respect to the theological approach to questions of war and peace. The principal lines of division already summarized in the chapter devoted to first impressions and employed as the framework for assigning individual campers to the various cliques and factions need not be recapitulated in detail. However, there is one point that deserves repetition because it bears directly upon the issues. The Catholic Worker bloc, it was suggested, regarded Camp Simon as an extension of the social movement of which they had been a part before coming to CPS. There was justification enough for this attitude in the fact that the ACCO was a creation of the Worker, an organizational front for its peace activities, and depended upon the parent movement for whatever funds, however insufficient, were obtained for camp operations.

This became a problem when the Catholic Workers in camp seemed to be exercising proprietary rights without giving due consideration to the interests or preferences of the other elements. The charge was often made, and in a variety of contexts, that the intention was to impose the movement's philosophy and standards upon the entire group. This gained added credibility in the charge, easily enough substantiated, of favoritism in camp assignments or preference for the Catholic Workers and others in the core supporter group when it came to detached service opportunities.

Several references were made to the case of Stuart Grant, a man listed on the Warner camp roster throughout its history but permanently assigned to "detached service" at the Catholic Worker House in New York City. Grant had been a member of the staff there until he was ordered to service; shortly after his arrival he was sent back, ostensibly to assist with the ACCO administrative work at its headquarters there. To make matters worse, the transfer was effected before the other campers were aware that such an assignment was available. Detached service opportunities in New York were always much sought after and became increasingly desirable with the passing of each month in New Hampshire. It is no surprise, then, that the decision to send Grant from Stoddard to New York was resented as arbitrary and unjust.* Later, when other choice assignments were giv-

*It was both, but the implication that it was also evidence of favoritism is less certain. In the course of a visit to Warner, Dorothy Day explained the assignment as a decision made entirely in terms of probable qualifications for the job. The fact that Grant was already familiar with the life at Mott Street (not an easy

en to reliable friends of the ACCO administration, they would be regarded as further evidence of favoritism.

However deep and real the differences between the various Catholic positions, there was one point of unity to provide a measure of stability when serious controversy arose. In spite of its faults, it was generally agreed that the ACCO presence in the CPS program should be preserved as an identifiable corporate Catholic witness against the war. Thus, while protests against administrative deficiencies or the physical shortcomings of the camp could usually be assured of support cutting across all lines of internal division, it was equally certain that something resembling a united Catholic front would emerge when it seemed a particular protest or proposed solution might jeopardize the continued existence of the camp itself. To an increasing extent this meant, at least in the Warner phase of Camp Simon's history, its Catholic identity was meaningful and operative in a defensive sense, a decisive factor only in the emergencies created by the non-Catholic or fallen-away Catholic elements. It should be easy enough to see that this was guaranteed to aggravate the already divisive potential and further weaken camp morale.

Open religious clashes rarely occurred. The Rafferty-Luzon exchange described earlier and, to a lesser extent, "the great *Salt* controversy" still to be discussed were the only instances I can recall. Nevertheless, there did develop a kind of covert religiously oriented animosity based on bilateral suspicion that had its hidden effects upon almost every issue that came along; the Catholics ever on the alert for some threat to the camp's Catholic identity and the others equally watchful lest they find themselves or their rights subject to manipulation by the Catholic administration and its supporters.

Because of this, differences which may seem petty in the telling seldom were. In the midst of a war that was to cost upwards of eighty million lives and cause immeasurable hardship to those fortunate enough to survive, complaints of a few conscientious objectors concerning inadequate diet, the lack of pay, arbitrary furlough restrictions, and the like seem scarcely worth mentioning. At Warner

---

life, she noted—getting up at all hours to deal with drunks, enduring the bedbugs, eating stale and moldy bread) made him an obvious choice. Perhaps so, but this did not satisfy the objection that volunteers should have been solicited before the final selection was made. Quite apart from the merits of the choice, the manner in which it was made contributed greatly to the already widespread suspicion and resentment concerning ACCO policies and intentions.

these things assumed an importance beyond all reasonable proportion, a fact that in itself can serve as a measure of the frustrations
and the sense of alienation ruling the lives of the men in camp. In a
broader context these trivial concerns and issues find added significance in that they reflected deliberate policies and actions of the
conscription authorities and, by extension, the nation itself—policies
and actions that, in their own way, represented a serious departure
from the very ideals the war was presumably being waged to preserve.

If the issues seem petty, the term controversy may strike some as
overly exaggerated. No blows were struck, though there were two or
three occasions when they were seriously threatened. The Selmon
diary describes the incident which came closest to actual violence.
Pat Rafferty, as ever the irrepressible jokester, had started a spitball-
throwing contest using pellets of bread, one of which caught William
Marsh* between the eyes. Marsh, an erratic and short-tempered fellow, retaliated by throwing a knife that barely missed Selmon himself. The latter grabbed the offender by the arms and "set him down
smartly" after which, the diary notes, "Bill was red in the face and
he was roundly jeered when it was shown that he threw a knife. The
tempers of the men are pretty much on edge. But Marsh, to my
mind, is just a sorehead." Sorehead or no, the Selmon explanation
was sound. Tempers *were* on edge that month (January 1943). Winter was in full sway; food was at its poorest; and the grievances concerning what the men considered an increasingly dictatorial exercise
of administrative authority were approaching their peak.

Selmon's own morale was none too high if one is to judge by the
tone of his diary entries for the entire Warner period. Never the detached or unemotional reporter, he grew increasingly impatient in his
references to what he called "the usual wrangles" that came to characterize camp meetings. "It pains me so much," he notes at one
point, "to listen to the quarrelsome factions of men throwing verbal
daggers at each other based on their different beliefs of Catholicism

*Marsh, one of our "wildman" truck drivers, was a confirmed hypochondriac
and might fit into either the oddball or loner classification. In another sense he
was in a class by himself, having been *paroled* to Camp Simon following conviction for violating the Selective Service Act in refusing to obey orders for induction into the military. Not a particularly popular man, he was one of Pat's favorite targets for the teasing and needling at which he was a master. Marsh, too,
must have had an especially unhappy life at Warner among his not always considerate fellow campers.

and what it dictates them to be. Another meeting where feeling ran high and names are exchanged with bitterness over questions which they think involve their religion. How stupid this all appears to me— I know this is just another cause for my great disillusionment in living at this camp."

Fortunately such incidents resulted in no real or lasting emnities. The principals in the more heated exhanges usually made up and apologized shortly thereafter. Even so, there was enough of a carry-over effect to produce roughly predictable rivalries and alliances with the result that even the most casual remark or criticism sometimes served as the flashpoint for the smouldering resentments or frustrations never too far below the surface.

The Governance Issue

The one continuing source of controversy basic to most of the others centered upon the manner in which camp affairs were to be governed. The battlelines had been drawn at Stoddard and, for all the high hopes of reduced tensions in the new and larger camp, it became immediately evident that the Warner experience would feature more of the same. Here again, with a population fluctuating around fifty-five or sixty throughout the six months of its history, it should not have been all that difficult to provide for the orderly and peaceful handling of daily affairs, and to create decision-making procedures leading to, if not consensus, at least a suitably high level of concurrence born of shared interests and mutual concerns. This was not to be. The root difficulty lay in the characteristics of the men themselves. Individualists all, each had his own idea of what policies should prevail and how whatever order and discipline might be required (and some, of course, rejected both on principle) were to be established and maintained. The shared interests, as we have seen, were not really shared; religious differences and differences within the various religious divisions made for a least common denominator of agreement involving little more than their basic refusal to accept service in the military forces. Mutual concerns were recognized, of course, but these too were usually translated into personal, even selfish, dimensions by the individual campers.

In the earliest Stoddard days, as Winchester reconstructs them, it was thought that whatever decisions were made should reflect the will of the group. This dream of governance by free and informed consensus faded before the influx of new men and the emergence of a substantial core of dissidents. After a series of meetings failed to produce anything like consensus on even the most trivial issues, sentiment grew for a change in favor of some system of representative camp government. It is probably at this point that the seeds of all the later difficulties were planted. This shift in emphasis represented the first significant departure from the founding Catholic Worker philosophy of personalism. The personalist ideal envisioned a system of self-government under which everyone would be alert to what was needed and ready to assume responsibility for doing what had to be done to meet that need. The purity of this ideal was already compromised to some extent by the acceptance of the will-of-the-group approach, but the two were not incompatible. In those instances where personalist judgment might not conform fully with the will, matters presumably could be resolved through further discussion leading to fuller understanding. Representative governance, however, though it too could be suited to personalist commitment, presented more of a challenge. Once procedures were established under which the individual became subject to the will of a majority, the area in which he could be certain of the freedom to decide and act on his own responsibility was seriously diminished.

The response of the camp administrators to the inability to achieve consensus was a move in the other direction, toward the monastic ideal of a guiding authority. Already at Stoddard, Winchester reports, the assistant director—not yet the Tony Saunders who was to assume that post and have so unhappy a time at Warner—noted the change in Director Larrowe's viewpoint as one of absorbing more fully "the CW principles of authority, trust in authority and not in the will of the group, not in counting noses." The director felt now that "the group decision is more of a compromise and therefore is that much further from what the truth would be. We should put trust in a leader to guide us and we should obey. Then we are likely to have the right answer."

It is difficult to conceive of an approach more unsuited to this particular body of men. The mere thought that they would look for, or even accept, a leader to guide them and then obey his guidance was so wide of the mark as to guarantee a widening gulf of ideological disagreement and an intensification of suspicion on their part. And this, of course, is precisely what happened.

A compromise of sorts was reached at Stoddard and this, it ap-

pears, was the governance structure transplanted to Warner. It provided for a rotating council of six members, each serving for six weeks.
This council was empowered to make decisions on camp business.
The weekly camp meeting was left with two functions: to review and
ratify or disapprove council decisions that had been taken and to discuss more basic camp principles and set broad objectives. However,
both the representative council and the camp meeting were to continue to operate on the will-of-the-group basis. This proved to be the
plan's fatal flaw.

The compromise had no more prospect of success than the director's vision of the wise leader. A group of men already so sharply
fragmented into interest groups by virtue of their differing beliefs
and who, under the constant attrition of the frustrations and alienation built into the Warner situation, were given to those usual wrangles at camp meetings could scarcely be expected to reach consensus,
even to ratify or reject actions on which their representatives had
reached agreement. My personal recollection is that this feature gave
way to direct majority vote shortly after the Warner camp opened
with the will of the group still honored in theory but ignored, or
at least suspended, in practice.

Meanwhile, in the December 1942 issue of the *Catholic Worker*,
Director Larrowe expanded upon his current philosophy of camp
governance.

*We are operating under a sort of functional authoritarianism. The Director is
ultimately responsible for the whole camp and so has supreme authority. Other
officers have authority according to their responsibility. The cook is responsible
for and has authority in the kitchen; the nurse is responsible for and has authority in the infirmary, and so on.*

*Responsibility and authority are inseparable, though they should be as decen-
tralized as possible; responsibility must be moral as well as financial and political.
We believe that discipline is essential and must, when necessary, be enforced. But
the spirit of government and of officials must be a spirit of love, of charity, of
understanding, of service.*

The *Worker*'s publication schedules being what they were, this passage raises an intriguing question of historical sequence. At the time
of the move to Warner, Larrowe was on extended stay at the Mott
Street House of Hospitality and, the record suggests, did not get to
Warner until mid-December. If so, what is presented here as a description of already established policy was actually an outline of in-

tention. Once arrived on the scene, he did attempt to put functional authoritarianism into practice with the only noticeable result of his efforts being the entirely predictable escalation in animosity.

It was a losing game in any event. In late October the welcoming letter to new assignees still spoke in terms of encouraging them "to pitch in and help on the jobs around the camp" but assured them they would be free to refuse. It professed a preference for a personalist approach of self-assumed responsibility over the duress of punishment or imposed discipline. Even the reference to the camp director's "power to say that the men must do all the work he thinks important about the camp, must even forego leaves or furlough if necessary" was coupled with assurances that "we leave the doing of 'extra' work up to a man's conscience. We do not try to force him to do that."

The shift to functional authoritarianism met its severest test on January 14 and 15 when the work siren sounded despite the obvious fact that inclement weather would not permit the men to go out on project.[1] The entire camp had been placed on "special detail" status by Director Larrowe and assigned to a variety of housekeeping and kitchen duties. It was announced that anyone discovered not doing the task assigned to him would be subject to loss of furlough time and that the director would be checking up on the men himself.

It was on this occasion that Lowell Bartlett had the confrontation he still remembers and resents. Assigned to washroom cleaning duty, he was ordered to do the work over when the director came through and discovered some dusty areas remaining. The fact that Bartlett was new to the scene, having arrived only nine days before, may have helped fix the unhappy event so indelibly in his mind. More significant in its implications, therefore, is the impression this particular exchange left upon others who learned of it and shared Bartlett's resentment. Thus, while Selmon's diary contains a number of references to his own difficulties with Director Larrowe, it is an offhand comment provoked by the Bartlett incident which provides the best indication of the campers' reaction to the work edict. Selmon noted, "If I would recognize the government of the camp, I would have protested at the Council and made this an issue. But I don't recognize the government because to my mind it is little more than a sham for the real dictatorial administration which exists through Dictator Larrowe."

So much for functional authoritarianism! The intervening years have mellowed Selmon's judgment a bit. Now he describes the "Dictator" as "an enigma," a man "who was disturbed over what he was searching for—and just was not certain where his position was." Crediting Larrowe with intellectual and administrative leadership, Selmon goes on to say "he never could sustain it in one given direction for any length of time . . . sometimes I thought he was for the rank & file camp men—at other times he gave the impression of representing the government policy." This is probably a more perceptive analysis than Selmon realized at the time. After all, every camp director must have learned at some point or other that his difficult position did incorporate both sets of obligations.

The personalities involved contributed negatively to the efficiency and acceptance of the camp situation. The Warner experience began at the severe disadvantage of suffering a leadership void with the director in New York for at least the first five or six weeks of its existence. By the time he returned with those more forceful notions of how the camp was to be administered from that time forward, morale had already reached a state of almost total collapse. During the intervening period it had fallen to Acting Director Saunders, himself an assignee, to make the decisions and assert such authority as he could muster, both tasks clearly beyond his means and temperament. Almost all remembered impressions of Saunders agree in describing him as sincere and devout but completely unsuited in personality for the challenge presented by the responsibilities thrust upon him. Some, more unkind, add the judgment that the deficiency extended to intelligence as well, but most recognized that, as one who was closely associated with him notes, those weeks must have been torture for him. Openly scorned by his more intellectual critics and mimicked by others for that "weird laugh" and other personal mannerisms, the task of helping to administer the conscription program he had once walked out from in protest must have been humiliation compounded. If Larrowe's return was greeted by the men with a sigh of relief, none could have found it more welcome than Saunders himself.

Director Larrowe proved more difficult for my respondents to characterize. The remembered impressions ranged from the frankly unfavorable (Bartlett's description of him as a "Catholic Quaker" and "second-miler") through Selmon's "enigma," and on to enthusiastic praise. One of the latter describes "a thoroughly extraordinary man—an excellent choice for Camp Director—a deeply spiritual person, keen insight and judgment, mature, aware, urbane (despite his faded blue work shirt and red neckerchief!), reasonably tolerant of personalities he had to deal with." The most balanced assessment presents Larrowe as a pleasant and calm person who looked older than he was, who "was one of us and yet he wasn't," a "good man with the difficult job of managing a camp of a great many non-conformists who often acted pretty childishly."

For what it is worth, this latter judgment approximates my own. I, too, remember him as a quiet, soft-spoken, balding man with a dry sense of humor that always seemed to border on sarcasm; a man from whom, largely out of my desire to avoid extra work, voluntary or not, I found it best to keep my distance. William Grandman's memory puts Larrowe in the camp context, seeing him with "his head tilted to one side, a half-mocking smile on his face as he spoke at camp meeting—blue eyes and skull-skin (through wisps of hair) shining in the light from overhead in those drab and gloomy cabins—still hear the tone of quiet resignation in his voice."

Ron Baxter, the camp clerk, adds a most significant observation. Clearly sharing the favorable view ("He combined a much higher degree of selflessness than I can remember in anyone else, with a wonderful sense of humor"), he goes on to say, "These qualities were perhaps more in evidence at Stoddard because by the time the community (Is this the right word?) was transferred to Warner the patience, firmness, forbearance, and good will with which Dwight almost always countered the childish and often loutish behavior of the dissidents had begun to wear thin." Baxter's observation finds unanticipated conformation in Larrowe's own response to my request for his recollections of Warner:

What single meaning of Warner? About Stoddard, many beautiful pleasant memories as not so pleasant—Christmas carols in the snow—skating on the frozen pond—Mrs. Hower—Mattano's humor—Torto's individuality—peeling apples together—Mr. Wilson—Bob Dunfey—Angus McNeill waking the guys with an accordion—Michael Trevor typing outside in the sun—friendships with many of the fellows. Warner I don't remember much—what I do remember is unpleasant.

Personality factors aside, the major criticisms of the Warner camp administration was that the exercise of authority was overly arbitrary and too much inclined to favor the Catholic campers, most specifically the Catholic Worker and chapel (or, to use Selmon's favorite description, the "die-hard") Catholics. Both charges are valid to some extent. Since one of the overriding concerns of everyone was to find a way of somehow escaping from the depressing camp situation, the slightest rumor of new detached service opportunities, however unfounded, would stir great excitement and hope. It was no small matter, then, that two men—listed and carried on the Warner roster though they never served a day in that camp—had been named to what were viewed as extremely desirable assignments in New York City, or that a third was assigned in December to detached service in Washington, D. C. To make matters worse, all three were inner circle supporters of the ACCO and the camp administrators. A sour-grapes reaction was predictable in any event, but there was more to it than that. The pattern seemed to give substance to the nagging suspicion that, first, information about other available assignments of this kind was being kept from the men and, second, individuals who did not support the ACCO and its policies might find their chances for detached service jeopardized as a penalty for their criticism or opposition.

Both fears were exaggerated, yet there was a reality factor to each that should not be overlooked. The ACCO was not in the mainstream of CPS and this, coupled with the normal inefficiency of its procedures, did mean that the men were not always kept abreast of developing detached service opportunities. And even when they were informed, Camp Simon assignees were at a disadvantage. Understandably enough, men in camps maintained by the mainstream religious agencies had a better chance of being chosen for any new special units to be administered by those agencies. Camp Simon assignees could hope for comparable priority only with respect to the Alexian unit, but its quota had already been filled. Then too, if new openings were to become available there, it was reasonable to expect that Catholic applicants would be given preferential consideration by the hospital administrators, a matter of no little concern to the non-Catholics and nonpracticing Catholics who knew they would require the recommendation of the ACCO to be given any consideration at all.

The assumption that detached service opportunities would be withheld or refused as a penalty had far less substance, though it is reasonable to assume that really obstructive elements would not have received much support for any applications they might make. But the appearance of arbitrariness was enough to feed camp resentment even where it was not justified by the facts. The much criticized

Washington appointment is a case in point. Documents reveal that
the appointment actually originated from the other end. The favored
individual's name had been suggested informally to the NSBRO as an
excellent prospect for the position of ACCO's liason officer, the suggestion offered by one of the other campers, a leader of the chapel
group, who happened to be visiting the Washington office when the
subject was raised in casual conversation. The NSBRO, acting on its
own, approached the individual directly to determine whether he
would be interested in the job. At this point the camper himself
sought the director's advice only to be informed by Washington
that the orders for transfer had already been approved.

It is certain that the director and the ACCO would have concurred
in the nomination had they been consulted in advance. The man in
question was one of the Catholic stalwarts, very competent and popular with campers of all factions. In the actual event, however, the
camp administrators seem to have been by-passed, a circumstance
that provoked an uncharacteristically sharp protest from Director
Larrowe. In a letter to the NSBRO he wrote:

*At the time I thought it was unfortunate that any individual should have been
mentioned. But I thought that before the position became a definite possibility
you would notify the camp and applications could be made. Possibly you would
require certain capabilities; certainly we, the ACCO, would. But the position
would be open to all those who qualified. Then it would be a matter of choice
by the ACCO or the NSB. This did not happen.*

What did happen, of course, was that many campers, including some
of the more reliable supporters of the camp administration, were disgruntled by what appeared to be another choice assignment arranged
in secret. Quite irrespective of the fact that an open selection would
probably have been made from a fairly restricted list of prospective
appointees, even those who knew they would not have qualified for
such a list saw this as one more cause for suspicion and resentment.
Larrowe, though his concern was primarily jurisdictional, took note
of these broader objections in his letter.

*The whole thing was so out of line with the usual policy of as much democracy
as possible that I hardly knew what to do. As you know, we have had plenty of
problems in this camp stemming from that very problem of democracy and representation. We don't claim to believe in democracy but the general impression
in camp is that the NSB does.*

We don't claim to believe in democracy. On the surface this may seem nothing more than a telling debater's point, but there is good reason to accept that statement's face value as an expression of administrative policy. Certainly there were campers other than Selmon who had come to regard the director if not as a dictator at least as someone determined to impose his brand of authoritarian order upon the camp and its members.

To repeat, no matter how open the applications for the Washington job might have been, the choice would surely have gone to a Catholic and, almost as surely, to a Catholic in full sympathy with the ACCO, its purposes, and its policies. After all, the position involved was that of designated ACCO representative at NSBRO headquarters, and such a restricted choice would have been fully justified. This is not to say that this thoroughly logical outcome would have gone unchallenged by the camp dissidents who, by that time, were quite sensitive to what they regarded as the effective disenfranchisement of all but the safest of Catholics. One of the problems the director probably had in mind as stemming from the overall concern with questions of democracy and representation centered on this precise issue: whether or not an individual's Catholicism and the *quality* of his Catholicism were to be criteria of eligibility for responsible policy positions in camp. This issue surfaced most dramatically in two camp meetings held in November and December (that is, before the director arrived at Warner) and took the form of proposals for a drastic new revision of camp governance structure and procedures.

The Selmon diary provides a detailed account of the sequence of events and the intensity of feeling aroused. The initiating event was the decision of Acting Director Saunders to discipline John Canory for leaving camp on a weekend when he was scheduled for normal rotation KP duty. At the first meeting the campers present voted to rescind the disciplinary order confining Canory to camp and went on to declare that the campers would henceforth mete out their own punishments and elect their own director and assistant director. A formal inquiry concerning the acceptability of the latter steps was directed to ACCO headquarters in New York.

Two weeks later a second meeting was convened to continue the action, this time featuring what Selmon calls "a great squabble" over whether the assistant director should be elected by the camp then and there and what the qualifications were to be. The argument soon narrowed to the single question of whether the post had to be reserved for a good, or practicing, Catholic. As Selmon describes the exchanges, the "dyed-in-the-wool" Catholics insisted upon this restriction while the opposition (including, though he does not mention the fact, some of the Catholic liberals present) argued that every camper should be eligible with the only qualifications being intelligence and the ability to understand and work with the men. The meeting degenerated into a flurry of name calling and other harsh exchanges, at which point it was adjourned in favor of a special camp meeting called for the following evening. At that special meeting, the diary notes, the restriction limiting eligibility to a practicing Catholic was rejected by majority vote.

There is no similarly detailed report of the affair from the viewpoint of the administration's supporters. Selmon, it goes without saying, saw it from the opposition's perspective. My own letters written at this time offer surprisingly little help in this respect. On December 31, three weeks after these meetings took place, I make belated reference to the episode with the observation that it had been an effort to "get" Saunders—which, of course, was true at least at the beginning. That letter also mentions the decision to hold an election but adds that the Saunders supporters (and I gather I was one on that occasion) succeeded in delaying a decision until he could be assured of a fair chance in the outcome. When the election finally took place (apparently the third meeting mentioned so briefly by Selmon), all the active Catholics who had been nominated for the assistant directorship withdrew their candidacies as a demonstration of nonrecognition of the entire proceedings. This action left the field to Carl Terry, a nominal Catholic of markedly liberal and socialistic leanings closely associated with the opponents of the camp administration.

With the return of Director Larrowe, Terry was declared unacceptable to the ACCO and Chuck Sterner was appointed to the assistant directorship instead.[2] There are no further references to the issue in my letters or in the Selmon diary, and it is possible that the matter never did reach formal resolution. The camp work records show that Saunders continued to be carried on administrative detail while Sterner was assigned to kitchen duty and other in-camp assignments. Terry remained on regular work project detail. A similar but somewhat less inflammatory contretemps arose in January when the director, acting on his own authority, selected two men to attend a New England CPS conference; once again there was a protest meeting and

an election at which Terry and James O'Donnell, a reliable administration supporter, were chosen to go instead. This time the director
approved the camp decision.

What might now seem like a tempest in a teapot was in reality
evidence of the rapid and progressive deterioration of relationships
among the campers, and between the campers and the ACCO administration. However one might choose to assess the blame, the results
were disastrous for the hopes and expectations with which the camp
had opened less than two months before. This nearly total collapse
of morale and the reasons for it may have played a major role in the
subsequent decisions of Director Larrowe, Assistant Director Saunders, and *all* the Catholic Workers—acting individually and not as a
bloc, of course—to leave CPS for military service. If this is a valid assumption, it must also be added that the legacy of bitter disillusionment was not theirs alone. Some, like Selmon, pointedly refused to
recognize or participate in camp governance from that time forward.
The greater number simply stopped participating with no explanation other than their unwillingness to subject themselves to seemingly endless, and usually pointless, debates over issues that were clearly
beyond the campers' power to decide.[3]

The most significant aspect of the governance controversy was the
difference of opinion concerning the role to be allotted to practicing
Catholics. A persuasive case could be made for both sides, but little
effort was made to keep the exchanges at the level of serious or even
rational dialogue. Instead, the administration's supporters rallied to
the defense of Saunders because they interpreted the effort to get him
as a move to undermine the Catholic character of the camp. The opposition, for its part, interpreted the eligibility restriction as an attempt to legitimize a second-class citizenship for non-Catholics and
nonpracticing Catholics and, in the process, to impose Catholic, especially the perfectionist Catholic Worker, values and philosophy upon
those who did not share them. It was, therefore, not so much a battle
over two different candidates, or even over the issue of representation, as an increasingly irreconcilable division reflecting a state of
mutual suspicion concerning motives and intentions that had long
since gotten completely out of hand.

The Food Issue

Fueling this division was the complex of more limited issues relating
to living standards at Warner, with the food situation dominant among

them. The others, though no less important, did not have the same immediacy on a day-to-day basis. There was, for instance, the failure to provide the qualified camp nurse required by Selective Service regulations. At least two men sustained axe injuries while on project, and two others required minor operations while under camp jurisdiction. This was no slight concern if one considers the consistently high proportion of men in the various sick classifications (sick in quarters, absent sick, and under infirmary or hospital care) which accounted for almost 1,200 man-days, or 13.9 percent of the total man-days at Warner. That this lack of professionally qualified nursing care was a crucial deficiency was acknowledged in the camp director's column in the February 1943 issue of the *Catholic Worker.*

Fortunately we have suffered no permanent injuries thus far, but I wonder what we will *do in such an event. The Government does not pay us, neither does it provide compensation even for injuries suffered on Government time. We are already beginning to feel the pinch of our poverty in the matter of medical and dental bills. Men have been in camp so long that dental attention is absolutely necessary. We have very little money, but are making appointments knowing that you will help us.*

Similar appeals for funds and contributions from the *Worker*'s readers mentioned the severity of the food crisis at Camp Simon. The adequacy of these appeals, however, was often challenged, partly because of the general atmosphere of suspicion that prevailed. Thus, the charge was frequently heard that the ACCO, because of its identification with the Catholic Worker movement and its basic philosophy, did not share the same sense of urgency on this score as the men in camp. Stated this bluntly, the charge is unfair; yet, here too, it was not altogether without justification. The movement, then as now, embraced the principle of voluntary poverty and advocated detachment from creature comforts of all kinds. Its houses of hospitality in the skid-row sectors of major cities were operated on the basis of freewill offerings of money, old clothes, unsold bread and vegetables, and response to special appeals related to emergency needs. The houses provided a daily fare of bread and soup made from those gatherings of vegetable discards, low-grade meats, and whatever other ingredients might come their way. The ultimate objective envisioned a decentralized and communitarian way of life to include farms where the needed produce could be grown, the wheat ground, the bread baked, so that the poor might be housed and fed.

It was no accident that this became the model for Camp Simon.

The ACCO was dependent upon the parent movement for financial support, and the situation could not have been otherwise even if the camp's leadership had not been committed to the movement's ideals and philosophy. The "apple diet" Dorothy Day recalls from her Stoddard visit was not imposed by that philosophy; it was dictated by the need to make full use of whatever was plentiful and available. The effort to operate a camp farm with the men expected to provide voluntary extra labor after project hours may have reflected the Worker's agrarian idealism, but it also happened to be the only hope for meeting food needs that were clearly beyond the financial resources of the ACCO. The fond dream of self-sufficiency was never fulfilled, of course, and most likely could not have been even if everyone had contributed to the effort to achieve that goal. That only an enthusiastic few were prepared to do so sealed its doom from the start.

Actually, even though the Stoddard farm project was a dismal failure, it did produce much of the food consumed at Warner. Once the supplies that had been brought along were gone, the camp diet became completely dependent upon whatever money was available in the always tentative budget. This was a certain formula for disaster, and it could have been no less so had Director Larrowe and his staff been prophets of hedonism and gluttony.

That they were in fact committed to a philosophy of life which stressed the spiritual rewards to be gained from self-sacrifice and detachment from worldly goods and pleasures seemed to lend substance to morale-destroying suspicions, and created a situation rife with mutual misunderstanding. Where, on the one hand, the campers resented being forced to endure Catholic Worker standards and life style, the camp administrators—Catholic Workers all—were perhaps too inclined to interpret the constant complaints and protests as shocking evidence of selfishness, possibly even insincerity. Those enthusiastic expectations of the welcoming letter, which had pictured Camp Simon as a training ground in perfection, became at one and the same time a confirmation of the suspicions of the dissidents and the background for the disillusionment suffered by the spiritually motivated men who had shared the dream.

One fact was incontestable: the food situation at Warner was desperate. The dire straits in which the Stoddard-Warner camps were caught became a matter of concern throughout the CPS system. The November 1942 issue of the *Catholic Worker*, for example, expressed gratitude to the AFSC's Campton camp for donating the entire proceeds from a guinea pig project in which some of its members had participated. The next month's issue included a similar acknowledgment to the Brethren Service Committee and the many camps continuing "to favor us with much thoughtful assistance." Several camps arranged for their members to voluntarily skip meals, with the money thus saved to be sent to the Catholic camp. Welcome though the assistance was, it should not be too difficult to imagine the effect it had upon men who were already bitterly conscious of the fact that they had become dependent upon the charity of others. Not only did they need regular support and gifts from those friends and family with whom they remained in good standing, they were also competing with the homeless derelicts of the Bowery for the meagre funds contributed by the readers of the *Worker*. Now, to top it all, these members of the largest and wealthiest religious community in the world found themselves obliged to accept the self-sacrificial offerings from other religious groups. It was not a situation amenable to a sense of dignity and self-respect.

The always critical food situation drew a variety of responses in camp. Supplemental food supplies, usually in the form of packages from home, were generously shared by some recipients, hoarded and consumed in secrecy by others, and, perhaps the grossest behavior of all, ostentatiously enjoyed by at least one to the annoyance and envy of his fellow campers. Indeed, some sense of the importance of the food issue may be found in the clarity and indignation with which this latter behavior was recalled by one respondent three decades later.

There was one obnoxious person in the camp who used to get a food package every week, and he refused to share his food with anyone. This wasn't too bad if he had the decency to have eaten his food in private, but he thought nothing of eating in front of everyone. I used to watch him fill his coffee cup with milk and sugar and put jam and butter on his bread. I watched sort of fascinated and with a touch of revulsion that anyone could have the gall and nerve to do such a thing.

Some memories linger!

Then there was pilfering. The appropriation of supplies for his own enjoyment by "Good Food Walt" Berryman has already been noted. His pilfering was an inside job since he served on the kitchen staff. Other campers conducted illicit late night raids on the pantry until this provoked the administrative responses of a public denunci-

(158)

ation and a padlock on the pantry door. These actions, as George Selmon confided to his diary, did nothing to enhance the director's standing in the affections of the campers. As for George himself, this keeper and killer of the camp's chickens was once so disgusted with an evening meal, consisting of a plate of beans, that he confessed to the temptation of appropriating one of his flock as a personal night-time treat.

It is important to note that there was not much that would ordinarily seem worth pilfering. The milk supply was probably the most common booty along with whatever else might be available in cans. Viewed in any perspective, it was not a healthy situation. It is well to remember that the pilferers were young, active men who were expected to do a full day's work and who, as a result, bitterly resented the inadequacies of the regular camp diet. For their part the administrators, keepers of a barely manageable budget, had to consider the fact that anything pilfered by the few could only reduce further the already scant provisions available for all.

Too severe a judgment passed upon the pilferers, however, must ignore the indisputable fact that theirs was no petty grievance. According to one former member of the New York house of hospitality, *the Camp Simon diet did not meet even the usual Catholic Worker standards.* As he recalls it now, "The food, I must admit, was terrible. There was not enough to go around. Coffee was served black and without sugar. Cereal was oatmeal with watery milk. And I recall the peanut butter sandwiches. It was all we lived on, or so it seems to me. I got so sick and tired of peanut butter that I could not bear to eat it for years to come."

Maybe it was not quite that bad. Thanks to George Selmon's diligence, we did have eggs occasionally and chicken almost every Sunday. The peanut butter regimen was occasionally supplemented by ersatz sausage for the sandwiches, and it seems to me now as if the Warner universe was bounded in a swamp of apple butter as well. With varying degrees of regularity the menu featured chopped meat for dinner, frankfurters with the omnipresent beans, and lamb stews. After Roderick, the Stoddard pig, was slaughtered, there was a good supply of pork, though, as Director Larrowe duly reported in his *Catholic Worker* column, the unfortunate beast had been permitted to go too much to fat.

This is not to deny the major thrust of the more dismal recollections. Things were bad at best, and they went from bad to worse in

the closing weeks of the camp's brief existence. A letter of mine
dated at the end of February rejoices that, "Today we are having
chicken—the closest we have come to a meat dish since Tuesday. And
I can't even remember what kind of bone stew we had then." Bill
O'Flaherty's unsettling memories of worms in the oatmeal and the recommended manner of dealing with them need no further repetition.

Food protests ranged from the humorous to the bitter to the
formal, and all proved equally ineffective. Robert Dunfey's shouted
contempt for the "pig bread" prepared by our amateur bakers became something of a camp joke. Leonard Mattano recalls the camp
cook who "made that great pot of ungodly soup-chowder with fish
heads, etc. in it and some character (I *am sure* I know who) put several old shoes in it, and he got sorta hot under the collar." Direct-
action protests of this nature were rare, though there were many
times when a meal on project or in camp was so bad that some of
the men preferred to go hungry.

More formal protests took the form of a continuing barrage of
petitions to Mott Street (the ACCO-Catholic Worker headquarters),
to the NSBRO, and even to Selective Service. The Swarthmore files
contain one such petition directed to Paul Comly French and dated
November 30, 1942. Apparently organized by Roger Tennitt (it requested that any response be sent to him), it bore nineteen signatures
and asked, "Can we have an inspection of the food in this camp.
There must be some standard by which this can be measured. Is it
not true that religious agencies that run CPS must agree to minimum
requirements laid down by Selective Service? The food problem in
this camp is apt to cause enough dissatisfaction to endanger the work
projects. P. S. What about a nurse?"

Tennitt's concern about endangering the work project must be
read as a rhetorical ploy, since the petitioners included campers noto-
rious for their noncooperative attitudes toward the work of national
importance to which they had been assigned. Tennitt himself, as we
have seen, had been on strike less than three weeks earlier. Somewhat
more significant, however, is the fact that except for Pat Rafferty—
and he was probably drawn in by virtue of his friendship with "the
New York crowd" who were represented in full force—none of the
active Catholics, not even one of liberal persuasion, signed that particular petition. This would appear to signify that the polarization
of camper opinion had reached the stage where the Catholics were
either not invited to sign or, if they were, had withheld support from

a petition they viewed as a dangerously disruptive move on the part of the outspoken opponents of the ACCO administration. If the latter, it would again testify to the overriding value placed on keeping the Catholic camp in existence even at the cost of continuing to endure the inadequate diet.

In any event, by December 28 something of a Christmas truce seems to have been declared, for Tennitt wrote a second letter to French informing him that Director Larrowe had returned to camp and had introduced some changes. "The food here is still unsatisfactory," he wrote, "especially in regard to project lunches. However, it is the best it has ever been at the present time."

Tennitt and his fellow petitioners probably did not know the full story behind the changes they welcomed. In his recollections of the unhappy Warner experiences, the former director describes an incident that reveals the dimensions of the problems with which he had to deal and, inadvertently perhaps, also provides a hint of his own position on the food issue.

The first vignette is of Wally North exploding and saying, "I won't feed these guys this junk. I'm going to buy the food from now on—and it'll be meat and potatoes—and stuff they need!" or words to that effect. I don't doubt he was right in wanting to feed them better—nonetheless the manner of the decision— revolt—hurt me deeply. I remember that. I had been holding the budget down because I felt we just didn't have the funds—and would go broke and lose the camp—the supervision of it—if we spent more. Wally felt the men worked hard— needed meat and cake and so on. Being a Catholic Worker he wasn't talking luxury—he was talking hearty meals. He finally moved—and I felt betrayed by a fellow CW. That's my memory.

Improvement there may have been, but it obviously did not continue. The protests resumed until, at long last, Selective Service made its own inspection of camp conditions. The documentary record confirms that the dietary deficiencies loomed large in the decision to close the Warner camp less than six months after the transfer from Stoddard. Though other considerations were involved as well, as we shall see, there is no reason to doubt that the inadequate diet would have been considered reason enough for Selective Service to act.

The Censorship Issue

The suspicion that Catholic, and in particular Catholic Worker, principles were being imposed upon the entire camp fed much of the resentment associated with the governance and food controversies. In both instances, the fear was exaggerated. What appeared to be a Catholic line was more of a defensive reaction, a response to the suspicion in the minds of the Catholic campers, justified to some extent, that the dissidents and disrupters wanted to have the camp removed from ACCO jurisdiction. Since virtually all the Catholics wanted to preserve their corporate witness against the war, they tended to rally around the administration when challenges or protests seemed to pose a threat to that objective.

On two occasions, however, the imposition of what was taken to be Catholic morality stirred intense controversy of a more general nature. One was a minor, rather comic, incident; the other had more serious implications. Both featured puritanical attempts at censorship and produced a split among the Catholics that found the majority aligned with the non-Catholic elements. The incidents were important enough at the time to merit detailed coverage in my letters as well as in the Selmon diary.

The first occurred at the end of January when James O'Donnell, the sober Coughlinite, took it upon himself to remove a recording of the "Strip Tease Polka" from the camp phonograph and smash it. In his judgment the lyric's plea of "take it off—take it off" was indecent, an affront to womanhood. The reaction was as immediate as it was predictable. In a letter written three days later, I described the camp as "seething with anti-censorship feeling." Three of us composed a petition and presented it to the camp council for action without much success. "Naturally, it was considered a matter 'too trivial' (in spite of the fact that one fellow had actually decided how the rest of the camp should handle their morals) and was shelved. But I did have my say about Puritanical morals!"

Selmon set about soliciting the opinion of Catholics like Chuck Sterner and Lou Swanson, highly respected core members of the chapel group, and reported to his diary that none had found the record offensive. He took his protest directly to O'Donnell who predictably offered him a pamphlet defending chastity. This merely intensified Selmon's determination to communicate his indignation to as many of his fellow campers as possible. As far as he was concerned, the affair "revealed to my mind what a narrowminded interpreter could do with Catholic doctrine and make it a source of plaguing the rest of the men in camp as to what they should and shouldn't play."

Before the adverse reaction to this incident could die down, the censorship issue surfaced again two weeks or so later in the *Salt* controversy. This third issue of the Camp Simon magazine, the only one to be attempted at Warner, had been in preparation for at least two months and was now ready for distribution in camp and circulation to the rest of CPS. Unfortunately advance word of its contents reached some of the more rigorist Catholics and provoked an unfavorable reaction. Proposals began to surface in bunkhouse discussions that distribution should be halted or curtailed. The controversy came to a head in yet another special camp meeting called to discuss the objections being raised to its allegedly anti-Catholic material. As was now customary at these meetings, tempers rose and the debate grew "hotter and hotter" (Selmon's description) until a climax was reached when Ray Murphy and a companion interrupted the on-going tirades with the dramatic announcement that they had appropriated all copies of the magazine and burned them! Chaos ensued, and the meeting came to an abrupt end.

The problem may have become moot, but a new and even more furious debate took its place. The two culprits revealed the next day that they had only hidden the uncirculated copies. The fact that they were hidden under O'Donnell's bunk did nothing to lessen the indignation provoked by this second attempt to impose censorship,*and the damage had been done. Selmon's diary notes that "several people had to retract statements they had made in letters. Lou Swanson made a public apology at the supper table to George Andrews after calling him a heretic the previous night."† As Selmon's reference to statements and letters suggests, feelings ran high enough after the meeting to evoke a frantic flurry of indignant petitions and protests.

*O'Donnell himself did not seem to be actively involved in this particular plot, though the possibility cannot be completely excluded. As for Murphy, he does not recall playing the leading part. It is possible, of course, that Selmon was reporting the events secondhand (he was, one should remember, boycotting camp meetings) and may be in error. I am inclined to accept his version as accurate, however. Typically enough, Murphy now explains that if he *did* play the part attributed to him, he assumes he must have done it as a lark, just to see Roger Tennitt "sputter."

†*That*, to say the least, was a reversal of form. Usually it was Andrews, the archtriumphalist, who made such judgments about his fellow campers who were not of the Faith or, if Catholic, too liberal. It is to be assumed that in this instance Lou's charge related to something Andrews had said in support of the move to suppress the contested issue. Swanson, though a leader of the chapel group, was much more liberal on almost any issue than Andrews, our "torchman for Torquemada."

That inveterate petitioner, Shelden Dennison, again teamed with Lowell Bartlett, posted an especially sharp denunciation of the would-be censors on the public bulletin board. Nor was such activity limited to the champions of free speech and fair play. Again according to Selmon, "Eugene Orton* is going around getting a petition to prevent the mailing of *Salt*. His prudish acts continue, and he continues to reveal himself as the prudish jackass he is."

Whatever motivated the Murphy prank—and it was an act entirely in keeping with his reputation for caustic Irish wit and one that also served to express his personal disgust over the pettiness and mean-spiritedness of the discussion he so dramatically interrupted—it is harder to understand what caused the initial offense. A careful review of what may be the only remaining copy in existence reveals nothing particularly threatening to the camp's Catholic image. True, only three of the eight featured articles and poems (accounting for less than five of its eighteen pages) were written by identifiably active Catholics: one was a carefully reasoned three-page summary of the just-war teachings; a second consisted of a single-page reflection on Christianity's promise for a war-torn world; and the third was the quarter-page statement of "The Fact" quoted in its entirety at the beginning of this chapter. In addition to these, Lou Schnittler, that nominal Catholic but avowed agnostic, contributed a couple of poems and a two-page description of a visit he had made to a Washington Catholic-operated hospice for indigent "colored" men. LeRoy Torto, another nominal Catholic who seemed to have no religious interests at all, was represented by an obscure short story written in what might today be termed absurdist style; the only offence it could have given would be to an average reader's literary sensibilities.

The most plausible clue to the strong opposition to the issue is found in the articles contributed by those prominent, non-Catholic intellectuals, Dean Farfether and Alvin Manton. Farfether's four-page essay dissected "the failure of CPS" and indicted the religious agencies (with major emphasis, it is well to note, on the peace church

---

*Orton, not previously introduced beyond the general reference to background Coughlinites, was one of the older campers, very spinsterish in appearance and manners, a dedicated "second-miler" and a chapel regular. In short, an administration supporter but not particularly popular. One of the other Coughlinites describes him as a faithful and diligent worker, "much misunderstood because of his idealism." Murphy, perpetrator of the "great *Salt* controversy" hoax remembers him only as "a fellow pamphleteer of O'Donnell's. Quite dull."

leadership) for their "indifference" to CO morale. Thirty years later, his analysis has lost none of its cogency and bite. Given the already tense Warner situation, this Quaker Marxist's critique might have seemed too radical in thrust and unworthy of a magazine published under presumably Catholic auspices. Manton's contribution consisted of three "Poems on God," and one of these may have been the cause of all the fuss and fury. (Manton, of course, missed all the excitement; he had been transferred to a hospital unit weeks before.) Anyway, I vaguely recall that one of the charges brought against the *Salt* issue had something to do with imputations of heresy and disrespectful references to the Virgin Mary. Strictly speaking, the Manton poems are guilty of neither offense. It is quite possible, on the other hand, that one of the lines ("Mary made God") could have carried improper theological overtones for more rigorous Catholics, especially our confirmed heresy hunters like Andrews. It is virtually certain, too, that Manton's reference to Mary as a "subtle Jewess" would be enough to upset campers of the Coughlinite persuasion.

Whatever the reasons behind it, "the great *Salt* controversy" marked the absolute nadir in camp morale. There would be other meetings and other disagreements, but none ever reached the same level of intensity or awakened comparable animosity. The recovered copies of the disputed issue were not distributed, but this was more likely due to the lack of funds to cover mailing costs than to the Orton petition or similar expressions of concern. Certainly, considering the desperate state of finances in those closing weeks, that would have been reason enough.

Besides, the focus of attention soon shifted to other concerns affecting the future of everyone. At the end of January, the day before the record breaking incident, the first hint was received that Camp Simon's days were numbered. By mid-February it had become evident to all that there would be no other ACCO camp to replace Warner and that the men would most likely be transferred to some camp under AFSC jurisdiction. The only hope for continuing an official Catholic presence in CPS apart from the Alexian unit lay in gaining NSBRO and Selective Service approval for some new detached service project under ACCO jurisdiction to which the Warner refugees might be assigned as a bloc.[4] If peace and serenity did not descend upon Camp Simon in its dying days, at least the strains and contentions between the various factions were moderated by the sobering realiza-

tion that the impending change would bring a complete and final end
to the corporate witness they had tried to establish at Stoddard and
Warner.

Pay and the Government Camp Issues

If all of the foregoing has convinced the readers that life at Warner
was a constant storm of petitions and protests, they are not far
wrong. The campers were extreme individualists, jealous of rights
they felt were being ignored or violated and hypersensitive to any
new inroads or threatened limitations further diminishing their freedom. They were also an extremely articulate group, registering well
above the national averages in educational background as we have
seen, and predisposed to elevate the most mundane differences of
opinion into major ideological confrontations. The isolation and the
emptiness of camp life provided the perfect setting for contention
and guaranteed that even minor incidents would be magnified into
major causes by the frustrations of the meaningless routine.

It would be a mistake to conclude from this, however, that the
men of Camp Simon were so completely self-centered that they were
unaware of, or did not share, the broader concerns that engaged conscientious objectors elsewhere in CPS. On the contrary, these issues
were regularly brought before the camp for discussion and, often
enough, were given a special coloration by the peculiar urgencies
of the local situation.

Foremost among these programwide issues were the continuing
agitation for pay and the creation of government-operated camps as
an alternative to those operated by the religious agencies through
the NSBRO. Support for the former was by far the more widespread,
but as things turned out only the latter objective would be achieved
and then not for the reasons advanced by its advocates. The two issues were so interrelated, however, that they deserve to be considered together.

One must return to the origins of CPS to comprehend the pay issue
in its full dimensions. As explained earlier, the approval of a peacetime draft presented the nation's pacifist leadership with a problem.
They were determined to avoid any repetition of the excesses of mal-
treatment suffered by men who refused service in World War I; and
when conscription again became the order of the day, they succeeded

in persuading the lawmakers to include a provision exempting potential registrants who, by virtue of their religious training and belief, were opposed to all war and military service. The men so exempted were to be assigned instead to work of national importance under civilian direction.

That objective accomplished, the next step was to assure that this provision would be honored in a way that would do credit to the peace witness they anticipated. It was in keeping with this thoroughly laudable intention that the pacifist leaders consulted with Selective Service officials and developed an alternative service program modeled upon the summer work camps conducted by the leading peace churches. However far from the ideal the reality would stray, there is no reason to doubt the sincerity of commitment on the part of the pacifists who were party to the arrangement at that earliest stage. Nor can it be denied that Civilian Public Service as that ideal had much to commend it.

The major peace church service agencies, acting with and through the NSBRO, assumed responsibility for financing and administering the alternative service program. The government's contribution was to make available camps formerly operated under the Civilian Conservation Corps and to reactivate the work projects associated with them. The two models fit together nicely, and Civilian Public Service was born.

It is not entirely clear which party to the arrangement was responsible for the decision that the men called into alternative service would not be paid for the work they performed. It was largely taken for granted by the men in the camps that the pacifist leaders were responsible. The additional sacrifice was to be a symbolic expression of commitment, an almost literal application, as it were, of the Scriptural injunction to the effect that a man compelled by another to go on a mile's journey with him should go a second mile of his own accord.*Such would be most clearly in keeping with the Mennonite response to governmental oppression, but it was a value incorporated into the traditions and belief systems of the other peace church de-

---

*This, of course, is the referent to the "second-miler" epithet applied to men who, by example and often by exhortation, advocated giving the best and fullest efforts and cooperation to the CPS work program. Another term for anyone so committed was "200-percenter." Both terms were employed as taunts and terms of derision at Camp Simon, but few authentic examples of either were to be found on the roster at Warner.

nominations as well. This is not to suggest that the no-pay policy derived solely from fundamentalist applications of the Christian Scriptures. One must assume that the various parties to the negotiations were sophisticated enough to be aware of the public-relations dimension to the arrangement. For the pacifists, this additional sacrifice would be public testimony to the sincerity of the men to be granted the IV-E classification; for Selective Service, it would help lessen the impact of any negative criticism arising from the recognition of conscientious objection in the first place.

From Selective Service's perspective, there was yet another advantage, though it is difficult to estimate how important this may have seemed at the time. The denial of pay for alternative service would operate to reduce the number of registrants likely to seek the classification. It is very important to bear in mind, too, that not only were the men assigned to alternative service to receive no compensation or family allotments, but that *they were expected to contribute toward the costs of their maintenance at the suggested rate of $35 a month.* Probably not many actually did so, but the expectation is significant enough in itself. This policy was obviously framed with an image of campers more affluent than those who actually were conscripted into the program; it also anticipated a greater measure of support from local religious communities than would be forthcoming.

But this was not to be the only, or even the most serious, departure from expectations. Whatever value or relevance the summer work camp model may have had soon vanished under the pressure of national and international developments. The anticipated twelve-month term of service was extended to eighteen months in August 1941, and before that year was out, American entry into World War II changed that to "the duration plus six months." The original plans to draft only single men in a limited age range were also abandoned. As manpower needs expanded, draft calls were revised to extend to men in older and younger age categories, then to married men without children, and finally to fathers as well. For the latter two groups especially, CPS, with its indefinite term of service without pay or financial support comparable to that given men drafted into the other services, represented an almost impossible option, one that required they either ignore their familial responsibilities or make themselves and their families dependent upon the charity of others.

The government that, after all, had established the legitimacy of conscientious objection could have acted on its own initiative to correct this cruelly unfair situation; and the pacifist leadership that shared responsibility for the burdensome arrangement should have recognized its obligation to promote the necessary revision. Unfortunately, this is not what happened. Congress was portrayed by Selective Service and the pacifist leaders as being adamantly opposed to any proposal for the benefit of the men in CPS—and there is no reason to doubt the accuracy of that assessment of the situation. Further, as far as the pacifist leadership itself was concerned, most either reaffirmed the commitment to the "second-mile" rationale or held back from speaking out for a rectification of the injustice out of concern for potentially adverse public reaction that might endanger the entire program.

The men of Camp Simon were particularly vulnerable to the injustice of the no-pay situation on several counts. It is not surprising, then, that they were almost unanimous in their support of the continuing demands for a change. William Grandman, by his own admission, was one of only two (Ron Baxter seems to have been the other) to vote against one of the many resolutions and proposals concerning this issue discussed at camp meetings. Some idea of the full extent of the problems faced by the campers is given in Director Larrowe's column in the February 1943 issue of the *Catholic Worker*.

An even greater need for which we beg your assistance is that of the men who have dependents. Again the Government refuses to assist them. There are no allotments made and the CO receives no pay to send home. Yet there are several men in camp whose families need help. One boy's mother is planning to sell some of the stock on the farm to pay the taxes. Another man's family is being placed on relief because his sister (the breadwinner now that he is in camp) has been injured and lost her job. And there are others who are running into debt to keep going. We must *help them. And we ask your help to do it.*

One crucial dimension of the problem, of course, is that while the other sponsoring agencies represented religious communities supportive of their conscientious objectors, the overwhelming majority of American Catholics were hostile toward their fellow-communicants who refused to "do their duty" in the nation's war effort. Men in the peace church camps were receiving a $2.50 monthly allowance to cover incidentals, but the men at Warner were denied even that pittance by the strained and unreliable resources of the Catholic Worker movement.[5] In its place the camp office had a cash box to which individual campers would have the opportunity to contribute and from which withdrawals for necessities could be made on an honor system basis. As the needs grew greater and the decline in morale made a mockery of the honor limitation, even this poor substitute failed to be of much help.

Men who had come from a distance faced the dismal choice of either foregoing even an annual or semiannual furlough home or avoiding all other expenditures to cover the cost of such visits. And most troubling of all was the nagging realization that not only were they reduced to total dependency upon the Catholic Worker and the responses to the director's monthly appeals for contributions, but whatever funds were obtained in that fashion were really intended to benefit the even more underprivileged members of society served by the houses of hospitality. That this had to be a serious psychological burden for men whose self-respect was already weakened by the almost universal and unconcealed disapproval directed against them should be obvious; and its effects, though not always recognized as such, undoubtedly contributed to the strains and tensions of life at Warner.

All the protests and demands concerning pay proved unavailing, whether the product of an organized camp vote or merely an individual appeal to the authorities. One rather touching example of the latter is a letter in the personnel files written by Robert Tantino, one of the "New York crowd" (though not as disruptive a force as most of the others), to Paul Comly French, the man in most regular contact with Selective Service. Tantino described the situation at home, stressing the extra burden placed upon his and the other men's parents by the need to help support their sons in camp. Explaining that this was not fair to them, he asked French for his own sentiments concerning the problem. In response, a lesser NSBRO official wrote,

The present mode of arrangement, with religious groups undertaking the maintenance of men in camp, eliminates the pay possibility. Some CO's, perhaps the majority, would not accept any pay for their work. However, the problem is a serious one and you may be sure that this office is concerned with it, particularly where it relates to the dependents of assignees.

All of which was true enough as far as it went. Since the Mennonites constituted the largest number of men in the CPS program and were firmly committed to the second-mile principle, this majority probably would have refused government compensation for the work they were obliged to perform. Wittner cites an editorial from one of the Mennonite camp papers that, though it does not deal specifically with the pay issue, clearly supports this conclusion in its declaration that "Civilian Public Service is a privilege! . . . We intend to serve our country to the best of our ability. And we intend to do that without the unjustified grumbling and complaining that has been evidenced among some conscientious objectors."[6] Unfortunately, both the NSBRO official and the Mennonite editorialist ignored the obvious fact that any CPS-men who did prefer "the present mode of arrangement" would always have been free to continue it on a voluntary basis. The issue at question was whether it was right to eliminate the pay possibility for others who were not willing or able to make that additional sacrifice.

Though others supported the demands for pay, it was the dissident elements in the various camps who were the most consistent in their agitation for a change. At Camp Simon, the principal spokesman was Farfether. His contribution to that contested issue of *Salt* stated the case in what for one so reserved and quiet by nature were unusually harsh terms:

> . . . *The religious agencies, the NSB in particular, opposed government camps; yet they would not give us the standard of material well-being (food, clothing, medical care, recreation, accident compensation, and perhaps wages) that we knew we would get from the government. Not only did we rebel against our involuntary poverty which made many of us slaves equally with conscription—not only did we hate the heavy didactic atmosphere which killed any opportunity for fun; we also began to feel that the Pacifist leadership was preaching an idealism which they themselves were unwilling to live. Leaders who arrived in Packards and who obviously were living very comfortably made us feel that an element of hypocrisy existed in the situation, and that our hardships were only for economy and public relations, not for any high-minded idealism. When we heard of hotel dinners in Washington between leading Selective Service officials and our own leaders, lost in admiration of each other's virtues, we came to feel that there existed an unholy alliance among the "bigshots," and that they cared little about our happiness. Being scolded when we were not "content with our lot" did nothing but make the split between us and our leaders even greater.*

The pacifist leadership was equally disappointed with the attitude of the protesters in the camps, though perhaps not as bitter. The French diary contains several entries that testify to his almost complete inability to see the pay issue in the terms set by his critics. On January 9, 1943, he returned from a New England CPS conference in a sadly disillusioned mood. As he saw it, the extent to which the government camp and pay issues had dominated the proceedings suggested that those present were too inclined to reduce everything to materialistic terms, forgetting that the service one gives is more important than the reward received. The impression that many of the men believed that the right of conscience could be established by paying people troubled him. The harshness of Farfether's judgment found a measure of justification in still another entry (December 22, 1942) in which French noted his gratification over the quality of his relationship with the Selective Service officials and the evidence he saw in this of the government's tolerance and understanding in its dealings with pacifists in the midst of total war.

The campers engaged in futile efforts to correct the inherent injustices of the alternative service program received little of this tolerance and understanding from Selective Service and not much more from the NSBRO or from French himself. The officials were far more sensitive to possibly adverse public relations than to all the protests from camp. And, one must concede, with good reason. There is little doubt that any action designed to improve the conditions of life for conscientious objectors would have provoked an instant storm of public disapproval. The press was more than ready to pounce on anything that could be interpreted as favoritism toward men who were not willing to fight.

Thus Arthur "Buggs" Baer, a nationally syndicated columnist, railed against "evaporated patriots who are about as much use as two tails on an iron deer" and dismissed conscientious objection as "a racket." The "Conscientious O" of World War I, as Baer remembered him, was a privileged character who "rested on his bunk, ate three squares a day, and read the best books" while Baer and the others like him bore the burdens and discomforts of military service. That fortunate fellow's World War II counterpart, he continued, had all those privileges and pleasures *plus* "radio to while away the overstuffed hours." The conclusion to be drawn was as simple as it was obvious: "there is no place in a boat for the punk who will not pull his weight."[7]

Such opinions were not restricted to jingoistic columnists. French's diary entry for May 14, 1943, reports a meeting with the publisher of a major Washington paper in which he persuaded her to suspend a series of articles it planned to publish opposing a proposed program

for training conscientious objectors to perform postwar relief and re-
habilitation work. She agreed to drop the articles, but only after she
learned to her surprise that the men in CPS were not paid. She had
been under the impression that they had been getting the equivalent
of military pay and related privileges while being spared the rigors
and risks of military life, and that alternative service was nothing
more than "the easy way out." The moral, for French, was clear: the
sacrifice of pay for services performed was a more important asset
than his vociferous critics in the camps were aware.

The conclusion he drew from the exchange is sound; but the question remains whether such an attitude should have been condoned,
much less used as an argument justifying a policy that, in effect, put a
public relations price tag on the exercise of the individual conscience.

Though the government camp issue was linked to the question of
pay in the minds of many of us, the two were diverse enough in their
implications and potential ramifications to warrant separate treatment. In essence the proposal was that a number of alternative service camps be established under direct Selective Service jurisdiction to
be administered either by the Selective Service officials themselves or
by representatives of the various government agencies for which the
work assignments were to be performed. Even the more committed
advocates of the government camp option agreed that only a small
minority would elect to transfer to such camps, but they insisted
that the right to do so should be promoted and supported by the religious agencies and their NSBRO representatives. Although there was
no assurance that men who did so elect would be paid for their labor
in such government camps, it was generally assumed this would be
the case.

In the second Stoddard issue of *Salt* (January 1942), Farfether
and Alvin Manton combined to present the case for the government
camp in terms that were mild compared to the tone of the discussions that took place at Warner the following year. Whether this was
evidence of rhetorical restraint in making a then unfamiliar proposal
more palatable, or whether the issue itself became more controversial
over the intervening months is difficult to say. In any event, the Farfether-Manton article was mostly positive in its thrust, a straightfor-
ward appeal set in terms of the democratic ideal. The government,
they argued, had an obligation to provide maintenance for those it
called into its service, and the COs who availed themselves of the
opportunity to serve in such camps would be fulfilling their social

responsibilities "within the framework of government and to make that government decent and democratic." (The latter theme would assume more confrontational overtones in later statements that emphasized instead the advantage to the CO to be gained by dealing with the war-making authority directly once the religious agencies were out of the picture and no longer serving as a buffer between the men in the camps and the Selective Service System.)

In the Farfether-Manton statement this advantage was recognized by inference in their criticism of the existing program as one designed to isolate the dissenting pacifist minority from the people and their government. Such isolation "makes it all the easier for war to be waged with a minimum of contact between the government and that minority." Four other criticisms had preceded this: (1) the established system relied upon "the economically privileged position" of those who financed the private program to provide for their independence from the government; (2) as the war continued, the financial burden of the camps might become too great for the private agencies to bear, thus making it advisable to establish a few government camps as a pilot experiment to prepare for the possibility that the government might be obliged to take the whole program over at some later point; (3) maintenance of the camp system was a drain on private funds better devoted by the religious agencies to relief work at home and abroad; (4) maintenance of a private system implied a distrust of democracy in that it "assumes that the representatives of the people made provisions for CO exemption and CO service only with reluctance."

That last argument was disingenuous on its face as was the objection at another point that the private administrative setup committed assignees "to a position of Christian anarchy in which they did not agree"; nevertheless, the complete case for the government camps, as they presented it, deserved more of a hearing than it would ever receive. It may not have been fair of its sponsors to attribute opposition to the government camp proposal to the presumed fear that private camps would be unable to compete in terms of efficiency and appeal. The pacifist leadership, ever mindful of the sad experience of World War I, deserved to be credited for other and more valid reasons with being unwilling to deal Selective Service directly into the alternative service game. Moreover, these other reasons would be confirmed in fact once a few government camps were finally established. These camps were introduced more as a punitive measure designed to control malcontents than as an effort to make the government more "decent and democratic."

The government camp issue did not win the same measure of broad-based support from the men in camp as the pay issue did, and many of those who gave their support did so under the misplaced confidence that such camps, once established, would provide compensation equivalent to military pay scales. Nor were all the critics of NSBRO and its policies so anxious to build closer relationships, especially confrontational relationships, with the war-making authority.

At Camp Simon, however, there was at least one rather surprising source of support. Warner's beleaguered Director Larrowe had gone on record in a letter to the NSBRO written from Stoddard on September 15, 1942: "I must ask that you do all in your power to have Selective Service set up a government-operated CO camp. I think that it is unfair for us, the ACCO, a religious group, to *demand* cooperation with our policies and acceptance of our standards from men who claim no religious affiliation."

The reasons, obviously, did not coincide with those of the proposal's proponents but were, instead, frankly keyed to a strengthening of administrative authority and legitimacy by providing other arrangements for campers who "base their pacifism on humanitarian, ethical, even political grounds" and who did not "always see their way clear to accepting our leadership. Since we are emphasizing voluntarism and the power of love and since we avoid coercion as much as possible, I refuse to use penalties and punishments as means of obtaining order and cooperation from those who disagree with us. I refuse until I can say that I have *tried* at least to obtain from them the alternative of a camp operated by the non-religious, civil authorities." This was written, it is well to remember, before the era of functional authoritarianism.

The logical conclusion to be drawn from this letter is that once government camps were available, the religious agencies would be free to exert more effective discipline over the men who chose to remain under their jurisdiction. Director Larrowe was honest enough to make it explicit.

I think that some coercion is necessary, but before using it, in the interest of fairness and democracy, I think that a choice must be offered to the men in camp. I think that they must choose to give their loyalty and obedience to the administrative agency. Before pacifists can discipline pacifists the disciplined must give their consent. If the government refuses to operate a government camp then we will be in the position of operating the only *type of camp the government will allow. In such a case it would seem to me that the CO who did not agree with the policies of the Administrative agency would have only the choice of jail. But it would be because of the government's decision not because of ours.*

In the spring of 1943, shortly after Warner closed, the first government camp was opened at Mancos, Colorado. Seven others would open in due course, although no more than five were in operation at any one time. In its postwar monograph on conscientious objection, Selective Service cites some of the arguments advanced by CPS advocates of the change in explaining why the action was taken. "Some assignees had expressed a desire to be transferred to Government camps to relieve the churches of financial burden. There were also those who wanted such transfers in order to have a better opportunity for expressing their aversion to conscription."[8] The step was not taken to accommodate the assignees' wishes, however. The monograph continues to make it clear that the dominant consideration, as always, was Selective Service's own interests. In the process, it provides a strong hint of how the alternative service camp program would have been operated had it been placed under their direct jurisdiction from the very beginning.

Against the advice of Selective Service, most church-operated camps were set up on a self-government basis. This gave each assignee an equal voice in camp government and resulted in an extreme degree of individual freedom outside of working hours. In fact about the only effective check on freedom during off-duty hours was the penalty against desertion. Many of the problem-type assignees had considerable education. They were well fitted by training and experience to argue their ways of life. Often they were more persuasive even than the administrators of the camp. Their early segregation in special camps would therefore have had some advantage to the operation of the entire camp program. Eventually, some Government-operated units were organized for the specific remedial purpose of segregation.[9]

One camp at Germfask, Michigan, was to gain special notoriety within CPS, and in the public press as well, as a "special camp for the maladjusted" (Selective Service's term) in which the malcontents and the noncooperators *from the government camps*, which had already served this function for the camps administered by the religious agencies, were segregated. This Germfask population, the ultimate distillation of CPS dissent as it were, became a center of resistance activism, a scandal to the news media but a delight to the other dissident, though less courageous perhaps, elements throughout CPS.[10]

None of the Warner intellectuals who had been so earnest in their agitation for government camps chose to make the transfer once they became available. Manton, by this time a member of a detached service unit at an Asheville hospital, was but a month or two away from applying for military service. Farfether had moved with one of the Warner remnants to the ACCO-sponsored Rosewood unit from which he, too, would "go I-A" before the year was out. The eleven Warner men who ultimately did end up in government camps were, for the most part, members of the Coughlinite, worker, and loner categories and none seem to have been involved one way or the other in the government camp issue at Camp Simon. Two actually found their way to Germfask: Joseph Brown, that solitary Negro who by then had compiled a file record which must have earned him a ranking among the top ten problem cases in all of CPS history, and "Silent Larry" Kenniston. Why he, one of the most unobtrusive of men, came to be numbered among this highly select collection of malefactors is an unexplained mystery.

All those fond hopes that government camps would open the way to some just compensation arrangements for men in alternative service were doomed to disappointment. The $5.00 monthly allowance then standard for the religious agency camps (up from the original $2.50) applied for the government camps as well. There were some advantages to be gained there, however. Once the government assumed full responsibility for the men assigned to its camps—including provisions for general maintenance, sanitation, housing, feeding, medical care, and work clothing—they enjoyed a higher standard of living than was true for most of the religious camps and, it goes without saying, incomparably better than the conditions experienced at Warner.

Selective Service even went so far as to try to arrange for the services of a chaplain at their camps, but in this they failed. Perhaps that is just as well. It would have been the final irony had they succeeded in obtaining the degree of ecclesiastical recognition so fervently and fruitlessly sought by the chapel group and others at Camp Simon. It is interesting to speculate whether this would have made the government camp prospects more attractive to former Warnerites or not. After all, man does not live by bread, even "pig bread," alone. My personal impression is that most, even the more ardent members of the chapel group, would have chosen to remain in the Quaker camps and units in which they were to spend the balance of their CPS careers. Here, they probably would have reasoned, they found enough of both bread and spirituality to make life more endurable than it would have been in the government camps.

It was not much more than endurable though. In their eyes, CPS was a form of incarceration for their conscientious beliefs, and so it would remain for that full duration and six months. Few if any of the men I knew at Warner would have shared the generally favorable summation of the CPS experience made by the authors of the Selective Service monograph. "Of great significance is the fact that the conscientious objectors of the system who according to their beliefs could accept only work of national importance did accomplish many major tasks. Likewise noteworthy is that on the whole these Class IV-E registrants performed such duty well." Even in their optimistic assessment, however, the authors are forced to admit that ". . . all too frequently there were individual conscientious assignees to the CPS camps and small groups of the same who were a source of deterring irritation to satisfactory operations."[11]

The men of Camp Simon, especially in its Warner phase, can probably be included in that latter company. To the extent this is so, I strongly suspect that most of them would regard the fact as something in which they can, in retrospect, take considerable pride.

Readers are cautioned to keep their expectations in reasonable check. By most standards, the events to be reported here would rate as rather minor incidents; the high spots, pretty low. Chroniclers of other parts of World War II would find little to celebrate in the Warner scene, nor is there much chance of matching the most prosaic war experiences of the ordinary GI-Joe. The men of Camp Simon had no opportunity to fix their personal history into the context of crucial battles. Certainly no romanticized memories remain of joyous leaves or liberties in foreign lands, or of the flower-throwing welcomes in newly conquered (or liberated) cities so regularly reported in the newsreels of the day. Mademoiselle from Armentières and Lili Marlene were not to be found in Concord, New Hampshire. Even if they had been, it is a foregone conclusion that they would have had little time or affection to spare for our bedraggled group of involuntary woodsmen.

George Selmon greeted the New Year of 1943 with a diary entry that, even after due allowance is made for his customary rhetorical flourishes, reflects the general tone of the campers' reaction to the Warner experience and their gloomy assessment of what the future was likely to hold for them. Meditating upon the "great din" of revelries and celebrations elsewhere, he contrasts that with the situation where in "the isolation of nowhere, in the god-forsaken hell hole of this camp we are all listening for something we cannot hear and looking for something we cannot see. In the whiteness and coldness of camp we are isolated and almost forgotten."

It is deceptively easy to write this off as an extravagance of self-pity by calling attention to the multitude of men in military service who were spending equally dismal holidays in even more desolate places scattered all over the world. For every serviceman enjoying the fabled hospitality of the Stage Door Canteen, hundreds more were already experiencing the privations and dangers of combat in North Africa and thousands upon thousands were greeting the New Year in military camps in settings every bit as uninviting as that "hell hole" on wintry Mt. Kearsarge.

To grant all this, and even to admit that the physical isolation and personal dangers experienced by men in the other services "on land and sea and in the air" were far greater than those suffered by the men in CPS, is to miss a very important point. These others could find some compensation in the satisfaction that came from knowing they had the spiritual support and backing of a nation united behind them and their service. The fortunate few at the Canteen were enjoying what was there for them all as a token of that nation's gratitude and honor. If knowing this could not completely balance the deprivations of the moment or significantly reduce the sadness of separation from their families and loved ones, it at least served to lessen the pain by making the sacrifice seem necessary and worthwhile.

There was no comparable consolation for the men of Camp Simon. If anything, the reverse was true. They knew their physical isolation was imposed upon them as a token of the even more pervasive psychological isolation they were obliged to endure as the price, or penalty, for refusing to surrender their individual consciences to the national consensus.

If the triviality and pettiness of the issues and controversies described here offer conclusive testimony to the essential emptiness of camp life and the unimportance of the work the men were conscripted to perform, a resumé of the events that broke the grey monotony of those days should serve to reinforce that conclusion. In the six months of the Warner camp's existence, there were less than a dozen events deserving even passing mention. That they are remembered today, and in surprisingly accurate detail, is far more significant than any claim to importance they may have had in their own right.

Each camper created his own personal breaks in the monotony, but these will not be treated in any great detail. Trips to Warner or Concord, the less frequent weekend leaves, and, in most cases, a rare trip home when sufficient funds and furlough time had been accumulated were highly prized as escapes from the dismal setting and

routine of camp life. To a degree these dominated the campers'
thoughts, first as plans to be made and afterwards as recollections to
be enjoyed. I have already mentioned how envious Midwesterners
like myself could be of the more fortunate Easterners (especially the
regulars of the Canory Express) for whom such escapes were so much
more accessible. For us the trip to Concord, about twenty miles
away, had to suffice. Not only did a day or a weekend there provide
a welcome, though fleeting, respite from the frustrations and mount-
ing tensions that were by now the Warner norm, but it offered the
promise of a decent meal, perhaps a movie, and, most important of
all, the experience of being among people other than those with
whom one was forced to share his daily existence.

Concord, New Hampshire! I am sure poems have been written
about its homely virtues, but anyone acquainted with that town will
appreciate how unlikely a candidate it is for the role of pleasure mec-
ca. Yet that is what it came close to being in our eyes. The Selmon
diary's account of its author's first visit there is almost comic in its
portentous observations, but this should not obscure its deeper significance. The ostensible reason for the trip was a visit to the dentist;
however, upon his arrival after the usual crowded and uncomfortable
journey packed in the back of the "White Ghost" panel truck, he decided to skip the dentist call and went to a movie instead.[1] "It seemed
as though I wanted to do something that was not prescribed for me
once I was away from camp," he explained and, the entry continues

*Toward evening I began to feel the melancholy of waiting to do something and
nothing to do. The gloomy interior of a neighboring beer joint in the railroad
station served to remind me vividly that I was waiting to go back to camp, to
a place where there were no hopes, no cause for any secret joy, no cause for
anything to lift what is left of me in the way of spirit.*

My own reaction to a first excursion to Concord, though much
less poetic, was no more favorable. In a letter I described it as "one
first-class flop." Unlike George, I chose to take an earlier bus back to
Warner rather than "walk the empty streets" on a Sunday in Concord. "Such is life," I somewhat ungenerously concluded, "in New
Hampshire. There is none. You can't tell a native from the statues
that are everywhere."

In spite of the inevitable letdown once one got there, Concord's
attraction remained strong. Passage on the White Ghost's regular
trips for provisions was always at a premium, especially on Saturdays

when a professed desire to go to Confession was often a convenient cover for making a pleasure trip, if so it can be described, at a time when any frivolous use of scarce gasoline was officially condemned.

Camp Visits

The individual and very occasional forays in search of the bright lights of New Hampshire's capital and the world beyond did nothing, of course, to improve the tenor of life at camp, except that every absence from a meal meant a little more to eat for the men who stayed behind. There the only breaks in the monotony, apart from the always argumentative camp meetings and whatever controversy was currently raging, were provided by visitors from the outside and the binges that would be sparked by the fortuitous availability of a bottle of wine or a few quarts of beer. (Since travelers returning from Concord often brought these jolly provisions with them, it isn't entirely true that trips to the capital had no positive effect whatsoever on the tenor of life back at the camp.) The visits were few in number and, except for one exciting weekend invasion by a bevy of young college women, usually involved the family or friends of individual campers. Very occasional visits of a more formal nature were arranged by the NSBRO or the peace agencies, and on one occasion Selective Service officials descended on camp for an on-the-scene inspection.

The strangest was an overnight visit by a young Quaker in military uniform, a corporal who presented himself unannounced and for apparently no other purpose than to recount his impressions of the military life and the difficulties he had encountered in his attempt to be transferred from full-service duty to noncombatant status in recognition of his pacifist beliefs. In Selmon's judgment he was a simple-minded person, somewhat mixed up in his attitudes and opinions. However, since he gave the definite impression that he would have preferred not being in the military at all, he was made welcome. Simple-minded and mixed-up he may have been, but he was assured of a large and eager audience when the announcement was made that he would be meeting with all interested parties after the evening meal to tell of some of the horrible things he had witnessed in the service. Those who gathered around in expectation of hearing lurid details of military brutality and the like were sorely disappointed when they were treated instead to a temperance lecture. The guest proved to be an ardent advocate of total abstinence and his promised revelations were a graphic presentation of the excessive drunkenness and its dire effects as he had observed them in the military setting. A disappointing or amusing episode, or both, depending on the time frame one chooses; few of us thought it funny then.

The young man left the following day, but the real reasons behind his visit remained a matter of speculation for several days. Selmon confessed that he was sorry for the man because he was so obviously confused and concluded that his purpose had been to dissuade men from leaving camp for I-A-O service. Other possibilities suggest themselves in retrospect. It may have been nothing more than a visit born of curiosity, a chance for this young serviceman to see for himself whether CPS camps were in truth the hotbeds of subversion and sedition they were so widely believed to be. Or it could have been a subtle attempt by the NSBRO or even Selective Service to cut down on the drinking for which, we liked to believe at least, Camp Simon had already developed an enviable reputation throughout CPS. At the time other equally farfetched explanations were given serious consideration, but nothing further ever came from the visit and it remained a mystery.

Some weeks earlier the camp's calm, such as it was, had been shattered by another guest. An older man with a heavy foreign accent arrived unexpectedly and begged for attention at the evening meal. He was searching, he explained, for his long-lost son whose last known whereabouts had been "some CCC camp in New England." Obviously persuaded that the Warner camp was still operating as part of that earlier forestry program, he implored his listeners to help him by providing any information they might have. He grew increasingly agitated in the telling of his sad tale and finally burst into tears and carried on in so distraught a state that several men had to leave the mess hall to keep from breaking into open laughter. Every attempt to quiet him down and convince him that the new situation had nothing to do with the former CCC program and that nothing could be done there about locating his missing son was to no avail and merely evoked a new outburst of emotional pleas for assistance.

It was not until later that night and the following morning that the truth became known. The heartbroken visitor was Dave Komiker's father, a professional heckler-ventriloquist-comedian well known on the Pittsburgh banquet circuit. He stayed on for a week or more, a source of continuing entertainment whenever new and unsuspecting victims—men returning from leave or the Mt. Cardigan crew reporting in to the base camp—were at hand. For each there was a different, but always convincing, impersonation.* As usual the most complete account of this event is to be found in the Selmon diary, but the number of former campers who included references to this visit in their questionnaire responses justifies ranking it among the three or four most memorable events at Warner.

The Moroni family's visits to their son and brother in the less than two months he spent in camp were special in another sense. Christmas 1942 was made memorable for those who were obliged to remain in camp by the holiday feast prepared by Mama Moroni, and the occasion was brightened further by the vermouth and strega provided by Joe's soldier-brother who was present in uniform. The normal diet being what it was, *any* meal prepared by a competent cook was an event to remember, but the lavish spread produced on this occasion (pasta, turkey, and all the good things to go with it) rated superlatives in any context. The crowning touch of extravagance and luxury—and one can only imagine the shock and dismay it must have caused the regular cooks and the camp administrators— was Mrs. Moroni's appropriation of the entire supply of chopped meat (intended, of course, as the main course for several future meals) for *dressing* for the turkey!

Other visits of the family Moroni (father, mother, sister, brother all descended upon the camp en masse) had been less enjoyable except for the opportunities they provided for sarcastic jokes and other humorous references to the overprotectiveness that, to cite but one example, had Moroni's father covering the washroom windows with paper and setting aside a kind of curtained shower stall to protect his son's modesty. The repeated demands they made upon the administration for special privileges and concessions (e.g., Joe also insisted upon using the supervisor's toilet instead of the common latrine) be-

---

*Strangely enough, my own recollection of this is vague. Though I was in camp for the full period of Mr. Komiker's stay, my memories all seem to be secondhand, the facts familiar enough but not in the sense of having been an observer or participant in the fun. My letters—and there were at least three or four written while he was in camp—make no reference at all to his comic performance. Still, whenever Warner veterans gather there is almost certain to be some mention of the Komiker visit and the various roles he played: for Henry Fallon, that of a visiting physician checking up on an old complaint; for Lou Swanson, that of an irate neighbor charging him with trespassing while cutting firewood at the Mt. Cardigan camp; and many others, each unerringly suited to the particular victim.

came a source of considerable resentment. It was perhaps fitting that, having provided the camp with its only true culinary highlight, the Moroni family took their son with them on holiday leave following the Christmas feast, a leave from which he never returned. On his physician's recommendation, he was placed on "absent-sick" status and remained so classified until he was given a medical discharge at the time the camp was closed.

None of the other visits, except for the weekend visit of the Smith girls to be described separately, matched the Komiker and Moroni episodes for their entertainment value. Some, as already mentioned, were more official in nature or purpose. The visit of two prominent Quaker educators who came to speak and offer the encouragement of their presence would be an example. That "encouragement of their presence" phrase carried deeper implications than one might at first realize. This was one more area in which the Warner campers perceived themselves to be, and in actuality were, deprived and disadvantaged. The major peace church agencies had well-funded educational programs under which prominent pacifists visited their camps with some regularity. The impoverished ACCO could not hope to provide similar morale-enhancing programs. Moreover, even if they could have found the necessary funds, there were few prominent Catholics who would have considered becoming part of such an operation for the benefit of conscientious objectors. Except for individuals familiar with the Catholic Worker movement and its paper, few Catholics knew of Camp Simon's existence; and, for those who did, it was enough for them to provide money to keep the men fed and clothed at least to minimal levels of existential necessity. The visit of the two Quaker dignitaries, then, was welcomed and appreciated as evidence that Warner, though not in the mainstream of CPS, was not being overlooked completely.

Another official visit of sorts involved the son of the Governor of New Hampshire accompanied by two attractive young women. This was not a sign of approval and support on the part of the state authorities, however. The young man's purpose in coming was to recruit applicants for a proposed special unit to be established at the Concord mental hospital. Any prospect of detached service, always interpreted as a welcome opportunity to get away from the camp setting, was certain to excite some measure of interest, so this was a welcome visit too. As it turned out, the Concord location failed to stir much interest among the men, and when it was finally approved at the end of January, the unit opened under AFSC auspices instead.[2]

Warner could not compete with the regularity or prominence of speakers attributed to the more affluent Friends, Mennonite, and Brethren camps, but it could call upon spokesmen for the ACCO. There were a couple of visits by Arthur Sheehan, the titular head of this Catholic Worker front, but the most important visit of this nature was the one made by Dorothy Day, co-founder and guiding spirit of the parent movement. Though she does not recall her Warner visit as clearly as the one she had made earlier to Stoddard, her appearance was more than just a significant break in the camp monotony or morale-boosting ritual. Coming one day after the tumultuous camp meeting at which the disciplinary action taken against John Canory had been revoked and steps taken to make the director and assistant director posts elective, her visit provided the opportunity for the various factions to air their grievances and, even more to the point, for the *real* authority behind the camp* to spell out the religious agency's response. It is not possible to ascertain whether her visit was arranged through some emergency summons; but even if this were not the case, it must have been prompted by the atmosphere of tension and the rapidly deteriorating morale that had been illustrated so dramatically the night before.

Dorothy Day's talk and the exchanges that followed in the question period were marked by the degree of frankness and directness with which she "told it like it was." When it was over, she had succeeded in winning the admiration and respect of all her listeners, chapel group supporters of the status quo and Marxist intellectual leaders of the dissidents alike. This does not mean that the latter elements were won over to an acceptance of the situation. Complaints about the food and the other deficiencies of Camp Simon life would continue and, at times, intensify after her departure. Nevertheless, as her multitude of admirers will testify, Miss Day brings a combination of moral conviction and simple good sense to any issue that is always compelling in its impact. And so it was at Warner. The critics, however just their complaints, began at a severe disadvantage

---

*This, at least, is the way the men in camp defined her role. Sheehan, Larrowe, Saunders, and the others may not have been, as one former camper suggests, her "vicars" in the strictest sense, but the description is not entirely out of place. As this former camper continues, "By this I do not imply they had no minds of their own, they agreed with her, but that they accepted her authority, came to her for advice, and almost always accepted her decisions as final."

when those complaints had to be addressed to this plainly garbed practitioner of voluntary poverty whose work on the Bowery, as they all knew, involved accepting a standard of living no better than theirs and doing so as a matter of personal choice.

The Warner camp file in the Swarthmore collection includes an extensive summary of the Day talk and her responses to the more challenging questions raised by the campers. An accompanying note explains that the account is based "on the notes taken by a member of the socialist group there who is very fair minded" (most likely Dean Farfether). The summary provides considerable insight to the other side of the problem that had taken so deadly a toll of camper morale. For obvious reasons only the major points can be touched on here, but even these suffice to add some balance and perspective to this generally adverse review of the Warner experience.

As far as CPS itself was concerned, Dorothy Day endorsed virtually all of the criticisms voiced by the men in camp. She agreed the camps were designed to make sure that conscientious objectors were tucked away where they could do no harm; the work assignments were useless and stupid, approaching in a sense the moral torture depicted by Dostoevski. Pressed by a questioner as to whether required work without pay was not slavery, she readily agreed that it was and added, "All conscription means slavery." As she had done on several occasions, she expressed her own conviction that CPS and the CO classification itself represented too much of a compromise with the war effort, that total noncooperation with the draft would have been preferable as a truer and more consistent witness against war and militarism. For herself, she had not favored assuming responsibility for the camp but had acquiesced in the judgment of the young men responsible for the Catholic Worker peace activities that it was important to have a Catholic representation in the program.

Despite these personal reservations she respected the men in CPS and believed they were making a more effective witness than were the men who had chosen noncombatant service in the military or even those who had volunteered for work with the American Field Service ambulance units. These latter, she felt, were sharing in the honor and glory lavished upon the soldier; the men in CPS, isolated and frustrated though they might be, could at least enjoy the satisfaction of knowing they were more of a problem for the government if only in that the very fact of their existence disturbed the unanimity of a nation committed to war.

Catholics by and large, she reminded her audience, were extremely patriotic, a probable result of their status as a minority religion and the additional pressure this put upon them to prove themselves good and loyal Americans. In her view they were an oppressed lower class group comparable to Negroes and Jews, quite unlike the situation in France where Catholics constituted an elite. The little support the Catholic conscientious objector did receive—from one bishop at least —reflected that prelate's personal support for the Coughlinite point of view and his personal animosity toward the British; it should not be regarded as an endorsement of the pacifist position they had taken.

This observation turned the discussion to a more specific consideration of the relationship between the Catholic Worker movement and Camp Simon. She had sensed some hostility toward the Catholic Worker in camp which she attributed to the peculiar mix of the campers themselves and the suspicion that "Catholic Worker ideas" were being imposed upon them. The religious (and nonreligious) mix in itself did not trouble her. Indeed, it was probably a good thing that it was not a purely Catholic camp if one accepted, as she did, Jacques Maritain's view that Catholics, Protestants, Jews, and others must learn to work with one another in a pluralistic framework. As she saw it, the situation at Warner, even with all its strains, was preferable to life in an army camp where, and here the reporter quoted her words directly, "There is no thought, no responsibility, no protesting, and people are no longer alive."

The other part of the problem, she continued, was more difficult. Ideas should never be imposed on anyone; hence it would be wrong to impose the Catholic Worker ideas on the campers, especially since so many were not ready for them. At the same time, a kind of situational imposition was unavoidable given the Worker's financial dependence upon a semiannual appeal to the newspaper's readers and its unwillingness to turn to outside peace groups for direct assistance to support the camp. As far as she was concerned, individual campers were not excluded from "going over the head of the ACCO" to make such direct appeals for assistance to the Friends or other outside groups if they were so inclined, but it would not be ACCO policy to do so. At that moment the Catholic Worker was $4,500 in debt, a normal condition for the movement; as a result the camp, too, was deep in debt with no funds available to meet some of its bills. To this extent, she confessed, the movement was imposing its philosophy;

the camp, like the movement itself, would continue as it always had by "trusting in God." A sufficiency of funds, she added, might even be harmful, bringing ease and satisfaction.

Turning to more specific complaints, she admitted they were valid too. It was simply beyond the camp's precarious resources to meet the stipulated requirement of such staff services as dietician, nurse, medical and dental care, and the like. As for the camp diet, she acknowledged its shortcomings, but it was clear she did not invest this particular problem with the same degree of urgency claimed by the protesters. It was, she felt, "adequate" though not "satisfactory," a rather obvious application of Catholic Worker standards of adequacy. She then extended this to a double reminder that things were much worse for starving victims of war in Europe and that the present difficulties suffered by the men could be a valuable lesson showing that many, even they, were profitting from conditions of exploitation that caused the war in the first place. She assured her listeners, however, that efforts were being made, and would continue to be made, to find the funds needed to improve the food situation at Warner.

The next questions focused upon governance and the quality of administrative decisions and procedures. The manner of Stuart Grant's selection for detached service at the New York headquarters was, she admitted, a corner-cutting decision made without consultation, but she was confident that the decision had been made solely in terms of promised efficiency. Turning to the broader and more immediate question of the campers' proposals adopted the night before, she took a hands-off position. She reminded her listeners that the ACCO was a separate part of the Catholic Worker and to illustrate the point she described the frequent arguments over things like space and the use of typewriters at the Mott Street office. As far as the structure of camp governance was concerned, she would prefer something along the lines of the Benedictine model with an authority-endowed leader guided by a council of advisors. However, since the camp was "only fifty percent Catholic" this obviously could not be imposed. Therefore, her only advice was that when differences did develop between Director Larrowe and the men, their best strategy was to "take up the issues again and again, fight them out, and wear him down until you do change his mind and reach some sort of agreement."

It was worth remembering, she thought, that the Catholic Worker did in fact allow far greater freedom than was true of other camps in the CPS program. At the same time they were being accused of excessive authoritarianism by the campers themselves, others were criticizing them for being too chaotic, even anarchistic, in the operation of the camp. Addressing herself specifically to the question whether rule breakers should ever be penalized by the camp administration, she answered in the negative, explaining that to do so would, in effect, make the ACCO an arm of the government.*Besides, she continued, the better way was to trust to persuasion and understanding, the approach they had always found preferable in dealing with drunks in the Catholic Worker houses of hospitality.

Though no issues were resolved, the evening with Dorothy Day had at least served the purpose of bringing them into sharper focus. Bitter controversy and even personal animosity would continue through the remaining weeks of the camp's existence, but the men now had a better understanding of their situation and were aware of the extremely limited prospects for any significant improvement. In one intriguing aside, Miss Day revealed a divergence of views at the highest levels of ACCO administration; as she put it, Sheehan and Larrowe differed in their approach to governance and there were "arguments enough to make me dizzy." Of course, she reminded her listeners, Sheehan had the easier part to come to camp occasionally and speak in broad generalities of greater freedom and autonomy. He did not have to translate them into immediate applications to particular problems, the task faced by Director Larrowe. In this connection, one other passing comment of some significance was her warning against allowing the camp affairs to be "taken over by an articulate few." Pseudodemocracy, she reminded them, all too often leads to arbitrary dictatorship.

After this evening the options were more clearly defined for everyone. The Catholic Worker was not trying to impose its ideas and values on the campers, but its belief in voluntary poverty, mutual aid, and the willingness to suffer lack of privacy, food, and other corporal comforts would continue to govern ACCO operations. Campers did not have to share or accept those values, but given this approach to the situation and the financial facts of life it produced, they would have to endure their effects. Either that, or arrange a transfer to some other camp.

*The recorder of this session added his own confirmatory note at this point, stating that there had been no actual punishments applied in camp, no matter what rule had been broken. The Canory incident was a departure from this practice, of course; but it, too, had been overruled by the camp meeting.

The Smith Weekend

Where the Day visit proved to be the most significant and illuminating, there is no question at all as to which was the most anticipated and enjoyed. This was the invasion on the last weekend in January by a group of pacifistically inclined students from Smith College. Organized by the fiancée of one of the campers, the affair had been a matter of intense planning and activity for weeks. The thorough housecleaning that had been so bitterly resented when ordered by the director was now undertaken, as the Selmon diary put it, with the kind of enthusiasm "only girls could inspire in the men." Even Roger Tennitt made himself and his rat's nest of a bunk presentable, surrendering for the occasion his personal rebellion against the bourgeois virtues of neatness and cleanliness. Firewood was gathered and stacked for the recreation hall barracks where there was to be dancing and such other festive entertainment as could be managed in that dismal setting, and a multitude of other mundane chores were performed without argument or complaint.

What to others must certainly seem a minor event should be placed in its appropriate contemporary perspective. In the context of the national efforts amounting to a crusade designed to bolster the morale in the armed forces, the sacrifice of one winter weekend by a group of eighteen or so female college students ordinarily would not merit more than casual note. Every town and city of any size had its USO or similar servicemen's center, and the entire nation was networked by committees of patriotic householders eager to outdo each other in providing hospitality for "our boys in uniform." There was nothing comparable for the CPS-man, needless to say. The servicemen's centers were closed to him as they were to other civilians, and as far as the general populace was concerned, once they discovered his reason for not being in uniform, they were uninclined to be friendly, much less hospitable.

It would be too much to say that the men of CPS were abandoned completely. There was a scattering of peace people in the larger cities ready to welcome "their kind" of serviceman, but such efforts were modest in scope and nowhere nearly as well organized as the facilities and services available to men in uniform. In Warner, for instance, there was one prim, elderly woman who made a practice of inviting the men in small groups for Sunday brunch or an occasional evening treat of cake and ice cream. She was not, it is well to note, Catholic;

to my knowledge at least, none of the Catholics in the Warner area made even the slightest gesture of friendship toward the camp or its inhabitants.

One of the few attempts to show some support for the men in CPS was a Hallowe'en dance sponsored by some Boston pacifists to which men in the various New England camps, including Warner, were invited. The idea for the weekend visit seems to have grown out of that affair. For the girls it must have represented a daring display of pacifist dissent in a social milieu that would surely regard such behavior as bordering on subversion if not, indeed, giving aid and comfort to the enemy. For the campers it was a rare and welcome opportunity to enjoy feminine companionship and, of much deeper significance, a token of the support and encouragement they craved.

It was, above all, an occasion for feasting and frivolity. The weekend began with a baked ham dinner on Saturday evening and ended with an unusually lavish version of the customary Sunday chicken. No less than eleven of the camp's feathered population were put to Selmon's chopping block in honor of the great event. Following the Saturday feast, the guests and campers proceeded to the recreation hall, which was a grim barracks building like all the others except for its great fireplace. It was the only time this facility would be put to such use; ordinarily when it was used at all, it served as the setting for Chuck Sterner's ad hoc indoor basketball games.

Apart from dancing to the camp phonograph, the planned entertainment for the evening consisted of a program of skits written, cast, and directed by Shelden Dennison. Dennison, who put aside his customary output of petitions and letters of protest to devote his full attention and talent to the task, fancied himself as something of a comic writer. The result of his efforts was a parody of Irving Berlin's Broadway success, *This Is the Army*, with its armed forces cast. Dennison's parody, entitled *This Ain't the Army*, purported to trace the CPS-career of a typical assignee ("Mr Jerk") from his orientation at the hands of a functionally authoritarian camp director ("Dwight Lagree") to the finale in which the hero is assigned to detached service as a participant at the peace conference along with Roosevelt, Churchill, and Hitler.

The few surviving pages of the script reveal a brand of humor best described as sophomoric, but the Selmon diary gives it a favorable review, noting that the dialogue and the situations were received with abundant laughter. My recollection agrees with this assessment; but in retrospect it occurs that this generous response probably should be attributed more to the campers than to their female guests. It is most unlikely that the latter would have been able to appreciate the inside gags upon which the skits were based, Dennison having used this parody as a vehicle for exploiting camp problems and satirizing the various divisions among the men. All in the spirit of good fun, of course, but there was also a biting edge to some of the characterizations and events depicted. The skits and song lyrics may even have provided something of a therapeutic release by reducing the camp's tensions, strains, and controversies to semihumorous statements with more than a touch of self-criticism. As the few lyrics introduced at various points in the present volume reveal, they made admittedly sardonic allowance for the more blatantly uncomplimentary stereotypes of the conscientious objector. Thus life as a woodsman was "better than no life at all," at once an expression of disdain for the unimportant work to which they had been assigned and a dour reference to the widely accepted notion that alternative service was a device for avoiding the risks of the battlefield. Similar self-directed irony can be found in the references to working without pay "simply because" and the suggestion that the men of Warner preferred to work and play "while the other fellows fight." With months of endless squabbles behind them, the characterization of life at Camp Simon as "taking the high road" and, given the record of low productivity on work project, the claim of "leaving a sawdust trail" anywhere were obviously intended to bring the house down—and they did.

The casting helped. Memorable scenes had Ernest Rider, the morose "Gypsy King," singing of the joys of woodsmanship while offstage assistants showered him with sawdust and woodshavings, a performance topped only by the finale which found George Selmon, the only Jew in cast or audience, stealing the show with his riotous portrayal of an unrepentant Hitler at the peace conference.*

After what may have seemed to the guests an almost interminable interlude, the dancing resumed and continued on into the early

---

*Dennison, a great admirer of Cole Porter, also included some lyrics striving after the "naughty double-entendre" touch of the master. One showstopper had Walter North, that most combative of the Catholic Workers, "in drag" identifying himself as "just plain Lil/ an ordinary . . . well/ they say that girls like me/ will go direct to Hell" and ending "a handsome sailor/ may tempt me/ I'll confess/ but I'm true to CPS." Fortunately none of our guests (and, more fortunate perhaps, none of the guardians of the camp morality) seemed to take offense.

morning hours. The enthusiasm of Selmon's diary entry proclaiming
the weekend a smashing success would have found unanimous agreement on the part of his fellow campers, one of the very few instances
when consensus on anything was achieved. It was all very innocent
and none of the friendships flowered into new romances, but the
memory and impact remained long after Warner's days had come to
an end. Maybe it was not much compared to the opportunity to
dance with stars and chorus girls, but given the norm of Warner existence it may have counted for more as a strengthening assurance
that they were not really as alone, as abandoned, in their stand as
it seemed in their more troubled moments of depression and doubt.
In early March some of the men would travel to Northampton for a
return visit, this time as guests of the girls; but by then the camp was
in the final stages of closing down, and that second weekend would
be little more than a faint echo of this gala event.

The Binges

For those who stayed behind, that March weekend proved to be the occasion of one of the wildest, and certainly one of the most unexpected, of the alcoholic binges that periodically shook the oppressive regularity of camp life. As a principal instigator, I can recall the incident very well. This is fortunate since Selmon, the usual source of such detailed accounts, was among those journeying to Smith and could only provide a secondhand report for his diary after it was all over. The departure of the Smith-bound contingent had left the camp even more desolate than usual with only twenty-five men remaining. To make matters worse a morning snowfall had developed into a promising blizzard by mid-afternoon, adding the possibility of being snowbound to our normal state of physical and psychological isolation.

All things considered, it seemed an eminently suitable time for me to produce a bottle of gin, a Christmas gift that I had been carefully hoarding for some such special event or emergency need. The bottle and I proceeded to the mess hall where the skeleton staff on weekend kitchen detail—Lowell Bartlett and Lou Swanson prominent among them—managed to produce a few lemons. In a remarkably short time, lemons and gin disappeared leaving four joyously inebriated men to prepare and set out the evening meal. Other campers may have wandered in and had a taste as well, but there was no doubt as to where most of the gin had gone. There was even less doubt when the remaining campers came in for their meal and found Bartlett, until then one of the quietest and most reserved of men, raging about, jumping on benches, and chanting wildly in what appeared to be the purest liturgical Latin. It was on this occasion and while he was in that state that he conducted the mock excommunication of George Andrews, his archopponent in the liberal *vs* rigorist theological debates in which they so regularly engaged.

By itself this binge would have been notable enough, but there was more to come. Swanson, that most respected leader of the chapel group, was enlivened to the point of nagging Tony Saunders, who was once again acting as camp director, for permission to use the White Ghost for a jaunt to Concord to continue the party. It was an impossible request: the blizzard had now been in force for several hours; the ban on pleasure driving was being enforced by local authorities; public relations, as always, had to be taken into account.

Nevertheless, in defiance of all logical expectations, Saunders agreed.

In his secondhand report of this wild night on the town, Selmon was impressed most by the fact that the participants included "some of the Catholic boys who are known for their intellectual outbursts but are unknown for their activities that might link them to the usual man-in-the-street (drinking, kidding around, and giving off the warmth of a human that could only show them to be humans)." The characterization was not entirely fair; as we have seen, these "Catholic boys" had been the instigators and not just go-along participants. Still there was validity to the essential point he was trying to make. This was one of the rare occasions at Warner where the lines of division that were usually so hard to surmount were literally washed away. Swanson, the chapel group stalwart, teamed with Farfether, the Marxist agnostic; Mattano, the revered artist, was there along with Bob Tantino, one of the camp comics; most surprising of all, even John Luzon, that most disruptive of the disrupters, joined the fun. (The fact that this macho womanizer had not gone to Smith may be further evidence of the "innocence" connected with that visit.)

At any rate, ten or more happily boisterous men crammed themselves into the back of the never reliable panel truck and headed out into the blowing and drifting snow. Before the evening was over, Swanson and Farfether, as unlikely a pair of rowdies as one could imagine, were thrown out of one tavern. Luzon, on the other hand, assured himself of a popular reception and a number of free drinks, by announcing at another that he was enjoying one last fling before leaving for military service "to get a couple of Japs." Bartlett was the biggest surprise of all. By this time gloriously drunk, he topped his extravagant performance in the mess hall with a rousing concert of songs delivered in the style of the Gay Nineties which, as Selmon heard the tale, "left the boys gasping for breath."

For some unaccountable reason the diary account failed to include the final, crowning touch. The snow had stopped by the time the White Ghost limped its way back to camp. As we approached the outskirts of Warner, someone noticed a red glow in the sky, and further investigation revealed a circle of leaping flames and heavy smoke in the vicinity of Warner's only industry, a lumbermill and former crutch factory. Well primed for heroism and overjoyed to have an opportunity to put their fire-fighting training to use at last,

the men rushed out to fight the blaze only to learn, to their discomfiture, that they were not needed, that the fire had been purposely
set to dispose of wood scraps and was well under control. One can
only imagine what the local inhabitants tending that fire in the early
morning hours must have thought of the sudden appearance of that
unruly and tipsy delegation of conscientious objectors. It is even
more amusing to speculate on the shattering effect the incident
would have had upon Selective Service and the NSBRO, both always
so sensitive to even the slightest risk of possibly unfavorable public
relations. Apparently it was never brought to their attention.

Here again, there are much more significant dimensions to the incident than the high jinks involved, more even than the evidence it
gives that these COs certainly did not fit the "goody-goody" or
"holy Joe" images popular stereotypes and more traditional pacifists
might prefer. Alcoholic binges and beer busts, the terms most generally employed by the men, occurred frequently enough at Warner to
justify the fond belief that the ACCO camp could lay claim to a certain pre-eminence on this score. Sometimes they took the form of
holiday celebrations. Thus, a pre-Christmas eggnog party, traditional
enough in inspiration, soon got out of hand and culminated in a wild
display of impromptu dancing, ranging from mildly disorganized
square-dancing to free-style jitterbugging by one of the younger men
matched by a hilarious stomp-dance put on by one of the oldest. A
week or so later, New Year's Eve drew another boisterous company
to the mess hall where they soon converted a series of hanging skillets
into an improvised chimes organ, beating upon them with a variety
of serving spoons to "ring out the old and ring in the new," Warner-
style. As midnight struck someone added what seemed a perfect
finale by pushing the button that set off the work siren, a celebra-
tory touch reportedly not too well received by either the townsfolk
or the project superintendent, since the siren also served as part of
the local air raid warning system.

The majority of the binges, however, could claim no such ceremonial justifications but were purely spontaneous events brought about
by the chance availability of a few quarts of weak beer, a bottle or
two of wine, or, more rarely, a shared supply of more potent spirits.
Men returning from furlough, a weekend trip, or sometimes just a
one-day visit to Concord would bring the makings and those fortunate enough to be their friends, or to just happen on the scene at the
strategic moment, would be invited to partake of the unexpected

bounty. Before the night was out the happied inebriates would parade through the bunkhouses banging on pots and pans to awaken their sleeping comrades—and providing, in the process, one more occasion for indignant protest and complaint at the next camp meeting.

One thing is certain. *Never have so many been able to get so drunk so often on so little.* A single quart of New Hampshire's low alcoholic-content beer could reduce three or four men to a state of relaxed good humor and set them off on a series of foolish frivolities that, by any normal standards, should have required hours of steady carousing. Though there is no way of testing this hypothesis, there is reason to believe that the inebriation, if it can be described as such, was more psychological than physiological. In other words, so disproportionate a response to such limited stimuli was simply one more effect of the prolonged deprivation and isolation marking the camp situation.

Other possible hidden implications may be even more significant. Beyond the release they offered the participants, these binges may have represented an affirmation of the campers' masculinity and, in an even subtler sense, their Catholicism. Only too aware that the first was disputed in the prevailing stereotypes of the conscientious objector and the second challenged, if not denied altogether, by the majority of their fellow communicants, these men were under constant pressure to prove (perhaps to themselves as well as to those critics) that they were as manly and as Catholic as anyone else.

The suggestion calls for fuller elaboration. Generally speaking, there was a pronounced moral tone to life in Camp Simon. The "barracks talk," while not utterly devoid of profanity and occasional resort to the more commonplace obscenities, was relatively innocent by most standards and certainly far more innocent than the standards generally attributed to the military environment. If patterns of speech and general decorum were not exactly monastic, they were for the most part markedly restrained and correct. One might occasionally hear stories and experiences centering upon real or fantasized sexual conquests and exploits, but these were clearly out of keeping with the general atmosphere and quality of discourse.

Pin-ups, reputedly the sine qua non of the serviceman's taste in decorative art, were not greatly in evidence at Warner. I recall that the Luzons, and possibly one or two others, had photos of this genre posted near their bunks. The artists, of course, featured nude figures in some of their work, but these were not likely to give offense and, in any event, were usually kept in the studio with its relatively restricted access. The few honest-to-goodness prudes in our midst may have objected (there was a nude Christ-figure in one of the paintings produced by our ranking liturgical artist that evoked some unfavorable comment), but this never became a camp issue, even in the context of the other attempts at censorship discussed earlier.

This generally elevated moral tone was not a result of formal rules and regulations. Indeed, as the strong response to the record breaking incident proves, any such attempt would have failed miserably and in all likelihood produced an almost automatic proliferation of pin-ups and earthy language. What was involved was a kind of *self*-censorship, a combination of personal values and consideration for the values of others. This was, after all, a group of men gathered together precisely because they placed a special importance upon moral and religious considerations and recognized the obligation to translate these into personal behavior. Even those who by background or temperament would have behaved differently in other settings or situations tended to avoid subjects and forms of expression that might affront the sensibilities of those who were more chaste or ascetic in their personal interests and manner. Those few, like the Luzon brothers, who did go out of their way to use earthy language or to flaunt their sexuality did so partly with the intent to shock and offend; for them this would be one more form of disruption, one more way to express their contempt for the idealism they rejected.

So it was that alcoholic indulgence, along with embellished reminiscences of past drinking exploits, might have served as a substitute for the other affirmations of masculinity that would have been inappropriate in the Warner setting. My further suggestion that the binges and beer busts constituted a kind of *religious* affirmation calls for an even more complicated explanation.

The men of Camp Simon, like conscientious objectors of all religious persuasions, had knowingly set themselves apart from the national consensus supporting the war effort. This, in itself, was not too great a burden because that act of social deviance was put in a religious perspective as at once an act of obedience to a moral imperative and a recognition of the proper order of priority. The conscientious objector, simply put, was denying to Caesar that which did not belong to him.

Firm though they may have been in their private conviction, they could not ignore the fact that their fellow Catholics, including the responsible spiritual leaders of the Church, not only failed to share that interpretation but actually reversed it. Their refusal to serve was viewed as a failure to fulfill the citizen's moral obligations as these were defined in the traditional teachings of the Church. Nor was this all. In what was perhaps the unkindest cut of all, they soon discovered that their status in the alternative service program in which they were to perform their work of national importance under civilian direction was again that of the small, alienated, dissident minority. Not only did they see themselves as outsiders in the Civilian Public Service program; they were *exploited* outsiders at that.

As we have seen, the program and its leadership were frankly Protestant in origin and commitment. ACCO participation in policy deliberations and decisions taken at the NSBRO level was little more than window-dressing. The three major peace churches called the shots and ran the show *as was clearly their right* since they provided the funds and other support without which the program would have collapsed. In all fairness it must be said that the dominance attributed to the peace church leadership was exaggerated in some crucial respects. On the camp scene, for instance, they made no attempt to impose or enforce rigid disciplinary controls or standards on a system-wide basis as they might well have done. Discipline and standards of expectation within the individual camps varied depending upon the respective sponsor agencies and, as was noted by Dorothy Day, under the ACCO they were remarkably relaxed.

On the other hand, it is equally undeniable that the peace church leadership was responsible for approving, and later maintaining, those aspects of the alternative service program that provoked the strongest dissent and opposition in the camps, including Warner. However the dissidents of other camps may have defined these issues, to the more articulate Catholics on the Warner roster the deprivations they resented were expressions of Protestant values and traceable to puritanical life styles and behavioral expectations. Going the second mile, a Christian ideal honored in Catholic as much as in Protestant teachings, became a term of derision directed against those who seemed willing to accept the injustices inherent in the system. The archetypal "second-milers" were the Mennonites, the largest and believed to be the most conformist element in the program, and the Friends, generally charged with being its ideological architects. The Brethren, the third of the major peace churches, were discounted or dismissed when major blame was being assessed.

Such, at least, was the view from Warner, and the charges were

true to some extent. The Mennonite camps and campers were models
of uncomplaining dedication to high levels of work output, qualita-
tively as well as quantitatively speaking, and exhibited an over-all
standard of performance the more rebellious Catholics rejected as
an all too willing compromise with the evils of conscription. The
Friends, however, were more the object of a love-hate relationship.
On the one hand, they were greatly admired for their liberalism and
especially for their history of major contributions to the cause of
peace; on the other, they were held responsible for providing the
summer work camp model for CPS and the supportive rationale upon
which the alternative service program was based. That most crucial
deprivation of all, the denial of pay, was ascribed, rightly or wrongly,
to the reputed affluence of the Society of Friends and its members.*

Both the characterization of the Friends as a group and the motivations ascribed to them ignored some important facts. Not all the
men in Quaker camps were Quakers, and not all the Quakers were
wealthy. By the same token, most of the active agitation for pay and
for the elimination of other injustices originated from and continued
to be centered in camps operated by the AFSC. Even allowing for
these, however, it could not be ignored that the men at the top, the
Quaker leaders most clearly associated with the NSBRO policies and
practices, did seem to confirm the unfavorable impression held by
the men of Camp Simon, and that was enough for them.

What relation does all this have to the binges? Far-fetched though
it may seem at first, indulgence in alcoholic beverages assumed the
characteristics of a Catholic resistance to the Protestant domination.

*The image of the well-to-do and comfortable Quaker carried over to the camp-
ers' assessment of the advantages presumably offered in camps operated by the
AFSC. That there were some very definite advantages was certain. Those camps
did have more complete and more competent operational staffs, including dieti-
cians and practical nurses. Medical and dental care was more readily available.
The diet was certainly better, though probably not as lavish in quality or amount
as the hungry men of Warner were prone to imagine. Finally, there was the
monthly allowance (originally $2.50, later increased to $5.00) which looked
very generous indeed to men who were receiving nothing at all. Nevertheless, it
should be added that these oft-cited comparisons did not lead to any significant
number of requests for transfers from the lower depths of Warner to the bright
promise of a better life in a Quaker camp. Even those dissidents and disrupters
who did not share the compensating interest in maintaining a Catholic presence
in CPS seemed, for some reason or other, to prefer the known shortcomings of
Camp Simon to the unknown problems they might have to contend with in
some other setting.

More than that, additional gratification was drawn from the imagined dichotomy between the more human Catholic and the world-denying, pleasure-rejecting Puritan. Ethnic overtones were involved to the extent that an equally imaginary confrontation of values between the heavily Irish and Italian Catholics and the WASPs presumed to inhabit the other camps put a premium upon living up (or down) to the wild reputation its members felt Warner had achieved.* Therefore, one could take added pride as well as pleasure in getting a bit tipsy if by doing so he reinforced his self-image as a loyal Catholic and, equally important, gained special recognition on this score from others in CPS who would take notice and, it was hoped, be scandalized.

Whether one accepts these affirmation hypotheses or not, the more proximate explanations of the pattern lose none of their force. These lie in the factors mentioned in several other contexts as the most conspicuous and consistent aspects of life at Warner—above all else, the utter boredom and deadly monotony of camp life. Affirmations of masculinity or religious commitment aside, the general situation was itself depressing enough to make it possible for a few quarts of weak beer or a couple of bottles of cheap wine to send at least six or seven men and a dog (the latter the only nondrinker in the party) parading through the bunkhouses, raising "holy hell," banging away on an assortment of pots and pans in the dead of the wintry night.

The Farewell Party

The final event, and the last and greatest of the Warner binges, was more organized and official than any of the others. Once it was definitely known that Camp Simon was to be closed and its members

---

*Like all stereotypes, the life in AFSC camps was probably nowhere nearly as puritanical and well-ordered as the men in Warner liked to imagine. The French diary has an entry reporting that official visitors to the AFSC's Powellsville camp had been disturbed by the amount of drinking observed there. Furthermore, in a January entry, he refers to criticisms by Selective Service officials of New England AFSC camps, including the suggestion on their part that the government ought to take them over "on grounds of incompetence in their management." One was quoted to the effect that "the barracks look like a farmer's pigpen and for the life of him he couldn't see why any problem with conscience was involved with keeping the barracks clean." The offending camps are not named. It may even be that the inspecting officials had their references mixed and that their complaints were really concerned with the situation at Warner, which fit their description in several respects.

transferred to a new camp under AFSC jurisdiction, plans were laid for a farewell party. Invited guests included the government project's supervisory personnel and, of course, Miss McLaughlin, our Warner benefactress. The target date originally set (it was Lent, after all) was St. Patrick's Day, but the affair was advanced a week because of the uncertainty of the actual date for the impending move. Possibly this was just as well. The camp was officially closed on March 18, 1943, the day after St. Patrick's feastday. Few men would have been in acceptable condition had the original schedule held.

As usual I shall draw upon George Selmon's diary for the detailed account of this closing gala. His entry begins with a comment on the fact that the mess hall was decorated, already a startling departure from the norm, and moves on to describe the banquet table loaded with "a prize burden of food" consisting of "profuse, deliciously roasted chicken, freshly-cut varieties of vegetables with mayonnaise, fruit salad, ice cream, and coffee."

The chickens, to add the inevitable but still tragic note, were the last survivors of the flock of 250 that had been counted among the transferees from Stoddard. The other culinary luxuries represented the cleaning out of the camp larder supplemented by the generosity of Joe Ikard, the jolly barber-assignee who had donated the money accumulated from providing his professional services to the campers. The camp cooperative contributed a sizeable portion of its undistributed rebate funds to purchase the beverages that were to make the event so memorable by creating an atmosphere of total release and good fellowship. For this one evening at least, all the discords and divisions of the weeks and months before would disappear.

The official festivities began with a cocktail hour featuring Ray Murphy's "Brooklyn Manhattans," a concoction consisting of roughly equal parts of bourbon and brandy mixed together in a dishpan. There had been an informal start an hour or so earlier, however, for those who had assisted in this task or were otherwise involved in the evening's preparations. The preliminary tasting session, using cereal bowls as cups, was a prelude that assured a nicely relaxed atmosphere from the very beginning. By the time the meal was over and the dishes cleared away so that Shelden Dennison, again the master of ceremonies, could introduce the scheduled speakers, both the atmosphere and the campers were much more relaxed, and the affair began to show unmistakable signs of getting completely out of hand.

Tony Saunders, still acting as director, limited his remarks to brief-

ly welcoming the guests and wishing everyone well. Mr. Wilson, the
project superintendent, followed with surprisingly sentimentalized
reminiscences of the experiences he and the men had shared at
Stoddard and Warner and expressed obviously sincere regret that the
association was coming to an end. His comments were received with
great enthusiasm, but this could be said of everything anyone said
by that time. Selmon shamefacedly confessed to his diary that in his
own exuberance he responded to the various speeches with shouts of
"horse manure," a lapse of propriety especially painful to his memory in sobered retrospect since he sat near Miss McLaughlin. This was,
he noted further, the second occasion on which she had been exposed to such unseemly behavior as a guest of the camp.

At this his offense was rather mild. Richard Wysacki, a lanky
mathematical genius of sorts and one of the camp's professed athe-
ists, topped George's uncouth commentary each time with very loud
correcting shouts of "horse *shit*." Selmon, still reflecting on the affront the general atmosphere of drunkenness and hilarity may have
caused the elderly woman, a veritable model of prim New England
spinsterhood, concluded, "Too bad. This is the price that must be
paid. And the prim prudes bit their lips in embarrassment." There is,
of course, no way of knowing what that good lady thought of it all.
It is to be hoped that she departed early, perhaps even before Dennison introduced Lowell Bartlett. Since his debut the weekend of the
Concord binge he had become something of a camp celebrity and
was called upon now to make a few appropriate remarks. Bartlett
had nothing to say; he had just passed out and was being carried to
his bunk.

The proceedings degenerated into a state of happy chaos. Noting
the delayed but escalating effect of the Brooklyn Manhattans, the
servers had wisely decided against producing the several gallons of
wine that were to have accompanied the meal. However, once the
formal party was over and the guests on their way, the campers who
remembered the wine gathered in the mess hall and were soon joined
by others equally concerned that the unused resources not go to
waste. Though my memory of the remainder of that truly riotous
night is clouded and confused, as my perception must have been by
then, some images are unforgettable.

The mess hall, for one, was reduced to a shambles as pots, pans,
cups, and other convenient utensils were commandeered by the rev-
elers who proceeded to throw them around, breaking much of the

crockery and several of the windows through which things were thrown. The ritual parades through the bunkhouses followed with more than the usual shouting, singing, and banging as the thoroughly inebriated men bearing flaming torches snaked their way through to awaken the fellow campers who had been prudent enough to retire early. Jimmy O'Toole, Selmon reports, was dumped from his bunk while Tony Saunders, in what must have been his last attempt to exercise ACCO authority, desperately, angrily, pleaded for order.

Thirty years later my sharpest recollections, reinforced by Selmon's account of the wild affair, focus on individual personalities. There was "Silent Larry" Kenniston, never one to call attention to himself before, issuing dramatic demands for silence so he could speak. When given the floor with a great show of formality, he simply smiled a beatific smile, declared, "I have nothing to say," and sat down. Selmon describes himself performing a wild dance in the midst of the kitchen melee with the "Gypsy King." As for that somber and moustachioed character, in the waning hours of that memorable night, he was observed running back and forth along the peaked bunkhouse roof clad only in his long winter underwear.

Once the party had gone out of control, there was nothing to do but let it run its course until the last celebrants finally surrendered to sheer exhaustion or to the stupifying effect of the wine. By ordinary standards, this too may not have been as much as it seemed. Most college fraternities can probably boast of more extravagant sprees following The Big Game. Even so, this farewell party at Warner was truly something special. As Selmon noted the morning after, this was "one of the rare times" when barriers of discontent, prejudice and disagreement were forgotten, and the Warner community was drawn together by what he described as "a surge of emotion and deep-throated laughter." In one of the purplest of passages in his daily journal, this devoted admirer of Thomas Wolfe launched into a peroration that might have put his literary idol to shame.

And so into the early morning hours simmered away this mass accumulation of hilarity, a gigantic valve of human emotion. Into the night faded away and forever this one apex of joy and a sense of brotherhood. These, the wild results of sixty frustrations and monotonies . . . into the mysterious doors of the past thrust by the ceaseless stream of time disappeared the polyglot of emotion, of deep, dark joy, and hope.

The style is embarrassing, even ludicrous. Yet in a very real sense the perception was accurate and the analysis sound. This *was* the apex, an evening distinguished by a quality of fellowship that Camp Simon had not been able to achieve before and was not to have the opportunity to achieve again. Nine days later, Camp Simon officially came to an end.

WARNER ROUSER

Over hill
Over dale
We have left our sawdust trail

                    (and the caissons go rolling along)

Split that oak
Slash that pine
Come on, boys, you're doing fine

                    (and the caissons go rolling along)

For we're all COs
In our working clothes;
Chopping will make the muscles strong.
So let's sing and play
All the live-long day
While the caissons go rolling along

                    (and they'll keep rolling)
While the caissons go rolling along.

Sung to the tune of the Field Artillery March.

9 *Exodus and Aftermath*

As part of a *This Ain't the Army* skit, the Warner Rouser was sung with enough spirit and gusto to have gladdened the field artilleryman heart of Colonel Kosch himself, but the words are equally well suited to the mood and rhythm of a dirge more appropriate to the chapter we now begin. One last flurry of indignant protest marked the Warner finale, but it was one that struck an uncharacteristic note of unity directed outward against what was believed to be a parting provocation on the part of the local representatives of the Boston and Maine Railroad.

The concluding weeks of the camp's existence were devoted to packing and organizing the departure for whatever destination would finally be chosen for the men by the powers of the National Service Board for Religious Objectors and Selective Service in Washington. As it turned out, the bulk of the camp personnel, with the exception of a few campers who were approved for individual transfers elsewhere or were granted physical discharges, was assigned to a new camp located at Oakland, Maryland, and administered by the AFSC. When the men arrived at the Warner station on the morning of March 18, their mood was a mixture of regret over a move so much farther away from New York and an almost eager anticipation of a new experience and the perceived good life of a Quaker camp.

That final problem was completely unanticipated. Apart from the usual hand luggage to be carried on the trip, the personal belongings of the men had been packed in cardboard cartons of greatly varying sizes to be checked through to the new destination. The stationmaster, citing his rule book, refused to accept the mountain of cartons because they did not meet the specifications governing size and quality of baggage to be checked. His position was that only items of trunk size would be accepted, that the smaller cartons would have to be carried on board by the men themselves. This was no small problem: some of the men had as many as eight such cartons, and the trip to Oakland involved a complicated change of trains in New York.

Tempers flared over this final indignity. Justly or not, the rigid application of rules and regulations was interpreted as an expression of the stationmaster's personal animosity to conscientious objection and to the Warner conscientious objectors in particular. Much heated discussion ensued until it was finally decided that the men would go on to Oakland without their belongings. The rejected cartons would be returned to camp to be crated and sent on by the skeleton crew responsible for shutting down the camp facilities.

So the exodus began with brief interruptions en route to bid farewell to fellows who were leaving the group for good or who had arranged to take earned furloughs before distance made it impossible for them to get home. The New York City connection provided a few precious hours of lay-over time and a last chance to visit the Village bars and the like before boarding another train for the long and uncomfortable overnight coach trip. As the destination neared, the view from the train windows grew increasingly uninviting and depressing. One letter, written the evening of arrival, noted glumly, "This afternoon, after Cumberland, we started on an uphill climb that went on through desolate areas, past horrible black scrawny trees. It was easy to see that Warner was 200-percent more 'civilization' than Oakland would be."

The first hint that Camp Simon would be closed had reached Warner at the end of January, but the news was not made official for another week or so. Ironically enough, the decision was based on precisely the two grounds that had formed the basis of so many protests and petitions. An official visit to the camp by Mr. Imirie, one of the few civilians at Selective Service but generally regarded as a mouthpiece for the military officers above him, convinced him, first, that the work project was not important enough to justify continuation and, second, that the camp's living standards, especially the diet, were grossly inadequate. The French diary at Swarthmore reports a meeting with Imirie's superior, the aforementioned Colonel Kosch, and Arthur Sheehan of the ACCO in which Kosch is described as insisting that the camp be closed because the men had not had suffi-

cient to eat. When Sheehan objected, Kosch introduced the further
argument that the local bishop was objecting to the presence of the
Catholic camp in his diocese.

The crucial importance of such objection, if true, should be obvious. In a later communication to Selective Service, Bishop Peterson disclaimed any desire to suppress the camp although he did
admit that the camp's presence in the Manchester diocese had given
rise to criticism which "placed my Church in a false light." In an
illuminating statement of his own position this bishop, who had been
identified as one of the few episcopal contributors to the camp,
wrote:

*The Catholic Church has declared that participation in this war is an essential
duty. While it respects the conscientious opinion of any individual who may
think otherwise, it does not make the stand of such individuals its stand. . . .
Personally, however, I admire the manly character of most of these objectors
and the sacrifices they are making for their convictions, even if I do not share
these.*[1]

Whether the bishop intended it or not, Colonel Kosch's impression
that he opposed the camp was more than enough to assure its demise. The hypersensitivity of the Selective Service officials to even
the most remote threat of adverse public relations was always a determining factor in policy deliberations and decisions.

The French diary records other efforts by the ACCO to obtain a
reversal of the decision, but by this time it probably was obvious to
all that the Catholic camp venture was at an end and any hope of
keeping it alive was futile. As far as the men were concerned, there
was little jubilation, even among the dissidents, over this official
confirmation of what they had been claiming all along. All now shared
the anxieties and insecurities concerning possible future assignments
and location. By this time, too, it had become fairly evident that, as
far as Selective Service was concerned, the more important or desirable CPS projects were either the large scale soil conservation operations and similar programs located in the more remote parts of the
country or the mental hospital units that were being opened in response to the growing demands from state authorities and pacifist
leaders alike. Neither prospect was attractive to most of the men of
Camp Simon.

For the Catholic campers, of course, there was an additional and
more crucial concern, the desire to maintain an effective ACCO pres-

ence in the alternative service program. Nor was this an objective limited to the chapel group and the other consistent supporters of the
camp administration. Even the maverick Catholic liberals who had
joined the dissidents in most of their petitions for pay, government
camps, and the like were now agreed that a serious effort should be
made to keep the Catholic group together, whatever might be decided or wherever they were to be sent. One of the immediate effects
of the impending end was the emergence of a formally organized
Catholic caucus that sought to marshall support for a reversal of the
decision to close the camp.

Practical enough to anticipate failure in this effort, the caucus proposed a set of alternative options as a fall-back position. One proposal
called for a Catholic induction center to accommodate Catholic COs
entering CPS and to enable them to develop and maintain a Catholic
identity. Others concentrated upon possible special assignments for
the Camp Simon Catholics as a group. Specific suggestions along this
line included a special service unit in Puerto Rico, expansion of the
Alexian unit, or the development of a new unit in some other Catholic general hospital; if none of these preferred possibilities material-
ized, it was hoped that a new state mental hospital unit under ACCO
administration could be established. Plans were also formulated to
spread the news of the impending emergency to all past and prospective supporters, financial or otherwise, in a desperate effort to preserve and, in the process, make more effective, a visible Catholic
peace witness that was now so clearly in danger of being lost.

The objective was only partly achieved. Though the few weeks
that remained at Warner were enlivened by a succession of rumored
and vague offers of such possible ACCO units, none reached the stage
of acceptance or approval. But the point had been made, and all the
agitation bore belated fruit in the subsequent approval of an ACCO
unit at the Rosewood State Training School for the mentally deficient, to which many of the Warner men were ultimately transferred.
Not only did the Rosewood unit establish a measure of continuity
with the Camp Simon history but, probably more important, it preserved intact the antiestablishment spirit and attitudes that had become so crucial an element of the Warner experience.

The Oakland interlude proved to be brief; in less than a month it
was learned that this camp, too, was to be closed and its members
moved to a still newer camp in North Dakota. Fifteen of the former
Warnerites opted to open the Rosewood unit which became available

at this time, but a majority of thirty-four were destined for the long journey West. Later seven of these would apply and be approved for transfer back East to Rosewood, but for most the separation was final. The physical separation, that is; the association between the Trenton "exiles" and the Rosewood "officials" was kept alive throughout the remainder of their service in CPS through the bonds of correspondence; for some the association would carry over into their post-CPS lives as well.

The Trenton remnant became something of a CPS legend in its own right. Shortly after arrival they commandeered a special bunkhouse for themselves, named it "The Casbah," and declared it off limits to all "200-percenters," posting a sign to that effect. Maintaining a pattern of studied resistance to CPS and its proclaimed standards, they succeeded in making life difficult for the local camp administrators as well as for the AFSC and NSBRO officials in Washington. The men at Rosewood were kept well informed about the Casbah activities and took much vicarious satisfaction from the reports of the rebellious exploits of their former campmates, in particular the accounts of heroic binges, which seemed to rival if not actually surpass those of the Warner era.

It is not the purpose of this review to give a detailed record of the post-Warner experience of the men who had served together in Camp Simon. It is enough to note that the subsequent history divided them into two groups roughly equal in size—twenty-two ultimately serving at Rosewood and twenty-five staying in the Trenton remnant. Both segments included a mix of the various subgroups identified in earlier chapters. Indeed, even though Rosewood was established as an approved ACCO unit* and in response to those urgent pleas for a continued Catholic presence, most of the chapel group and other stalwarts chose not to go there at first. The initial Rosewood contingent consisted mainly of Warner dissidents—Catholic liberals like Bartlett and Dennison, the Quaker Farfether, and the disrupter Luzon brothers were included. Only after the seven transferees from Trenton rejoined the group six months later did the unit develop a more "orthodox" religious and ideological coloration. This initial mix undoubtedly had much to do with establishing the Rosewood spirit, which would culminate in the move to formally withdraw the ACCO from the CPS program.

*Trenton, like Oakland, was under AFSC jurisdiction.

To make the record clear, a brief statistical recapitulation is helpful. Although fifty-eight of the Warner men were officially transferred to the Oakland camp, three were permitted to continue in their special detached service status in New York and Washington. One man was continued on "absent-sick" status at home. Three other men had been transferred to units of their choice—Ron Baxter and Richard Wysacki to a New England AFSC camp, and Henry Benjamin, Camp Simon's studious volunteer infirmarian, to a hospital unit in Rhode Island. Joe Moroni was given a physical discharge in lieu of transfer.

A month or so later, when the Oakland camp was closed and the more decisive separation of the Warner personnel took place, thirty-four were assigned to Trenton and fifteen opened the Rosewood unit. The three "ghosts" on the previous Warner roster were now

administratively separated by being placed on formal detached service status, and four others were approved for transfer to other camps
of their choice or to detached service. Finally, in what was a shock
to all who knew him, friend and foe alike, Tony Saunders, the long-
suffering acting director of the Warner camp, left CPS to enter military service. For him the circle was now complete: the only man who
had once suited action to words by actually walking out of the Stoddard camp in protest against conscription now would enter the army
on a full-service (I-A) basis. Though officially assigned to Trenton,
two other men—Joe Burt and Walter North—would also decide to
apply for reclassification to military service and never make the trip
West. Like Saunders, they had been active in the Catholic Worker
movement before their Camp Simon days.

For twenty-three, the transfers to Trenton or Rosewood would be
their final CPS assignment; twenty others would have at least one
more change of location (this included the seven who would go from
Trenton to Rosewood) with another seven having two or more additional transfers ahead of them before the end of their CPS careers.
For most of them this happy event lay years ahead; others, as we
shall see, would be discharged earlier for a variety of reasons.

Taken together, the seventy-five men ever assigned to the Warner
roster would spend a total of 2,124 months in alternative service.
Eighteen served a year or less while forty-six spent more than two
full years in CPS—thirty of them, more than three years and six, more
than four. Twenty-eight months was the average span of service for
the entire group, but the *modal* span was forty-one months. Had the
fifty or so men waiting at the Warner station for the train that would
take them on the first leg of the journey to Oakland been aware of
the fact that they faced an average of two more years of unpaid service, it is likely the hassle over the baggage would have seemed less
crucial.

As indicated, the majority would be in the program considerably
longer than that two years. More than thirty had almost three years
ahead of them; Steve Bentley, though he did not know it then, was
destined to earn the dubious distinction of being the last Warner man
to gain his release—thirty-eight months later. The disparity between
the average and modal length of remaining service is explained by the
number of early discharges for reasons other than the normal demobilization procedures adopted by Selective Service at the end of the

war. Since this early discharge pattern differs in several highly significant ways from that shown for the CPS population in general, it deserves more detailed comment.

According to the Selective Service monograph, approximately 70 percent of the 11,950 men assigned to CPS stayed in the program until demobilized.[2] For the Warner assignees, however, the comparable figure shows only a minority (30 assignees, or 40 percent) of the original 75 serving out their full time. Since the Selective Service enumeration includes categories of early discharge in which no Warner men were included (e.g., 30 men died in service, and 184 were granted occupational discharges), the 30 percent disparity actually *understates* the true differential. The two Camp Simon men who ultimately received dependency discharges match the 2 percent level reported for CPS as a whole.* Two others left CPS in protest and were prosecuted as delinquents; they represented only half of the 4 percent rate reported for the total CPS population.

The really significant differences lie in the figures for defection to military service and medical discharge. Both have more than merely statistical implications for this study.

The sixteen Warner men who were to request reclassification to the armed forces virtually *trebled* the rate reported for the entire alternative service program. According to the monograph

A total of 905 registrants, or between 7 and 8 per cent of the objectors who were assigned to CPS camps, were later reclassified by local boards at their own request into classes available for armed service, or went directly into the Army and Navy through volunteering.

. . . Complete statistics are not available but those at hand indicate that two-thirds of the registrants leaving work of national importance for armed service

---

*Dependency discharges were not easy to get. A December 22, 1941, letter in the file of Warner's Henry Benjamin written by A. S. Imirie of Selective Service in response to his request for release on grounds of dependency reads: "In view of a recent administrative ruling by the War Department and this headquarters that *no consideration will be given to the discharge of any other than those physically disabled or incompetent*, no further action will be taken on this case." The emphasis is added. It is perhaps appropriate to note that the two such discharges that were recorded for men who had been on the Warner roster were not granted until late 1945 and early 1946 respectively. Since it is generally known that dependency releases from military service, though few in number, were possible, this is one more area in which the conscientious objector seems to have been subject to discriminatory treatment under Selective Service policies and practices.

asked for non-combatant duty. The other third went into service without reservation.[3]

On that latter point, too, the Warner pattern departs from the general, though the small numbers involved preclude claiming any statistical significance for the fact. More than half (nine of sixteen) of the men who requested military reclassification chose "service without reservation," thereby relinquishing the status of conscientious objector that they could have retained under the I-A-O limited service classification.

There is no way of knowing for certain why the Warner assignees' rate of defection was so unusually high. Neither the personnel files nor the NSBRO records contain information bearing upon such individual changes of heart. Even the authors of the monograph, despite their presumably fuller access to the post-CPS records of the men who made such choices, limit themselves to tentative explanations.

. . . In general the men simply stated in writing that they were no longer conscientious objectors or that they were no longer opposed to non-combatant duty in the armed forces. Sometimes they offered additional information. Some said that their assignment to an objector camp was through misunderstanding; others indicated that they felt out of place in camp, were not conscientious objectors at heart or did not like the idea of working without pay.[4]

At Warner it was taken for granted that this latter concern, coupled with family needs and pressures, had accounted for the sudden and quite unforeseen departure of Andrew Flood, the only married man on the roster. The Selmon entry for February 14, 1943, records his quiet exit and notes, "His wife must have exerted much pressure on him—the matter of money—and the prospect of a difficult existence after the war must have convinced Andy that it would be difficult for him to live with his wife. Hence his enlistment in the Air Corps." There was less room for speculation in the case of Will Gannon, a powerfully built and universally well-liked Irishman. A Boston fireman before his induction into CPS, he left shortly after the transfer to Warner for the Navy where he was assigned to fire-fighting instructional duties.

Three others were to leave the Warner camp for military service. Two had actually requested reclassification before coming to camp and left almost as soon as they arrived. The third, Bob Monaghan, had a more checkered career: at Stoddard he had been one of the Canory-Luzon circle of disrupters, reputedly one of the wildest of the wild, until his transfer to the newly established Alexian unit; his subsequent return to the camp setting, presumably a disciplinary transfer at the hospital's request, was short-lived. A few days after his enthusiastic welcome from his former cronies, he left camp announcing his intention to request reclassification to I-A-O.

Twelve of the sixteen who ultimately defected to the military were Catholics though only eight would have been described as active, or practicing, Catholics in the Warner setting. In both respects they reflect the camp's religious distribution. One point of more than passing importance, however, is that *all* of the men who had been associated with the Catholic Worker movement before coming to camp were among those eight actives.* It is perhaps too much to assume, as some did at the time, that this mass defection of the Catholic Workers can be explained entirely in terms of their disillusionment with the type of men and behavior encountered in the ACCO camps, but there can be little doubt that such disillusionment was a contributing factor. After all, if the personalist philosophy and the spirit of sacrifice extolled in the welcoming letter had been realized in practice in the camp setting, the Camp Simon history would have been far different and far more satisfying from their point of view. As it was, the apparent collapse of the corporate witness "their" ACCO camp was intended to provide would have been disappointment enough to turn them against the CPS program itself. It is true that the collapse *was* brought about in large part by the unwillingness of the majority to accept the idealism of the welcoming letter and by the constant complaints about the discomforts and disadvantages imposed by the Worker's normal state of poverty.

From another perspective, however, the really surprising thing may be the persistence of those devout Catholics who did *not* leave

---

*This included Stuart Grant, the camper whose arbitrary assignment to the New York Mott Street headquarters had caused so much dissension. Some time after May 6, 1943, he was ordered back to a CPS camp, at which time he elected to seek reclassification to I-A-O instead. There is some question as to whether Dave Komiker was actually involved in Catholic Worker work before coming to camp; if he was, he would be an exception to the generalization stated here. Dave was transferred to Oakland and then to Rosewood, from which unit he was discharged for medical (psychoneurotic) reasons in August 1943. Finally, even though he was not an assignee at the time and, therefore, not included among the seventy-five men on the Warner roster, Director Larrowe, when assigned to CPS some time after Warner closed, followed the Catholic Worker pattern and volunteered for military service instead.

for military service. Such service, it will be remembered, was more
compatible with their church's standard theological interpretations
of Christian responsibility and, as the war escalated in ferocity and
reports mounted of the crimes ascribed to the nation's enemies, all
must have had second thoughts about the war at some time or other
and doubts as to the moral legitimacy of the deviant stand they had
taken. Paul Fitzgerald, one of the men who left for the army almost
as soon as he arrived, had been one of the original founders of PAX,
the forerunner to the ACCO. In a personal letter solicited by me for
this research he develops this theme in terms that must have been
familiar to the Catholics who decided to remain.

*You must remember that the thinking of most of us, indeed our statuses as
COs, were a product of non-war thinking. Few of us were pacifists, except for
Dorothy [Day] and a few others. Most of us were products of a time when
Thomism was all . . . when a position on a moral matter was strictly a matter of
applying our philosophies to a particular event. And yet, until World War II
came about, there was no particular event. So you can see that the actual outbreak of the war threw some of us into an agonizing necessity for making decisions. The circumstances of the war (remember, this was at the time and we
had no chance for the 20/20 vision of hindsight) made it most difficult for a
moral decision. If we had been pacifists, it would have been a different story.
But, again, remember we had no clear-cut theology for pacifism; the years between World War II and the Vietnam war provided that. We had to contend with
the murderous attack on Pearl Harbor, Hitler's treatment of the Jews, etc.*

Fitzgerald's point is both valid and critical. Lacking the recognized
theological justifications and practical support available to the peace
church objectors or recourse to the political-philosophical ideology
and traditions of pacifism that brought others into CPS and sustained
them in their commitment, it is not altogether surprising if a higher
proportion of Catholics decided to leave because they "felt out of
place in camp" or "were not conscientious objectors at heart."

But there is another factor to be taken into account in this discussion of defections to the military, even though it relates more directly to the question of the number and nature of physical discharges to
be discussed below. Before the individual who requested reclassification was actually inducted into military service, he had to pass the
regulation medical examination. Theoretically, of course, this should
have made no difference. The same physical standards were supposed
to apply to men inducted into alternative service; in fact, their conscientious objection was to come under consideration only if they

would otherwise have been eligible for I-A status. In actual practice, however, these standards were regularly, and sometimes grossly, ignored. Men who never would have passed the military's physical were routinely ordered to report for induction into CPS.

While for obvious reasons there is no evidence to support the conclusion, it is entirely possible, and in some cases almost certain, that some of these requests for reclassification to the military were simply a roundabout way of gaining the exemption from service to which the individual was entitled. As already noted, the personnel files were usually closed with the notice of reclassification to I-A or I-A-O and do not include information bearing upon subsequent disposition. From other sources, however, it is known that *at least five of the sixteen* Warner men who requested reclassification were rejected as physically unfit for military service. A sixth man who also volunteered after requesting discharge from CPS for an arthritic condition was subsequently turned down by Selective Service, thus lending further plausibility to this explanation.

Some might dismiss the overtly discriminatory application of physical standards as a minor matter, or even justify it on the grounds that the rigorous demands of military life were not likely to be matched by the demands made of men in alternative service. The consequences of physical weakness or incapacities in the fighting man would be considerably more of a threat to the nation's survival than the same physical failings in a man assigned to clear away the "blow down" timber in the New Hampshire woods. Or so it could be reasoned.

The reasoning loses much of its force if the comparison is made instead to the vast majority of men in the armed forces who are never engaged in actual combat or other front-line activity. But the most compelling rebuttal of all to that easy rationalization has to do less with physical capacities and more with considerations of moral integrity and fairness in the application of law and respect for individual rights. If men were not to be assigned to alternative service unless or until they would have qualified for military service, policies that did in fact make an invidious distinction in service availability were at best hypocrisy and at worst a form of persecution of a deviant minority. And these, there can be no doubt whatsoever, were the policies that prevailed.

It is not easy to assign responsibility for this. Possibly in most cases, the guilt lay with medical personnel responsible for the pre-

classification and preinduction screening examinations or with local
draft boards which put men who were clearly unsuited for military
service on a I-A induction schedule merely because they had dared
to declare their opposition to the war. In a 1945 appearance before
the House Committee on Military Affairs, Colonel Kosch touched
upon this point in his discussion of the 1,271 medical discharges
that had been granted by that time. Noting that there had been no
preinduction examination other than that by local board physicians
in the early stages of the administration of the alternative service program, he admitted that the conscientious objectors did not go through
the same process as men inducted into the other services. The result
of this, as he put it, was that "we got a great many men into the service who, if they had been given an Army examination, similar to that
given men going into the service, would never have been accepted at
all." The situation apparently called for a touch of sick humor, for
Kosch continued, "We got a great many men who were disabled. We
had to meet the train with an ambulance and haul them to the hospital to keep them from dying before we could get them back home
again." Humorous or not, his obvious exaggeration should not obscure the critical saliency of his more serious conclusion that "the
physical condition of the men we had to accept in the early stages
was much worse than that of men going into the armed forces."[5]

Unfortunately the Kosch testimony did not elaborate upon how
the procedures had been changed after those early stages, nor did he
explain why it was so difficult or took so long for physically unquali-
fied men who had been inducted into CPS to gain their release from
service. As previous reference to some of the Warner men in this category has shown, he was not above personally overruling qualified
medical judgment on this score and, even where approval of discharge was finally forthcoming, an additional delay of several weeks
or even months was not unusual.

The Selective Service monograph tells of one death by drowning,
which was ruled a suicide in the coroner's verdict, and notes that
"discharge had already been recommended because of psychoneurosis severe, with anxiety and hysteria." Such tragedies might easily
have been more frequent. In May and November of 1944, after his
transfer from Warner to Trenton, Bob Tantino was described as "definitely schizophrenic" and "close to the breaking point" by a medical
examiner for a state mental hygiene society. Colonel Kosch, acting
on the advice of the Selective Service Medical Division—which, as far

as the record indicates, never conducted an examination of its own—
rejected the recommended discharge. As it turned out, the discharge
had to be granted a year later anyway when the recommendation was
renewed with presumably greater urgency. Similarly, a September
1944 diagnosis of "psychoneurosis severe which is of permanent nature," reinforced a month later by the report that he no longer had
full control of his bodily functions, brought Henry Blazek a physical
discharge from the Trenton camp; but not until two additional
months had passed. If this is the pattern that prevailed in the case
referred to by the monograph, what was recorded as suicide might
better be described as criminal irresponsibility on the part of Kosch
and his associates.

To return to the question of discharges for reclassification to military service, it is entirely possible that men faced with such obstacles
and delays and who had good reason to believe they could not meet
regulation physical standards honestly applied would find it to their
advantage to apply for such reclassification in anticipation of rejection by the military services. In this way they would win their release
with much less difficulty and sooner than if they were to try to go
through normal channels.

Those more normal release and discharge procedures did account
for the separation from alternative service for reasons of physical disability of 1,566 men, or 13 percent of all men ever inducted into the
CPS program.[6] Once again the Warner figures are dramatically different: no fewer than twenty-five of the men ever assigned there—*exactly
one-third of the total*—were ultimately discharged on these grounds.
Five such separations occurred at Warner before the transfer to Oakland. Walter Bruce had arrived at Stoddard in August 1942; an October physical revealed a heart defect that precluded strenuous work of
any kind. Though this is one of the cases that might come close to
fitting Kosch's "emergency" exaggeration, it took two months to discover the problem (during which time Bruce might have been asked
to perform all sorts of strenuous work) and it was to take another
two months before his release came through. In January 1943 the
long awaited discharges came for three charter members of "the
walking dead" contingent—Mark Roselli, Bob Dazurak, and that
bearded sunworshipper with the mysterious back affliction, "Utopia"
Marlon French. The fifth and last to go from Warner was Joe Moroni;
the closing of the camp on March 18, 1943, was also the occasion for

his official discharge though, as already noted, he had been home on "absent-sick" status since the end of the Christmas holidays.

There was another aspect of the Warner physical discharges, taken in total, that holds even greater significance. It is one which is likely to provoke misunderstanding and perhaps even serve to confirm for some one of the less complimentary stereotypes of the conscientious objector. The records, even incomplete as they are, reveal that the majority of the separations granted (at least eighteen of the twenty-five) were attributed to psychoneurotic disability. Since I have included in this figure only those cases where the fact was specifically recorded—and these, it is well to note, do not include Dazurak and French whose strange appearance and behavior earned them a place in our oddball category—even this strikingly high proportion may be an understatement.

Understated or not, it is certain that it exceeds whatever proportion may have applied for CPS as a whole. Selective Service provides no information at all relating to the number of discharges of this nature, but it is sufficient to note that the Warner rate (24 percent of the total roster) almost doubles the proportion of all separations for reasons of physical disability of any kind reported in the monograph.

To what extent does this reflect the long-term impact of the hectic, near chaotic, quality of life at Warner? Or, to turn the question around, to what extent did that quality of life reflect the concentration of men with a predisposition to mental instability, of which their extreme individualism and intensity of commitment may have been but symptoms? The latter becomes a particularly tempting hypothesis when we note that all the principals in what has been designated as the disrupters group, as well as two or three of their more peripheral associates, are included in this number. That it is not fully explanatory becomes clear when we consider that at least three of the staunchest supporters of the ACCO administrators, as well as several of the steady and reliable worker category—both described as forces for stability in camp affairs—are included as well.

Regardless of whether psychological instability or predisposition to such instability were factors in the Warner experience, it is still appropriate to ask to what extent the actual psychological breakdowns are attributable to that experience or to other traumatic experiences encountered in their post-Warner CPS careers. It is a complicated question and one impossible to answer with any degree of confidence. Nevertheless, some of the possible answers relate quite directly to points made earlier in this study. On an admittedly impressionistic basis, for as always they reflect my own personal recollections supplemented by the remembered impressions provided by the respondents to my questionnaire, it would seem appropriate to separate the men discharged on psychoneurotic grounds into three major groups.

First would be the men who came to camp with rather clear indications of psychological problems or abnormalities. Consider the "Submarine Captain." Surely some medical examiner somewhere ought to have had misgivings as to his eligibility for military service or, for that matter, service of any kind. My potato-sorting crony, Dave Komiker, though certainly a much more affable and helpful member of the Warner community than Blazek, was so simple and childlike in his behavior as to justify a similar conclusion even without calling into question the personal revelation that had brought him into CPS.

To state the obvious, that the breakdowns subsequently suffered by these two and others like them cannot be attributed entirely to their CPS experience must not obscure the equally reasonable inference that these experiences could have done them no good. Instead, they probably aggravated the original problem and contributed to the severity of the breakdown when it finally came. At that the record could have been worse; there were others on the camp roster— Jimmy O'Toole, the "Pepsi Kid, " comes easily to mind—who were quite as unsuited to service, military or alternative, and yet managed to carry on without a serious breakdown. In Jimmy's case, he endured for a total of forty-seven months before receiving his discharge under the regular demobilization procedures in January 1946.

So much for the men who may have brought their psychological difficulties with them. There were others who undoubtedly faked or exaggerated their mental problems to gain early release. In one sense, this was malingering carried to its extreme; in another, it was simply a matter of being smart enough, and willing, to go through an open door. This was especially true for the men at Rosewood, a unit which produced no less than four cases of acute depression in a single six-month period. The twelve-hour shifts on the Rosewood wards were depressing enough to produce such traumatic effects upon hypersensitive personalities, and we cannot exclude the possibility that what may have appeared to be fakery was in fact genuine. But one cannot overlook the circumstances that found the men working under and with staff psychiatrists who were clearly inclined to regard conscientious objectors in general, and this group of conscientious objectors in particular, as psychologically unstable almost by definition. Or so it seemed to us. It was a relatively simple matter then, for a man to suddenly exhibit the classic patterns associated with acute depression or some other clinically aberrant behavior and obtain the staff's professional recommendation for discharge on those grounds.

The potential for misinterpretation mentioned earlier is at its highest here. It is impossible to say how many of these breakdowns were authentic; some must have been while others, however convincing the symptoms, were not. In a few cases, the conditions may have been authentic enough but minor, and the breakdown was more a matter of amplification. Everyone had sufficient cause to be depressed, and each new crisis of this nature was a most unsettling experience for the other men in the unit. To discover that a friend, ordinarily one of the liveliest and jolliest of men, has suddenly locked himself in his darkened room, refusing meals and rejecting all contact with his fellows, was not an experience to be taken lightly. Even where there was good reason to suspect that the victim was really putting on an act, his friends shared the concern that the hospital authorities or Selective Service might opt for institutionalization instead of the hoped-for release.

It worked the other way as well unfortunately. The individual who had actually slipped over the line into episodes of paranoia or depression might have been denied the support or assistance he needed and should have received simply because his symptoms were not taken seriously enough by the others. Indeed, as time went on, the Rosewood unit became so inured to such breakdowns (six of the original fifteen were discharged on psychoneurotic grounds) that each release when it finally came through was generally regarded more as an award for acting ability than conclusive evidence of mental disability.

Our attitudes toward those who chose to escape through that open door were at best ambivalent. On the one hand, once it appeared that a comrade wanted out badly enough to make the attempt, the others were ready to share his relief and joy when the coveted papers arrived. At the same time, however, few could deny experiencing an undercurrent of resentment which gained strength as the successes multiplied. Envy may have been a factor in this, I suppose, but far more troubling was the awareness that each success threatened to

diminish the witness of those who remained, if only to the extent
that it seemed to confirm the widespread assumption that conscientious objection was linked to mental instability and, consequently,
not an option deserving serious consideration by more normal people.
In this sense, each new discharge on psychoneurotic grounds added
to the burden of alienation and strain borne by those left behind.
Nor was this simply a matter of increased acceptance of unfavorable
stereotypes. Each new breakdown, even the most dubious, posed the
question of one's own ability to continue in a constantly deteriorating
situation without putting his mental health and stability in jeopardy.

Let us not mistake the fact: many, perhaps all at some time or another, would see this as a definite possibility. With this we come to
the third possible explanation for the high incidence of psychoneurotic discharges among the men originally assigned to Camp Simon.
It would be foolhardy to deny that there were men who suffered the
CPS equivalent of combat fatigue, authentic breakdowns caused by,
or dangerously intensified by, the mental attrition created by the
CPS experience itself. At various points in this review of Warner's
history, reference has been made to the multidimensional pattern
of alienation built into the situation and the destructive impact it
had on camp morale. It requires but a slight change of focus to translate this into the destructive impact it must have had upon the individual psyche. At Warner most of the men were still in the early
months of their CPS careers; it was only as the weeks stretched into
months and years, and the national consensus in support of the war
deepened and spread into all areas of life that this sense of alienation
would intensify and take its full toll. Different men would deal with
these accelerating strains and tensions in different ways. Some found
relief in quiet adjustment and resignation to whatever was to be. Others, by contrast, took an almost perverse satisfaction in forcing issues
to demonstrate that they were at odds with the world and drew a
measure of psychological strength from that. All were exposed to the
steady accumulation of the effects of this alienation until much of
their initial idealism was soured by cynicism and bitterness. In the
most extreme or more sensitive cases, severe psychological trauma
was always a possible, even a likely, result.

We can carry this one more step beyond these general observations. Though all conscientious objectors to World War II suffered
some measure of alienation, the argument has been made here that it
was more complete for men assigned to the Catholic camps, deprived

as they were of any formal official encouragement or any other support for their stand on the part of the religious community with
which they were (or had been) affiliated. If the general argument
holds, it would go far toward explaining why such breakdowns were
more common, proportionately speaking, in their case than was true
for the CPS population as a whole. Even after the closing of the Warner camp brought improvement in the physical aspects of their existence, e.g., better diet, minimal allowances instead of none, access to
medical and dental care, the alienation and, even more important the
awareness of alienation did not lessen to any significant degree. If
anything, the added strain of being indigent Catholics in a camp
sponsored and paid for by Protestant agencies added still another dimension of alienation to the burden they already bore.

Obviously, there is no way at this time to measure the impact or
balance the effects of these aspects of the CPS experience upon the
specific individuals involved. What can be established is that Warner
was a special case in terms of the extent to which men assigned to
that camp would ultimately leave the program for reasons of defection to military service or mental difficulties sufficient to justify
their separation from alternative service. One prominent member of
the Warner camp community, when asked for his assessment of the
reasons behind these facts, suggested a combination of ideological
selection intensified by a process of self-definition in response to the
peculiarities of the camp situation. He begins with the observation
that the rare Catholics (or ex-Catholics) who took the CO position
had to be individualists of the highest order even to the point of being eccentric and, in some cases, borderline neurotics. Even those
who were not in the latter two categories had put themselves under
pressure from Church, family, and friends for taking so deviant a
stand and this "might have led them to think of themselves as 'odd'—
neurotic—and so have become so." The final complication came from
the camp situation itself. As he saw it, the experience of living in isolation with other men of this type would have fostered and exaggerated any neurotic tendencies that may have been latent in them.

It is a plausible scenario and thoroughly compatible with the explanations I have advanced here. Unfortunately that is all it can be.
In any event, except for the few who left or were discharged from
the Warner camp, these speculations are of merely peripheral concern
related more to the aftermath of Camp Simon's history than to that
history itself. It is a reasonable enough assumption that the experi-

ences of those few unhappy months laid the foundation for the defections and breakdowns to follow—in some cases as much as two years later—but this, too, is something that cannot be traced or validated on the basis of the limited records that are available. We are left, then, with little more of substance than the striking disparity between the patterns of separation for these men and those recorded for the general CPS population, a comparison that adds further weight to the claim that this particular camp and its history were special enough to justify the attention given them in this volume.

As has been stressed in several contexts, Camp Simon was special in a number of important ways. It was the only Catholic camp. In addition to this, and partly as a result, its particular circumstances, most specifically the poverty it was obliged to endure, set it apart from the other camps in the system. Though most CPS camps shared this third characteristic (with the possible exception of those under rigidly orthodox peace church jurisdiction), Warner's assignees represented a concentration of individualists, including some extremely well-educated and highly articulate individualists. Finally, and in this Warner *was* different from most other camps, these men were provided with a setting and situation in which their individualism had virtually free rein because of the ACCO's unwillingness and inability to institute or enforce restraints upon it.

A final evaluation of the CPS experience and the meaning it may hold for us today is the subject of the concluding chapter. It is well to note at this point, however, that this very uniqueness of Camp Simon enhances rather than diminishes its value as a basis for making such evaluation. In its often tumultuous history, the Warner camp provided the most tangible evidence of the crucial shortcomings and basic failures, in theory as well as in application, of the alternative service program.

The real aftermath, which began with the departure of the Warner men from the Warner station, is not limited to a resumé of those later stops along the way—Oakland, Rosewood, Trenton, and all the others. It carries on beyond their discharge for whatever reason and their return to the civilian life that had been interrupted by their assignment to work of national importance under civilian direction. Curiosity, if nothing else, would prompt some questions concerning what has happened to these men in the almost thirty years since Steve Bentley's discharge wrote the finish to that chapter of their lives.

A comprehensive review of their later careers and accomplishments would require a more intensive search and pursuit than was attempted for this study. A few partial answers are provided in the information furnished by the twenty-six men (actually twenty-seven if we include me) who cooperated by responding to my questionnaires. Since some forty men could not be located by my admittedly ad hoc methods, and a half dozen or so of those who were reached failed to respond, this information cannot be taken as representative of the entire group. Even so, some of these partial answers are of sufficient interest and possible significance to merit a brief summary.

Three or four of my respondents mentioned the death some years ago in an auto accident, of Frank Hackner, a slightly older member of the worker category and a man best remembered, by me at least, for his sputtering indignation over the inadequacies of the Warner diet. His particular complaint was the cooks' reliance upon onions as a filler, a matter of such annoyance to him that his complaints delivered in a voice whose pitch raised as his anger mounted became a staple of camp humor. Since this study began I have heard of three other deaths (Alan Survich, Will Gannon, and LeRoy Torto); and it is probably safe to say there have been others among the original seventy-five whose deaths are unknown to me or my informants.

Perhaps the most striking thing to be noted from the personal data provided by those who did respond is the extent to which this already well-educated group of men have added to that distinction in their post-CPS careers. Fifteen of the twenty-seven had resumed or completed their education, eight of them reaching the Ph.D. level and several going on to postdoctoral study as well. Especially noteworthy is the fact that three (Shelden Dennison, Bill O'Flaherty, and Paul Sartov) who had apparently terminated their education at the high school level entered upon college studies after their discharges and continued through to the Ph.D. For them the CPS experience had truly been the opening to an entirely new life. To put these educational accomplishments in their proper perspective, it is well to note that veterans of CPS were not eligible for the educational benefits provided the veterans of the other services of World War II. That they had to be the product of their own initiative and effort makes these accomplishments all the more remarkable.

Occupationally, the respondents are, as the educational record might suggest, disproportionately represented in the professions: the

eighteen who would be so classified include nine teachers (eight at
the college-university level), three men in publishing or editing, two
priests, two artists, one professional photographer, and one lawyer.*
The nine remaining include three who have retired and a scattering
of various blue- and white-collar occupations such as civil service
(post office, fire department), union official, sales representative, and
building engineer. One man who had come to Warner from the Catholic Worker's Mott Street House of Hospitality returned there after
the war and is still active in the movement.

Sixteen of the twenty-seven respondents married, and two of them
(one a Catholic) became divorced. Of the twelve who reported having
a family, the majority have three or more children; two reported sev-
en and Ray Murphy topped the list with twelve! The nine who re-

*This distribution, it is well to note, is probably biased to a considerable degree
by the manner in which the respondents were obtained. The admittedly haphazard procedure—starting with friends with whom I had maintained contact and
getting further leads to others from them—produced a total of thirty-two potential respondents. It was only to be expected that these communication links
would reflect the shared interests and, to some extent, professional associations
(three, for example, are professors of sociology) of those reached in this manner.
However, even allowing for this methodological bias and assuming that the former campers who could not be reached by this procedure probably do not fit the
educational and occupational patterns described for those who were, these distributions are impressive in their own right. They reveal that *at least* 11 percent
of the total Warner roster have achieved the highest academic degree and *at least*
24 percent entered the professions. (Though they are not included in these distributions, for example, I know of others—two artists and a federal judge—who
could have been added had they chosen to respond to the questionnaire.)

The following is a roster of the former campers who did respond and their
occupations: Lowell Bartlett, retired elementary school teacher; Ron Baxter,
editor; Walter Bruce, philosophy professor; Joe Burt, Catholic Worker; Shelden
Dennison, sociology professor; Henry Fallon, retired building engineer; Dean
Farfether, program specialist, UNESCO; Paul Fitzgerald, editor; Will Gannon,
fireman (since deceased); William Grandman, sociology professor; Dan Kerrigan,
newspaper delivery supervisor; Robert Langner, priest; Alvin Manton, secondary
school English teacher; William Marsh, photographer; Leonard Mattano, artist
and curator; Walter Montorwicz, hotel administrator; Raymond Murphy, lawyer; Walter North, union official and politician; James O'Donnell, retired postal
worker; Bill O'Flaherty, sociology professor; Pat Rafferty, construction machin-
ery salesman; Paul Sartov, philosophy professor; Tony Saunders, priest; Lou
Schnittler, professor of social work; George Selmon, artist and researcher in
graphic design; Chuck Sterner, philosophy professor; Lou Swanson, editor and
publisher. In addition to these there were responses from former Director Larrowe and Arthur Sheehan of the ACCO (since deceased).

mained single probably constitute a higher than expected proportion (even allowing for the two priests) if compared with the general population, but whatever this might mean would require more intensive analysis than can be attempted with the data at hand. So, too, with the question of current religious affiliation and commitment. In those cases where a conclusion can be drawn on the basis of the responses, most remain what they were: with one exception, the fifteen active Catholics are apparently still active, and six of the non-Catholics give no indication of change. Two non-Catholics (Ron Baxter and Robert Langner) have converted to Catholicism, and one of these has become a priest; however, this may be less of a change in religious ideology than it appears since both were already active in the chapel group at Warner. A change in the other direction is reported by one of Warner's more active and articulate Catholics, Lowell Bartlett, that leading member of the Catholic liberal faction, who now rejects any belief in supernaturalism and Christianity.

The questionnaire responses are only slightly more helpful with respect to post-CPS involvement in organized peace activities, an area, the reader will recall, in which the Warner assignees ranked relatively low. The situation does not seem to have changed. The largest number report either no involvement at all (seven) or only limited involvement (eight), and most of the latter activity seems to have been limited to opposition to the war in Vietnam. The various Catholic peace organizations that have come into being since the war* have not attracted much support; only five make any explicit reference to them. Moreover, of these five only one seems to have assumed anything approaching a leadership role in any of these groups. The more traditional peace groups (War Resisters' League, Fellowship of Reconciliation, SANE) are mentioned by seven, and here too only one seems to be actively engaged at any policy-making level, though additional provision might be made for the former camper who holds a career staff position with UNESCO.

Slight though their own participation in peace movement activities might be, several volunteered the information that their children have been more active than they. At least seven of the former campers' sons registered as conscientious objectors to the Vietnam war,

*Most notable of these are the Catholic Peace Fellowship (affiliated with the Fellowship of Reconciliation) and Pax Christi/USA, the American section of that international Catholic peace movement. The Catholic Worker movement, of course, continues to maintain its pacifist stance.

and one other refused to register for the draft.* The extent to which the fathers' wartime witness may have been a factor in the sons' decisions not to serve is again impossible to determine. Two of the fathers made a point of stating that they deliberately avoided influencing their children in this matter, even though in both cases the children did take an active role in opposing the war. Another made the point, no doubt valid, that his own background as a World War II objector made it easier for his sons to gain the CO classification; but even he did not go so far as to suggest that his example inspired the sons to go and do likewise.

The reasons offered for not being more active were interesting. In four cases at least, there was dissatisfaction with the tone and direction of the more recent antiwar movement. As one put it, "After the Communists and other violent people and groups took over the peace movements for their own uses, I avoided them like the plague." A similar sentiment finds expression in the statement of another that the Catholic peace group he had belonged to for a time was "getting tangled in affairs not related to a peace movement." On the other hand, still another attributed his lack of involvement to his judgment that most peace groups were "too wishy-washy."

Most, however, explained their nonparticipation in terms of individual temperament. Their personal disinclination to get involved in any organizations or organized activities is an attitude obviously consistent with the Camp Simon history. These men were, and apparently still are, individualists par excellence; and there was little in their CPS experience that would induce them to change in this respect. If anything, the endless hassles undoubtedly confirmed for many the futility of organized activity for peace. Just as their preinduction background revealed virtually no involvement in the peace movement as such, it is clear that, once their alternative service was behind

---

*At least two reported that their sons had gone into military service. In one particularly tragic case, the father's permission had been required for an underage enlistment, and the boy was killed in a service plane accident. It is entirely possible that others also had sons who entered military service but did not volunteer the information. Most of the references to CO-sons came in response to the specific inquiry concerning the respondents' own peace activity. The question read: "How much have you or your family been involved in peace activities or organizations since leaving CPS? (Please be as specific as possible here in giving examples of such involvement. Have any of your children become COs or engaged in any other form of overt "resistance" to the war in Indochina?)" Unfortunately there was no similarly direct reference to possible military service.

them, they simply resumed their preference for individual commitments held in private.

This is not true of all, of course. A few carried their witness against the war into the peacetime setting, using various means to awaken the Catholic Church to what they held to be the pacifist implications of Christianity. To this extent they did contribute, however indirectly, to the significant change that has taken place in Catholic attitudes and teachings concerning war, peace, conscientious objection, and related issues. How much of this change can be attributed to their postwar efforts directly is beyond the scope of this study. Much more to the point is whether and to what extent this change can be related to the Camp Simon experience. That is the question to which the next, and concluding, chapter is addressed.

There are several different contexts in which a final evaluation of the Camp Simon experience deserves to be placed. First and most obvious, of course, is the extent to which it succeeded in being the witness against World War II the men intended it to be. This consideration expands quite naturally into the broader question of whether or not Civilian Public Service itself fulfilled the purpose for which it was established. A third context shifts the time frame to the present by raising the question of what impact, if any, this miniscule, loosely coordinated, and almost unprecedented Catholic witness against war has had upon the current redirection of Catholic approaches to the morality of war. Finally, though closely related to this, is the intriguing question of the extent to which this opposition to World War II can be linked to the much more broadly based Catholic opposition to the war in Vietnam.

As far as the first context is concerned, we are limited again to the information provided by the former campers who responded to my questionnaire. They only represent a segment of the total Camp Simon population (a segment that does not include the Luzons, Canory, and others whose motivation was suspected of being more self-centered than ideological), and this could be viewed as a fatal limitation. An equally good argument can be made, however, that in this case omission enhances rather than reduces the usefulness of the sample because those who had a definite witness in mind are best qualified to judge whether or not their expectations had been fulfilled. Be that as it may, an open-ended question asking whether these former Warnerites would do it over again produced some very revealing answers.[1]

Surprisingly enough, no one answered the question in the negative, including the four men who had left camp for military service or the one who walked out and was subsequently prosecuted for violating the conscription law. (All five, incidentally, indicated that they would do everything over, leaving as they did and still justifying the position that had brought them to CPS in the first place.) Two of the responses were somewhat indecisive in tone; and one respondent preferred to respond in the form of a general letter rather than complete the questionnaire, and he, unfortunately, did not respond to this question. Inasmuch as these three were most closely associated with the college boy-intellectual group—Alvin Manton, Ron Baxter, and Dean Farfether—this indecisiveness was quite in keeping with the preference for abstract generalizations over specific applications charged against them in the old camp controversies. Ten others made it clear that, although they had no second thoughts about their refusal to serve in the military, they probably would not accept the alternative service program as it was then structured. Even William Grandman, one of the very few to oppose the demands for pay at Warner, has modified his views on this score.

No second thoughts about being a CO. I have some second thoughts about alternate service without pay, although at the time I shared the enthusiasm and idealism of service donated (?) to one's countrymen.

I have never tried to judge the CPS experience or my opposition to war in terms of "worth" or personal difficulties—nor can I really do so now. It is one of those circumstances where one "chooses" the only thing to be done. The difficulties, though real, are really irrelevant in making and living with a necessary decision.

This theme of unshaken confidence in the rightness of their stand was repeated over and over. It ranged from Pat Rafferty's characteristically political judgment ("Definitely! History bears out my position more and more every day. WWI led to WWII, Korea led to Vietnam, and V.N. will lead to Mid East very shortly.") to Paul Sartov's deeply philosophical statement.

I would do it again immediately. CPS was a place to grow spiritually and spiritual growth is "worth" physical difficulties. Opposition to war is the will of God *and therefore an intrinsic value. As an intrinsic value opposition to war (as the will of God) was both a worthwhile experience and also a goal of life.* *

The absence of second thoughts should not be dismissed as easy self-justification. Usually it was a careful, even deliberate judgment. Ray Murphy, never known for his humility in camp, revealed an almost self-deprecatory note in his response.

I believe that what I did was right, and that war is wrong. My rightness was more a combination of callowness and luck rather than perception and virtue. Nonetheless, I believe more people are coming to realize that war is an unacceptable means for settling disputes among men, much less Christians, and in time, not too distant, it will be as outmoded as slavery.

The questionnaire consisted of a listing of the complete Warner roster with space provided after each name for the remembered impressions of as many of the individual campers as possible. A second open-ended question sought a composite evaluation of all the Warner campers taken as a body.[2] Though the value of the responses was reduced by some confusion traceable to the wording of the question itself, several themes were advanced with some consistency. There was agreement, for instance, that, with the possible exception of a very few dubious ones, the men they had served with in camp were sincere in their conscientious objection. Several, however, went on to challenge whether the question itself was appropriate, whether anyone can (or *should*) presume to pass judgment on another's commitment. Most of the positive affirmations went beyond the question to include a note of comparison. One confessed, "In checking off the list (as I have done in one sitting) for the first time in 30 years, I am really astounded by the essential solvency of the group's moral integrity. . . . I am certain that the level of sincere men was as high if not higher than any other group I have been personally aware of, including the seminary."

The confusion arose in connection with that part of the question that asked whether COs "as a category" are particularly susceptible to "personality maladjustments or other forms of 'deviance' " and

*Sartov was the only member of the Orthodox Church at Warner. Greatly respected for his quiet and steady demeanor and reliable work, he seldom entered into camp discussions and never, as far as I can recall, took active part in any of the controversies that arose. Possibly because of this, his characterization of CPS as "a place to grow spiritually" comes as something of a surprise.

whether the respondents felt there was any evidence of this at Warner. Several interpreted the reference to deviance as relating specifically to departure from sexual norms (they knew of none) instead of
to its broader sociological usage extending to any conscious and intended departure from statistical or behavioral norms. As far as "mal-
adjustment" was concerned, most took pains to assert that whatever
Warner's record in this regard might have been, it was probably no
worse than would be true for military units or other similarly select
and segregated populations. Some responses took general society as
the basis for comparison. "No more maladjusted or deviant than any
cross-section of society," wrote one of the men who had left camp
for service in the armed forces. Others narrowed their frame of reference to specific groups or the special context of the time, the latter
asking, in effect, "Maladjusted to what?" Leonard Mattano's analysis
cut across most of these lines of emphasis and, in the process, confirms the image he left of the mild and melancholy seer.

*I don't know who was sincere and who wasn't. It was a time of world-wide in-
sanity. I think Warner's population may have been very much like a good or
similar cross-section of an Army outfit of Draftees. Less violence—fights, etc.—
but the usual depressions, fits of tempers, frustration, etc. Any camp life with
its disruption of men's normal work or profession leads to discontent. I always
felt the War would last 10 years and wondered what would become of me when
it was over. I think I was often more depressed than most. Looking back now I
think CPS was rather easy in view of what happened to P.O.W.s in the Pacific or
to the Jews.*

   The truth is, as we have seen, that the Warner level of maladjust-
ment, at least as measured by its rate of psychoneurotic discharges,
was considerably higher than for most cross sections of the general
population, the army, or, for that matter, the rest of CPS. Several
comments showed some awareness of this possibility and advanced
tentative explanations echoing those advanced in the preceding chapter. George Selmon, though he agrees with his good friend, Mattano,
that "as a category the personality maladjustments were no greater
than for other people," expands upon this to say, "However, the
kind of life in camp to which they were confined, as unnatural and
unfulfilling as it was, could breed an unusual amount of maladjustments." He concludes on a positive note of confidence that once
these special circumstances were removed, the maladjusted individuals were able to return to a normal pattern of living, presumably

freed of their problems. The same note of optimism is present in the more narrowly focused observation of another who wrote,

I think the men at Warner were mostly very sincere Catholics *who believed in what they were doing. Mostly idealists. And the confusion, the stresses in and out of camp, lack of support by outside Catholics caused them to warp a bit. Most adjusted normally when discharged.*

This notion of a temporary personality warp may be as good an explanation as any. Whether all of the victims did respond so well to their return to civilian life is, unfortunately, something on which no reliable information is available.

It may be nothing more than the softening effect of passing time, but the most striking quality of these responses is the consistently favorable evaluation of the personal associations formed at Warner. Over and above the testimonials to the sincerity of the men already noted, there is high praise for other characteristics that, the respondents feel, were demonstrated by their former colleagues: moral commitment, perseverance, intelligence, generosity. So consistently laudatory are the assessments of the group that one tends to forget that they refer to a body of men who spent six unhappy months to-

gether in an atmosphere of almost constant bickering and, sometimes, more serious controversy.

Walter Bruce, now a professor at a prestigious university, is "convinced that some of the men I knew at Stoddard and Warner are the most admirable men I have ever met." Another responding in the same vein (though he does except Canory and the elder Luzon; he had left camp before the younger Luzon arrived) describes the Warner group as one "with whom it was pleasant and at times inspiring to live and work." It can be assumed, of course, that these complimentary comments refer most particularly to the closeness of ties within the several major cliques and subgroups and may not apply without some reservations to the Warner personnel in toto. Even if this is true, the consistently favorable evaluations should not be dismissed too lightly. The very fact that such memories can be associated with a setting so often charged with hostility, that lasting friendships could have been formed in such an atmosphere, has to be counted as a positive factor in any evaluation of the Camp Simon experience.

Few of the men would have foreseen this at the time as a likely result of their brief and generally frustrating sojourn in the New Hampshire woods; yet the assessment made by Robert Langner is probably not unique. In reflecting upon his dominant memories of the camp in which he served for barely three months before being transferred to a detached service unit, he begins with a reference to the scenic beauty of the countryside and "the excitement of paying something for my convictions for the first time in my life." He then turns to the memory of "the surprising psychological and sociological variety of the types of people I encountered there," noting that he had expected "only an intense Catholic Worker type" and found himself surrounded instead by "an inexplicable menage . . . artists, eccentrics, totalitarians, etc." Most significant of all, however, is his statement that

. . . the most enduring friendships of my life were made in a place where I stayed perhaps the shortest time I have ever stayed in one place—you and Ron and Lou and Pat particularly, although I've had contact since with Bill O'Flaherty and Bill Grandman and Lou Schnittler and Paul Glick and Lowell Bartlett and Joe Burt and Walter Montorwicz. I guess this is the most important thing about it all—and it seems to me that it says much more than merely that sharing an unpopular position produced strong feelings of kinship. I've shared unpopular

positions with other people at other times without this kind of empathy and fraternity.

It would be impossible to overstate the importance of this reflection, though its full significance may not be obvious in the mere reading. That litany of eleven names constituted *a full sixth or more* of the entire roster of the camp at the time he left, surely a strikingly high proportion to be included in a lasting friendship circle. It is unlikely that all the former Warnerites could cite as long a list, but it is even less likely that many emerged from the experience without having formed some close and lasting ties based on what Langner describes as "empathy and fraternity."

Such friendships, then, constitute one plus for the Camp Simon experience. Added to this would be whatever personal satisfaction every former camper can take from knowing that he had not contributed to the worldwide carnival of death and destruction. In the final reckoning these may be all the Catholic COs of World War II can count against the months and years of frustration and alienation spent in CPS. If today some might credit them with having contributed to significant changes in Catholic teachings or behavior, there was nothing at the time to offer the slightest promise of such developments. Their witness against the war, such as it was, was divided and often confused; for the most part it went unheard and unnoticed. If, by sheer accident, their existence and their message came to the attention of their ecclesiastical leaders and fellow communicants, it was all but certain both would be studiously ignored or indignantly rejected. To make matters worse, there was always the nagging suspicion—for some, indeed, the outspoken conviction—that their acceptance of alternative service as it was then constituted involved a surrender of rights and integrity; that their intended witness had been transformed into an unworthy compromise with the military system and the values that they had set out to oppose.

"Reduced to essentials, " Robert Ludlow was to write in the January-March 1946 issue of *The Catholic C.O.*, a sometime quarterly edited by the men and published under Catholic Worker auspices, "CPS is a program of involuntary servitude without compensation, nothing more than a program of slave labor offered by the State as an alternative to outright imprisonment." The rhetoric may be strong, but it echoed the official action of the ACCO in its October 30, 1945, statement formally withdrawing from membership in the NSBRO and "from all further responsibility for or participation in the administration of the Civilian Public Service program."[3] The statement initiated and approved by the Catholic men still serving in the program at the time declared,

Very soon after the opening of our New Hampshire camps it became generally evident that most of the men directly concerned with the program, the conscientious objectors themselves who were attempting to present an effective rejection of war, were strongly opposed to the situation wherein the traditional pacifist leadership allied itself with the military in administering conscription, one of the most essential phases of the war effort. Nevertheless, in the hope that it would be possible to work out the difficulties and ultimately bring about a fair and honest interpretation of the status of the conscientious objector, we continued our membership, although financial limitations forced the closing of our camps. These hopes were never realized.

The statement continued with a strong denunciation of the alternative service program and, with it, the sternest of rebukes for those who made it possible.

Instead the program degenerated into a system of punishing a minority under the guise of a democratically-given opportunity to fulfill alternative service and, in so doing, establishing a precedent whereby other minorities could conceivably be similarly punished by enforced and unpaid labor under the actual direction of those most interested in silencing their voices. Not only did the religious sponsoring agencies, including the ACCO, continue their cooperation; but, in effect if not in intent, they assured the program's "success" by cushioning and absorbing whatever protest the men in camp managed to shake loose from their resulting burden of disillusionment and frustration.

Having made their point the authors of the statement added a rousing rhetorical flourish: "These men would rather rot in concentration camps than bear arms in an unjust war. But if slavery is the price they must pay for conscience's sake, let us not disguise the fact!"

The ACCO withdrawal, dramatic though it may have been, came too late in the day to have any noticeable impact or, indeed, put anyone to the test of its daring challenge. After all, the ACCO, despite its status as one of the four founding agencies, had always been more of a liability than an asset to the alternative service program, the extra part that never did fit in and, moreover, kept breaking down. The AFSC, for its part, continued until the following March as it had announced it would, at which time its remaining units and camps were turned over to Selective Service administration. The other major religious sponsors carried on until the end. But even granting the lack of effective impact, the official nature of the statement had to count for something. In the eyes of the former Warnerites who had initiated the move, it was assured a measure of attention well beyond the organization's actual influence and role. If nothing else, it would put concerns and objections that might otherwise have been muted or ignored firmly on the historical record. This it accomplished, of course, though the measure of success depends on who is reviewing that historical record. The Selective Service monograph, for instance, ignores the withdrawal action, the statement, and its charges.

The question remains: Were the repudiation and those charges justified by the facts? This brings us to the second of the four contexts chosen for this evaluation. My personal judgment is that they were; but this, too, is not very surprising. Like Ludlow, I helped write the Rosewood statement. If the perspective provided by the intervening years might modify the rhetoric, the basic conviction remains that opponents of war should not have cooperated with Selective Service to the extent they did.

The issue cannot be resolved as simply as that, however. For one thing, it ignores the positive aspects of CPS, its intention and its actual accomplishments, and they should be acknowledged. Since some of these have already been considered in some detail, a brief recapitulation will suffice to put the issue in better balance. A simple reference to the pacifist leadership as allying itself with the military in administering conscription does not do full justice to the representatives of the peace churches and other traditional pacifist organizations who were involved in the negotiations and discussions out of which the church-administered alternative service program emerged. Their intentions were generous and sincere, and their efforts were directed toward what appeared, at the time at least, as the best interests of the men who would be called to service in that program.

As the leadership saw it, placing the sponsorship and administration in the hands of those favorably disposed toward conscientious objection would guarantee that there would be no repeat of the World War I situation in which men who rejected military service suffered the harshest of treatment in disciplinary camps and military prisons. Furthermore, not only would the proposed arrangement spare the new generation of objectors similar abuse and hardships, but it would provide them with the real alternative of serving society constructively instead of learning and practicing the arts of war. Even that most questionable decision to commit prospective objectors to a period of service without pay can be understood (though still not justified, perhaps) as yet another demonstration of altruistic commitment, especially since it was assumed it would be a short-term sacrifice limited to a year at most. In this respect another expectation strayed even farther from the future reality. The men who would be locked into the program would not fit the image of the religiously motivated, service-oriented and relatively affluent types usually associated with the summer work camps chosen as the model for Civilian Public Service.

Failed expectations aside, a fair evaluation must credit CPS with fulfilling the good intentions of its founders in a number of important ways. Valid though the criticisms and protests issuing from the camps unquestionably were, the hardships and injustices they were protesting did not match those endured by the World War I objectors. Clearly then it accomplished one purpose. Similarly, however short of the "work of national importance" ideal the actuality may have fallen, much that was done, especially in the mental hospital and more glamourous special units, did have lasting benefit for society. And in a more profound sense, even the severest critic must agree that *all of it*, including the waste of talent and effort represented by the Warner project, was still more worthy of their endeavors than the most likely alternatives: participating in the war they sincerely believed was forbidden them or spending a number of even more unproductive years in prison.

When the definitive history of the peace movement of World War II is finally written, the record may well show that the prison witness was not totally unproductive. Some significant first steps toward effective prison reform can be credited to the pressures exerted through hunger strikes and other forms of protest organized by the pacifists behind bars.[4] And once the war was over and these men were returned to freedom many of the more dedicated leaders of the postwar peace movements would come from their ranks. In fact, given the disparity of numbers, their leadership contribution may even have been proportionately greater than that attributed to the veterans of alternative service. Nevertheless, after making due allowance for these, the more pessimistic expectations were not completely groundless. Men buried away in prison were clearly more isolated from the general population and had even less opportunity than their counterparts in CPS to make known their opposition to the war.

Futile though the efforts may have been, CPS in theory offered the semblance of such opportunity. If the major share of the responsibility for the failure to produce a more effective peace witness lies in the flaws structured into the system, this cannot be taken as a total explanation. The men in the program—and this certainly includes the men of Camp Simon—deserve some of the blame. Had they been more willing to concentrate on the positive aspects of the program and less upon its injustices, and less inclined to impute unworthy intentions and bad faith to the pacifist leadership, a more understanding and lasting partnership might have been achieved between the two generations of pacifists. For their part, had the religious sponsoring agencies and the NSBRO been more responsive to the very real concerns voiced by the critics of the program and joined in the effort to obtain pay and government camps for those who wanted them, much of the original promise of the alternative service program might have been salvaged.

In any event, CPS could have been the inspirational witness the pacifist leadership had intended if Selective Service and the Congress (and, of course, behind Congress the war-intoxicated public) had been willing to meet their part of the bargain fully and honestly. Instead, as we have seen, the two basic principles upon which the alternative service was based—that the work was to be of national importance and performed under civilian direction—were distorted and circumvented until they became little more than a grotesque farce.

In fairness, some allowance must be made even here for situational considerations. It is probably too much to expect that military officers (especially military officers assigned to desk duties who might have preferred a more direct part in the great crusade) could have seen these issues from the perspective of the deviants who rejected the military service itself as well as the whole structure of military traditions and values. If Paul Comly French was too easily impressed by the tolerance displayed by General Hershey and other officials with whom he had to deal, his observations were not entirely without basis in fact. These men could have been much more restrictive in their policies and far less tolerant in their attitudes. One need only consider Stafford's account of the attitudes of nonmilitary government employees on the work project cited at an earlier point. It is reasonable to suspect that similar sentiments must have been shared by Selective Service officials in their private views and conversations concerning the conscientious objectors over whom they had been given virtually unlimited authority.

To admit, however, that things might have been worse is not to justify what they were permitted to become and, much more to the point, *what Selective Service clearly intended them to be.* To them, the conscientious objector *was* best handled if no one heard of him; he *was* subject to their unchallengeable authority twenty-four hours a day, regardless of his constitutional rights and privileges; there *was* no obligation on their part to provide service opportunities suited to his talents or desires; and, above all, whatever work he would be required to perform *was* secondary to their own demands for discipline. True, they knew that even if Selective Service were to recognize the injustices protested by the men and moved to correct them, Congress would never have approved recommendations for pay or other concessions and the general public, ever sensitive to anything that might appear to favor or coddle men who refused to "do their duty" would have given Congress its wholehearted support. Of course, the issue was never put to the test because things developed just as Selective Service had intended all along.

The basic wrong, as Dorothy Day kept insisting, was conscription itself. Once a system is approved under which some men are given the power to sit in judgment upon other men's consciences or to determine what those others will be permitted to do with their lives and talents, freedom is violated; and with each new directive it is further diminished until, in a state of emergency, real or concocted, or over a span of generations, freedom can be dispensed with altogether. The danger may seem moot to us in this day of the all-volunteer military, but the appearance is deceptive as long as the Selective Service System is permitted to exist even on a stand-by basis.

Some might argue that the more liberal practice employed with respect to men approved for alternative service during the Vietnam war years refutes this pessimistic evaluation. After all, they were permitted to seek out their own work assignments and were even paid for that work at the prevailing rates. If, as it developed, local draft boards were reluctant to approve any but the lowest paid and least palatable jobs, this seems not to have been imposed by Selective Service policy. It is entirely possible that these improvements mean that Selective Service officials learned some lessons from the organized dissension and open disruption that marked most of the camps operated under its direct jurisdiction in the closing months of the CPS program.

Encouraging though these signs may be, it would be well to interpret them with caution. It is also true that contingency plans have been developed for the resumption of a full-scale camp program for conscientious objectors[5] along with efforts to reestablish some measure of religious agency support and administration, should the present stand-by status give way to a resumption of full-scale operations. At this point there seems to be little likelihood that peace church agencies would be too receptive to the opportunity to become involved again, directly or indirectly, in the administration of any part of a conscription program. If this resolve holds, all those protests and petitions, including the ACCO statement quoted above, will not have been in vain. At the very least, this reticence suggests that, in spite of all the positive aspects mentioned in the earlier evaluation, the religious agencies have come to share the conclusion that CPS was a failure when measured against the original intention to make of it a worthy and effective witness against war.

The third context for evaluation and, from the Catholic perspective, the most crucial poses the question, To what extent did Camp Simon in both its Stoddard and Warner phases (and, though to a lesser extent, in the Alexian and Rosewood units as well) have meaningful impact *upon the Church*? Considering the importance placed on maintaining a Catholic presence in CPS as a corporate witness, to what extent was it accepted as such? There was never much expectation of official ecclesiastical endorsement or approval, of course; but as far as the campers themselves were concerned (at least the active, practicing Catholics among them), they had made that witness *for the Church* and *in the name of the Church* because, as they saw it, its responsible leaders had failed to recognize the obligation to oppose the war. To what extent, the question remains, was this claim to be "doing the work of the Church" respected or even noted by Catholics on the outside?

The answer is not encouraging. Whatever semblance of theological or ecclesiastical support the Catholic CO might claim was largely of his own creation. No matter how much encouragement he might take from the latest papal statement denouncing the war and calling for an early end to the slaughter, he could not ignore the fact that the encouragement lay entirely in his own interpretation of those statements and that it found no echo in the response to those appeals by the designated spiritual leaders of the American Church. The reports of new cities "taken out" or other equally tragic acts of war actually became a source of twisted intellectual satisfaction in the evidence they gave of what Pope Pius XII had described as "the brutality of the methods of total war, which tend to pass beyond every just limit and every norm of Divine and human law."[6] Others may not have recognized the fact, but to the Catholic CO that description and those reports combined to confirm the rightness of his stand against the war. His fellow Catholics, however, remained unconvinced and unimpressed. On the rare occasion when he did seem to make some headway—one former camper still remembers being told by members of a monastery he was visiting that they shared his objections—any attempt to carry the argument to the logical conclusion that such considerations outweighed the traditional obligations to render obedience to legitimate authority fell on deaf ears.

It must be borne in mind that a corporate witness against war such as the Catholics of Camp Simon were presuming to make was an altogether new phenomenon in the American Catholic Church. In the course of its longer history, of course, the Church Universal had encountered similar displays of pacifist commitment, but these had either been shunted aside as the work of heretical sects or incorporated into the ecclesiastical framework as individual callings and, where larger numbers were involved, religious orders. Even the few Catholics who refused to serve in World War I cannot be viewed as a true precedent; each had represented a separate and individual objection and gave no indication of intention to give witness for the Church as such.[7]

This does not mean that the principles on which the act of conscientious objection was based were new or unknown. Between the two world wars Catholic peace movements of some size and signficance had emerged on the European continent—in Germany, France, Belgium, and England. The Catholic Worker movement which appeared on the scene in 1933 was the only comparable force in American Catholicism, and its influence was quite limited. The only competitor for the honor was the Catholic Association for International Peace (CAIP), an affiliate of the hierarchy's National Catholic Welfare Conference, but this organization was more peace oriented in name than in program and practice. Its principal objective, laudable enough as far as it went, was educational in that it sought to familiarize American Catholics with the internationalist implications of papal social teachings. In its publications and conferences, however, it studiously avoided giving the slightest suggestion of pacifist overtones or emphasis.[8]

Given the background of almost total ignorance of the pacifist implications of the Roman Catholic faith, the enthusiastic support for the war that began with the "act of infamy" at Pearl Harbor was entirely predictable. That a small group of Catholics chose not to accept the nation's call to arms was neither understood nor well received by their fellow communicants. Note has already been taken of the denunciations and deprecations encountered at draft board hearings and the less overt but equally disconcerting patterns of unfriendly avoidance by the Contoocook parishioners. And assuming there was any basis to Selective Service's impression, the "insistence" of the local bishop that Camp Simon be removed from his diocese was merely one more step taken to stifle the intended witness and assure that any impact it might have had upon the general Catholic community would be minimal at best.

The Catholic C.O., the "quarterly" journal that appeared at highly irregular intervals from September 1943 to the winter of 1948, was one attempt to remedy the situation and bring the message to a wider audience; but, it proved to be another exercise in futility in that, funded as usual by the Catholic Worker movement, its influence was limited to an already committed audience.[9]

This clearly negative assessment of over-all influence does not mean that the Camp Simon experience must be written off as a total failure. There is evidence that it can be credited with a delayed impact far in excess of any reasonable expectations its members may have had. By its mere existence this dissident minority succeeded in raising questions that otherwise would probably not have been raised, questions that would assume their full significance once they were freed of the emotional and existential pressures of an on-going war.

This American Catholic opposition to World War II, we must remember, flawed and feeble though it certainly was, represented the only organized peace witness of its kind in the entire Catholic world. Men were being executed in Germany for refusing to fight in Hitler's wars[10] and there were Catholics among the recognized conscientious objectors in the few other countries that made some provision for such a stand; but in neither case was there any indication that these were more than purely personal acts of individual resistance. It is a nice irony that credit for establishing a common Catholic witness and a sense of group identity belongs to Selective Service and the much-maligned "collaborationists" and to the compulsion of conscription. This was a blessing not recognized at the time.

Anyone conversant with the dramatic changes that have taken place in the Roman Catholic Church since the end of World War II will agree that few are more impressive than the changes in its teachings related to modern war and conscientious objection. To an extent far beyond their most extravagant hopes, the position taken by the Catholics who served at Warner has suddenly become eminently respectable. The repudiation of war, rather than the search for justifications, has become the dominant thrust of contemporary theology. Even in the context of traditional just-war formulations, the edge now lies with those who hold that the specified conditions for such a war, if honestly applied, can no longer be fulfilled. Frankly pacifist interpretations based on literal or inferential applications of Scripture reject even the theoretical possibility of a just war and are taken seriously and accepted by highly respected members of the theological community. This, it will be recalled, was the moral position dismissed as unorthodox by all but the Catholic liberals at Warner.

The major impetus for this astonishing shift in direction and emphasis was the pontificate of Pope John XXIII with his encyclical, *Pacem in Terris*, the watershed document. The Second Vatican Council with its call for an "entirely new attitude" toward war and its explicit condemnation of area-destroying weapons and tactics as "a crime against God and man himself" elaborated upon the Joannine theme. The pontificate of Paul VI gave convincing evidence, not least in his dramatic pilgrimages of peace, that the trend is not likely to be reversed. From 1968 when he instituted the annual January 1 observance of a "Day of Peace," Paul issued a series of statements that justly would have been taken as explicit approval for the stand the men of Camp Simon were taking in that grim winter of 1942.

Rome's lead has been given some application in the United States. The American hierarchy has issued statements endorsing the principle of selective conscientious objection and recommending amnesty for men forced into exile by their unwillingness to serve in the Vietnam war. Compared with the refusal of the Washington bishop to intercede on behalf of men denied their legitimate rights to parole, this is a significant change. But such statements hold more pragmatic meaning as a reflection and ecclesiastical validation of the dramatic increase in the number of draft-eligible Catholics who sought and obtained classification as conscientious objectors. McNeal reports that, as of September 1969, they numbered almost twenty-five hundred and represented more than 7 percent of men so classified.[11] All Catholics in CPS, including those who never came under ACCO jurisdiction, barely constituted 1 percent of the total CPS population. But even this comparison falls short of providing the full measure of the change that has taken place. Other Catholics for whom conscientious objection and alternative service represented too much of a compromise refused to register and turned instead to more active forms of resistance—and most incredible of all, they were joined and supported in their resistance by priests, nuns, laywomen, and a host of other draft ineligibles intent upon making an effective witness for peace.

It would be premature to suggest that Pope John and the Vietnam war have succeeded in converting Catholicism into a peace church as that term is generally applied to the Friends, Mennonites, and Brethren. Still the shift in posture was significant enough to cause spokesmen for more traditional elements of the peace movement to confess with some amazement that, at least with respect to the war in Vietnam, the peace "action" was to be found in the Catholic community. A far cry, indeed, from the record of World War II. Those of us who shared the task of editing those occasional issues of *The Catholic C.O.* had more modest expectations. As the masthead put it "We hope that war will be overcome through the Church, and even if, after two thousand years, this hope is still unfulfilled, we still hope and go on knocking at the door like the importunate man in the Gospel." Today that hope, though still unfulfilled, seems almost prophetic.

It would be immensely gratifying to be able to attribute the progress that has been made to the Camp Simon witness. Simple honesty forces the admission that the real explanations lie elsewhere and are at best remotely and indirectly related to that experience. Unquestionably the most important factor is the lessons learned from World War II, especially those relating to the cost in lives and resources, the destruction of entire cities, the perversion of the human spirit in the distortion of truth and escalation of hatreds. Taken together, these represented a quantum leap in scope and intensity over all previous wars and rendered any serious attempt to fit them into the neat categories and conditions of traditional just-war morality ludicrous if not obscene.

Most specifically, the culminating atrocities of what Paul VI had characterized as the "horrible massacre" at Hiroshima and the bombing a few days later of Nagasaki proved so offensive to moral sensibilities that many Catholics have become "nuclear pacifists," rejecting any and all wars in which the use of such weapons might be contemplated. This position found a measure of official confirmation and extension in that condemnation of area-destroying acts of war referred to earlier—the *only* condemnation, it is well to note, issued by Vatican II.

Other lessons learned from World War II have contributed to these changes in moral teachings on war and peace. Most fundamental, perhaps, was the question it raised concerning the relationship between religion and the secular milieu or, reducing the question to individual terms, the ever-present tension between the roles of *believer*, subject to the moral dictates of conscience and the teachings of the Church, and *citizen*, subject to the authority of the state. Seldom has the issue been reduced to sharper focus than in the failure, or inability, of German Catholics to refuse to support or participate in the clearly unjust wars initiated by Hitler and his Third Reich. All the carefully detailed conditions spelled out in the traditional just-war morality proved inapplicable and unenforceable; popular theologians advised the Catholic faithful that this decision could only be made after the war when all the facts were available, and bishops called upon their flocks to fight "for Folk and Fatherland" as a Christian duty.[12]

In short, the nature of the modern state combined with the nature of modern total war have revealed the inadequacy of those traditional teachings and have forced the opening to the entirely new attitude called for by the Fathers of Vatican II. The Catholic conscientious objector of World War II anticipated this change, and, easy though it had been to ignore him and his position while the war was in progress, his proposed answers now begin to receive more serious attention. Not everyone would share the judgment expressed to a former member of the Warner camp that he and the others had played the role of prophet, but the term is not altogether inappropriate. If it is taken to imply that those who refused to serve were directly responsible for the crucial changes in theological stance and interpretation that have developed since, it would be claiming far too much. On the other hand, if it refers to nothing more than the recognition that their stand anticipated, and may even to some extent have prepared the way for, a more unambiguous commitment to peace and nonviolence among important segments of the Catholic community, the Warner witness was a prophetic witness. It met the test of the two characteristic notes of the prophetic tradition: it affirmed, and exercised, the competence of the individual conscience to pass ad-

verse judgment on the acts of principalities and powers; and it insisted that, by doing so, it was fulfilling moral obligations that should
have been recognized by all.

It is here we find the essential link between the Catholic peace witness of World War II and that more extensive Catholic resistance to
the war in Vietnam. There were other links as well, of course. At the
most superficial level would be the contributions of those, admittedly a disappointing few, from the Warner generation who participated
in the Vietnam resistance—speaking at demonstrations, contributing
to the various defense funds, counselling prospective conscientious
objectors. If nothing else it was now impossible (though some local
draft boards still tried) to deny that Catholics could legitimately
claim classification as conscientious objectors under the law. The
simple fact that there had been a Stoddard, a Warner, and an ACCO
was indisputable proof that they could. A more positive link lay in
the readiness of participants and leaders of the new resistance to
admit that they had gained their first insights into the incompatability of war and the Christian teachings from learning about the works
and examples of the objectors to the earlier war.

But having said this much one must also note some very fundamental differences between the two generations of the Catholic
peace witness. For one thing, the "conspiracy" of the 1960s was political in its orientation to a degree not found among the men at
Warner except, surprisingly enough, for the Coughlinite element. Not
all of the latter were as open or outspoken as Pat Rafferty in his admiration for "the other side," but their fervent opposition to Bolshevism, to say nothing of the anti-Semitism they shared, gave rise to a
certain measure of sympathy for the Axis powers and their leaders
that foreshadowed in its way the identification of some Catholic
opponents of the war in Vietnam with the defined enemy. That the
comparison incorporates a complete turnaround in ideological thrust
—the Coughlinites would certainly have had no sympathy with the
supporters of the NLF and vice versa—is obvious enough; yet in both
cases the political dimension of the opposition to the respective wars
was paramount.

This is not to say that the difference between the two generations
on this count was absolute. If the refusal to serve in World War II was
almost exclusively religious in motivation in most cases, it also carried
incidental political overtones in its anti-British and anti-Roosevelt
sentiments, its demands for a negotiated peace instead of the official-

ly proclaimed policy of unconditional surrender, and its references to broader social justice issues used to point out the inconsistencies between professed war objectives (e.g., the famous "Four Freedoms" of the Atlantic Charter) and the grim actuality of American racism at home and the imperialism of her allies abroad.* By the same token, the predominantly political actions and proclamations of the Catonsville Nine and the other aggregations of Catholic activist opposition to the war in Vietnam were not exclusively, and probably not even primarily, political in the usual sense but, at least as conceptualized by the participants, necessary and inescapable expressions of their religious convictions.[13] However, once due allowance is made for the common elements in both positions, there remains enough of a contrast in emphasis to produce a difference in mix substantial enough to justify treating the two witnesses against the respective wars as different in kind and not only in degree.

Nothing illustrates this more convincingly than the disparity of mode between them. The Vietnam resistance stressed a commitment to activism which found expression in its draft board raids, intentionally obstructive sit-ins, and similarly aggressive acts against the war-making authority. There were even passing suggestions of sabotage and kidnapping as options, we are told, but it is questionable how seriously they were considered. There was nothing comparable in the Catholic opposition to World War II. The so-called absolutist objectors, most of whom chose the prison witness in preference to alternative service, may have considered and, in some instances, even attempted direct action to disrupt the war effort, but this was not part of the Warner experience and would not have been approved by most of the campers. The issues and controversies that occupied our attention were generally linked to the injustices of CPS and conscrip-

---

*Sometimes, in fact, the rhetoric employed was a direct foreshadowing of what was to come a generation later. Thus, in the Winter 1948 issue of *The Catholic C.O.* Robert Ludlow writes, "I do not believe in reformism or political means. I believe in radical non-violent revolution carried on by direct action, utilizing first and foremost the spiritual weapons of prayer and penance alongside techniques such as the general strike to effect worker ownership of the means of production and distribution and the abolition of acquisitive class society." This paragraph could have come from some of the literature circulated by the Fathers Berrigan and their supporters to explain and justify the actions taken at Catonsville and elsewhere. Other social-justice issues on which the Warner objectors took a stand were the rights of labor, the abolition of poverty, racial equality, and freedom for India.

tion; our actions more likely to take the form of written protests and petitions. The World War II objectors were not silent about the excesses of the war, but neither were they inclined to organize or support efforts to disrupt the war effort.

Stated in this fashion, the Vietnam era resisters have the edge in heroism and consistency of purpose. Unfortunately they also fell prey to a kind of elitism that threatened at times to undermine the effectiveness of what should have been a united peace movement. Conscientious objection and alternative service were downgraded to a status of a "cop-out" by young men who refused to register or who participated in the ceremonial destruction of their draft registration cards. More restrained forms of dissent against the war—petitions, peaceful picketing, letters to political officials and newspapers, and so on—tended to be dismissed by the activists for whom anything short of tax refusal was almost equivalent to open collaboration with the Pentagon. A halfway or lukewarm opposition might be tolerated, but it was not enough to earn full admission into the more activist community of the "saved."

There is much to justify such an attitude, but a far stronger case can be made for welcoming and honoring *any* refusal, no matter how minor, to go along with the war effort. This difference in perspective and expectations is based upon differences in experience. Self-serving though it may be for a veteran of Warner to make the point, there is a significant difference in social contexts to be entered into the equation. Active or outspoken opposition to the war in Vietnam may never have engaged the majority of the American populace, and certainly not at first, although the weight of opinion may have shifted in the later stages of the war. Still the war was sufficiently unpopular to provide a cushion of tolerance, if not acceptance, for such opposition. The public indignation stirred by a Catonsville was as much a response to the *manner of protest* as to the protest itself. World War II, in contrast, was a highly popular war. Unlike the pattern of reaction to Vietnam, the longer that war continued and the greater its costs in dollars and casualties, the more complete and intense the national consensus supporting it became. Under the circumstances, a decision to stand apart and oppose that consensus required as much soul-searching and deliberation (perhaps as much courage too) as the more contemporary decisions to invade draft board offices and burn their files.

But heroism should not be the measure in either case. The fact that the so-called Vietnam conspirators could count on a community of support to applaud and encourage them ought not to detract from the authenticity of their witness and the inspiration it provided others. Nor need their predecessors suffer any pangs of guilt because what was radical in the social context of their day may suffer by comparison to what has been accomplished since. The one thing necessary, a refusal to support what they considered an unjust war, brings the two witnesses together. For both it came down to "choosing the only thing to be done."

Out of the wealth of slogans and posters opposing our most recent war one is particularly pertinent here: What if they gave a war and nobody came? As a question it made much more sense in the Vietnam context than it could ever have made in World War II when they gave a war to which virtually everyone came running. Only a ridiculously small percentage of those called to take part refused, and an even smaller percentage of these were Catholic. From this tiny share came the men who served at Camp Simon.

In the final reckoning their record is a mixture of achievement and failure. As a witness against the war, it was probably more the latter. In their isolation they had absolutely no effect upon the course of the war. On the individual scale, of course, it was a successful witness if only in the sense that they avoided contributing to what they regarded as the war's immorality. This was no small accomplishment, but unfortunately it was diminished and to some extent distorted by the unpleasantness of the camp situation and their response to it. It fell short of the corporate witness they intended it to be. Camp Simon in its Stoddard and Warner phases did represent a formal Catholic presence in CPS, a presence continued in a slightly modified form as long as the ACCO maintained jurisdiction over the Alexian and Rosewood units. But the most to be said for that presence is that it was more a matter of appearance than substance, and it ended abruptly with the end of the war and the termination of the alternative service program. There was no real corporate unity to carry over into the postwar world where its influence would be so sorely needed.

As far as CPS is concerned, the mixed but essentially negative assessment already suggested needs no further extended discussion. Some worthwhile objectives were set and achieved, but the cost was probably greater than it had to be and, even if not, more than should have been paid in any event. Pacifist collaboration in military conscription, even indirectly and at a distance, was doomed to be a losing venture from the start. One hopes this sad lesson will be remembered should any effort be made to reconstitute such a program in the future.

The two remaining dimensions, as we have seen, are much more difficult to evaluate. It is the unprovable judgment here, that the Catholic opposition to World War II, while it had little or no impact at the time, has had a delayed impact of considerable significance to the Roman Catholic Church and its developing new morality of war and peace. All the other factors of greater immediate importance—for instance, the escalating evils associated with war and nuclear war in particular—that have forced a reassessment of traditional just-war teachings have been given a sharper focus because there was this Catholic witness against World War II to serve as a frame of reference. My personal experience is illustrative. In 1957 I received my first invitation to address a Catholic audience on the subject of conscientious objection, and the purpose, quite clearly, was to introduce that audience to an off-beat (lunatic fringe might be the more apt description) point of view. If today that situation has changed and conscientious objection is recognized as a legitimate, even preferred, option for the Catholic called to service in a war, it is partly because there *were* conscientious objectors at Warner and elsewhere who, in a sense, created the possibility. Even those not yet ready to see the men of Camp Simon as prophets must at least credit them with being pioneers.

Which brings us to the final dimension. Obscure and indirect though the relationship may seem, the Catholic peace witness to World War II did contribute something, even if only the support of a precedent, to the vastly more significant and effective opposition to the war in Vietnam. Most of the young Catholics who chose alternative service or resistance and exile were probably quite ignorant of the Catholic opposition to their fathers' war. Many of them, given their more political orientation, would not have approved of the refusal to "fight Hitler" if they had been aware of that earlier witness. Making all due allowance for both the ignorance and the probable disapproval, I would still insist that enough of a continuity can be established to justify the conclusion that merely by being there the objectors of the 1940s helped prepare the way for the resistance that developed a generation later. It remains to be seen whether these later opponents of war will do a better job of carrying their peace witness into their postwar lives and activities. Thus far the prospects are not promising.

In the last analysis it makes little difference if the links between the two generations can be shown to be direct or indirect or, indeed, if one prefers to deny that there are any links at all. Every witness against war must be judged by its own record and taken in its own social context in terms of what those who made it set out to accomplish.

As far as the World War II witness is concerned, the concluding sentence of the Wittner book I have cited from time to time offers one such judgment: "In a society grown accustomed to the mass extermination of human life it led the assault on the forces of death." That image of leading an assault presents the objectors of World War II in a more active mode than they may deserve; for most, and this was certainly true for the men of Camp Simon, it was enough simply to reject participation in the war "they" were giving. But even so passive a contribution should not be underrated. In 1961 a young German writer drew a troubling parallel between the Nazi atrocity of Auschwitz and the American atrocity of Hiroshima. In both he found a common factor: the horrendous capacity for justifying the mass destruction of living human beings. Any mind capable of formulating such justification, he decided, had to be corrupt. And he went on to add, "This corruption is general."[14]

So it is. So it was in Vietnam. So it was in the war which produced the two events he joined together in reaching his pessimistic conclusion. It ought to count for something then that, in the face of insistent demands and an almost total consensus in support of that war, there were men who refused to accept or share those justifications. If they accomplished nothing else, they at least prevented that general corruption of mind from being universal.

This descriptive analysis of the social backgrounds of the seventy-five conscientious objectors ever assigned to the Warner camp makes no claim of any statistical significance for the distributions or that the interpretations based on them are in any sense conclusive. The data, obtained from the personnel files of the National Service Board for Religious Objectors on deposit at the Jane Addams Peace Library of Swarthmore College, are complete and valid as far as they go; but the population is obviously too small and the range of information too limited to support anything beyond simple proportional presentation and comparison.

As noted in the text, there is virtually complete homogeneity on the factors of sex, marital status, and race. All of the assignees were male; only one was married; only one was a Negro. Some of the questionnaire responses referred to one of the older members of the camp as an American Indian, but confirmatory evidence of this is lacking in the official records.

Religious Affiliation

Sixty-one of the seventy-five assignees were identified as Roman Catholic, and the ethnic origin indicated by the names of several of the eight men who indicated "no religion" or "none" on their Selective Service forms would suggest that they, too, may have been baptized as Catholics. The other six religious affiliations were Methodist, Unitarian, Society of Friends (Quaker), Episcopal, Orthodox (but "inactive"), and Jew (in this case, however, religious preference was indicated as "War Resisters' League").

Preinduction Residence

Place of origin, by regional distribution, shows forty-eight men coming to camp from the Middle Atlantic states of New York, New Jersey, and Pennsylvania. Six others originated from the New England region, and the remaining twenty-one from Midwestern states (Wisconsin, Minnesota, Illinois, Michigan, Indiana, Ohio, Missouri). It can be assumed that this preponderence of Easterners made the New Hampshire location somewhat desirable in the eyes of many campers. Even so, it is likely that the designation of the camp as Catholic and the prevailing Selective Service assignment policies were the principal selection factors as far as place of origin was concerned.

Sixty percent of the men came from cities with populations of one hundred thousand or more, and slightly more than a quarter from places with populations of twenty-five thousand or less. Only five indicated a rural, or farm, background. Here, too, one may relate this to the well-established fact that Roman Catholics are a predominantly urban population—indeed (and this is probably borne out by the regional distribution figures as well) principally metropolitan in character. The difficulties of adjusting to so alien a setting, particularly when coupled with the special disadvantages imposed by the financial straits of the camp and the ACCO administration, must be seen as a factor contributing to the morale problems encountered throughout the camp's brief existence.

Age

The age range of the men assigned to Camp Simon was governed by Selective Service induction priorities and policies. For the six months of the camp's operations, the progressive expansion of induction susceptibility to older (and, somewhat later in the war, younger) men, married men, men with families, and so on, had not yet taken effect. All but six of the Camp Simon men were in the 22-to-36 year range at the time of induction; three were 20 years of age; and the remaining three were 37, 39, and 42 respectively. The mean age was 27.3 years, and the median, 26. The modal age, however, was only 22 years—again more an effect of induction schedules than anything else. The disparity among these three measures of central tendency suggests a pattern of chronological maturity that might be of some significance. Such maturity, it can be assumed, would be essential to the development of so individual and principled a decision as a refusal to comply with the call to military service.

Indeed, the fact that the majority of men in this particular group were obliged to make and persist in that refusal without the support and encouragement available to objectors from other religious communities might have placed an even greater premium on chronological maturity. Some confirmation of this can be drawn from previous research (Gordon C. Zahn, "A Descriptive Survey of the Social Backgrounds of Conscientious Objectors in Civilian Public Service During World War II" [Ph.D. diss., Catholic University of America, 1953]). There it was found that in a random sampling of men in Mennonite CPS, 77 percent were less than twenty-five years of age; the comparable figures for the other peace churches were 72 percent for the Brethren and 63 percent for the Friends. But only 37 percent of the Warner assignees were that young. If it is unwise to draw any definitive conclusion from this clearly impressive difference, it would be equally unwise to ignore the possibility that taking a deviant stand on religious principle *without* the support of the religious community (in fact, in the face of its obvious disapproval) calls for the independence of judgment and persistence usually associated with chronological maturity.

Education

This is another social background factor on which the Camp Simon men differ dramatically from the general population and from their fellow CPS-men as well. According to a 1940 study by Adrian E. Gory and David G. McClelland ("Characteristics of Conscientious Objectors in World War II," *Journal of Consulting Psychology* 11 [1947]: 245–57), 24.4 percent of the American population had graduated from high school and 10.1 percent had attended college at the time the alternative service program was in operation. The sixty-one Warner men who had completed high school constitute 81 percent of the total, and forty-three (57.3 percent) had some college to their credit. Actually, twenty-three of these had completed four years or more of college; six already held the master's degree at the time of induction; and one was awaiting his Ph.D.

Again, it would be too much to suggest that these figures, however dramatic the comparison, establish a causal connection between educational attainment and conscientious objection. The military services, even though one assumes their educational distribution would most likely approximate the national levels, could certainly claim their share of high school and college graduates and, given the disparity in size of the populations involved, these would outnumber their counterparts in CPS several times over. More to the point, if we were to incorporate the educational levels that must have applied as far as the Mennonite and Brethren camps were concerned—both drawing more heavily from rural populations than did the Warner camp—the overall averages for CPS would find the differences greatly reduced. The most that definitely can be said on this score is that the men of Camp Simon constituted a highly educated group in the main. From this we may infer that their position against war and service in war can be attributed in part to the application of that superior level of educational achievement and, to the extent the two are related, intellectual capacity leading to the very crucial and controversial decision they felt called upon to make.

Before leaving the discussion of education as a social background factor, note should be taken of some rather suggestive internal differences related to religious affiliation and age. A comparison of the Catholics, both nominal and active, with the non-Catholics on the Warner roster reveals that the former appear to have the educational advantage, 84 percent of them having completed high school as against 71 percent of the others. The discrepancy disappears, however, with respect to college background: the proportion here is 57 percent for both.

The age-educational attainment comparisons are more striking. Of the fifty-one men who were twenty-nine years of age or less when inducted, forty-six (90.2 percent) had completed high school as compared with fifteen of the twenty-four (62.5 percent) who were thirty or older. The proportions reporting some college were 62.7 and 45.8 percent respectively.

Combining all three factors, one finds that the non-Catholics aged twenty-nine or less ranked highest in educational attainment (15.1 years completed); Catholics of the same age group were second (13.7

years); Catholics thirty and older came next with 12.8 years of education completed, and the three non-Catholics in the older group brought up the rear with only 9.3 years of schooling to their credit. The numbers, again, are much too small to justify any claim to statistical significance. Nevertheless, they do reveal an important potential for differences in perspective and difficulties in communication that did in fact materialize in the camp setting and, one must assume, contributed to the sad state of camp morale.

Occupation

As might be expected for so relatively young a collection of men, most of the Warner campers had not settled into a definite occupation or career at the time they were inducted into service. The first point to be noted here, then, is that the educational attainment summarized above actually *understates* the true state of affairs; no less than fourteen identified themselves as students at the time of induction. This represented the largest single occupational category on the Selective Service forms, matched only by the same number describing themselves as engaged in clerical or managerial occupations. Factory and general labor accounted for thirteen, and artists and writers represented the only other double-digit occupational category with eleven. Seven men had been employed in service trades and six in the civil service (postal workers, fireman, and the like). Six others had already entered upon professional occupations in teaching and the law. Three men listed their affiliation with the Catholic Worker movement as a social service occupation. Only one was a farmer before his assignment to camp.

Even allowing for the tendency on the part of some who had been engaged in what are generally regarded as lower status occupations to speak deprecatingly of the college boys and intellectuals (often enough, they were called pseudointellectuals) in their midst at Warner, the occupational factor did not constitute a significant source of division or dissension. Those who had been accustomed to hand work seemed to respect the head work achievements of the others; and these, in turn, were fully conscious of the essential contributions made by the former to the maintenance of even a minimal level of existence for all. After all, preinduction diversity made little difference at Warner; there everyone had been reduced to the same level of meaningless activity for "the duration and six months."

It is possible, of course, that the men who came into CPS from a manual labor or factory background may have had a psychological advantage in that their frustration threshold might be higher than for men who, having prepared themselves for more significant social contributions, encountered greater difficulty in adjusting to the Warner work regimen. This may account for the fact that the workers were less frustrated and, consequently, less likely to assume an active role in the issues and controversies that dominated so much of the camp experience. This is highly speculative and not supported by any tangible data.

Peace Activities

The final background factor to be summarized here relates to previous involvement in peace organizations and activities. The information included in the personnel files of the Camp Simon men makes it very clear that they had little or no past connections with what is usually referred to as the organized peace movement.

The reliability of the data on which this conclusion is based is not secure. The informational items regarding such factors as religious identification and affiliation, age, education, and occupation were obtained from responses to specific questions on the Selective Service forms. Any information relating to past participation in peace works or activities was deduced from incidental references volunteered by the registrant, usually as supplemental evidence of the sincerity of his claim. It is quite possible, therefore, that some affiliations that may have had a bearing upon an individual's decision to refuse military service were not volunteered on some of the forms.

Be that as it may, only twenty-nine such memberships or affiliations were mentioned *for the entire group*. The Catholic Worker, the ACCO and PAX—all of which were essentially the same in origin and sponsorship—received eleven mentions. Ten men listed the nondenominational Fellowship of Reconciliation, and the nonreligious War Resisters' League was mentioned by four. Single mentions went to the Wider Quaker Fellowship, the Episcopal Peace Fellowship, the Pacifist Action Fellowship, and something called the Catholic Students' Peace Society.

An even better illustration of the low peace movement involvement is the fact that fifty-four (72 percent) of the Warner assignees volunteered *no organizational affiliations at all*, and of the twenty-one who accounted for whatever involvement there was, sixteen indicated only a single affiliation.

With all due allowance for the possibility that the responses on this item were incomplete, it seems safe to say that whatever peace movement background these men may have had before coming to camp was so slight as to be of little or no positive influence on their decision. Here, too, we may have a key to some of the problems encountered at Warner. Had this not been the case, had there been a deeper involvement in peace organizations and activities and a closer identification with the Catholic Worker sponsors or even the more traditional peace groups, there might have been a deeper and more durable commitment to the alternative service program and its purposes. If not this, there might at least have been less of a disposition on their part to see themselves as outsiders in the CPS setting—and victimized outsiders at that.

Notes

Part One

* This lyric, like the others used to introduce the major sections of this book, was featured in one of the skits prepared for the visit of some Smith College girls to the Warner camp (see chapter 8). In the last line of the lyric, popular stereotypes of the conscientious objector notwithstanding, the term "gay" was used in its 1943 connotations—i.e., as high-spirited, joyous, or cheerful.

1. First Impressions

1. Patricia McNeal, "Catholic Conscientious Objection During World War II," *The Catholic Historical Review* (April 1975), p. 232 n.
2. The Warner camp file, for instance, contains a blistering letter from a published author on the West Coast demanding that his assignment there be cancelled because he refused to have anything to do with anything Catholic. That this man was even considered for assignment there illustrates the desperation of the Camp Simon situation. It was normal practice, at least then, for Selective Service to assign inductees to camps on their respective sides of the Mississippi for reasons of economy.
3. Several friends told me of interviews they had had with my FBI investigator. In one instance, the woman being interviewed expressed indignation over such a procedure and told him, though I was away from the city at the time, he should wait and ask his questions of me after I returned from vacation. To which he replied that I had returned the previous day and that he had known when I left and where I had been!
4. I am indebted to Harold P. Winchester for permitting me to use his incomplete manuscript for information relating to the Stoddard phase.

2. A Witness Unheard and Unwanted

1. The quotation is attributed to Rev. Richard Klaver, O.S.C. of St. Paul writing in the July 1941 (?) issue of the *Crozier Missionary*. It was answered in an

"open letter" published in the first issue of *Salt* (January 1942), the Stoddard-Warner camp journal published three or four times in mimeographed form.

2. The Catholic was not alone in this situation. Other religious denominations that tended to take a distinctly unfavorable view of conscientious objection included Lutheran, Morman, Russian Orthodox, and—for obvious and special reasons—Judaism. It should be noted, of course, that these are generalizations. Under the stress of the war's events and wartime propaganda, it is likely that a given congregation of a denomination described here as neutral might be quite hostile to a member who chose to oppose that war. By the same token, it is conceivable (though I confess I know of no such instance) that a given Catholic parish might have taken a favorable or supportive stand behind one of its sons who chose to enter CPS rather than accept induction into one of the other services.

3. The promise, I have been told, was not always kept. Some men who were classified I-A-O by their local boards apparently ended up in the infantry. Since Selective Service did not keep these military records separate from those of full-service inductees, there is no way of determining how often this may have occurred or under what circumstances. Selective Service estimates that 25,000 men were inducted into noncombatant service under the I-A-O classification. Selective Service System, *Conscientious Objection*, Special Monograph no. 11 (Washington, D.C., 1940) 1:127.

4. John Leo LeBrun cites Arthur Sheehan, General Secretary of the ACCO, as confirming this assumption. Another contributor, as recalled by Dorothy Day in a personal communication, was Bishop Peterson of Manchester, the diocese in which both the Stoddard and Warner camps were located. Occasional reference has been made to Bishop Shaughnessy of Seattle as a third benefactor, but his support may have been intended more for the Catholic Worker movement than for its pacifist front. See LeBrun, "The Role of the Catholic Worker Movement in American Pacifism, 1933–1972" (Ph.D. diss., Case Western Reserve University, 1973), p. 127. The McNicholas quotation is on p. 90 of this work. McNeal, apparently drawing upon information provided by Sheehan adds Bishop Karl T. Alter of Toledo and Archbishop Francis J. Bechman of Dubuque to the list of episcopal donors. Patricia McNeal, "Catholic Conscientious Objection," p. 236 n.

5. *New York Times*, 9 October 1944, p. 3.

6. One such speech is found in the *New York Times*, 31 October 1941, p. 4. The endorsement of such aid for the Soviet Union has a particularly direct bearing upon the position taken by at least one of the Warner factions. According to Rhodes, the McNicholas position was actually initiated in Rome by Pius XII for the specific purpose of relieving American Catholics of whatever scruples they might have concerning military aid to Russia. McNicholas was selected, Rhodes suggests, because "he was known for his reserve and political neutrality, and he could not be accused of having succumbed to governmental pressure." Interestingly enough, he goes on to note that Bishop Shaughnessy, one of the other reputed contributors to the Stoddard-Warner camps was scheduled to give a broadcast attacking Russia, a broadcast that was cancelled after the McNicholas statement was issued. Anthony Rhodes, *The Vatican in the Age of Dictators (1922–1945)* (New York: Holt, Rinehart & Winston, 1974), p. 263.

7. Published by the Catholic Worker Press as a pamphlet in 1941.
8. In that 1935 article Furfey sets forth an imaginary debate between Christ and a patriot. The pacifist argument was based, not on the just-war theory but on "the Christian's calling to a kingdom of love and peace which takes precedence over his calling to obedience to the state." As McNeal sees it, "With that single article the American Catholic peace movement was born." McNeal, "Catholic Conscientious Objection," p. 227.
9. William D. Miller, *A Harsh and Dreadful Love* (New York: Liveright, 1973). See especially chapters 10 and 11.

3. Background and Beginnings

1. There was another factor involved. The camp program was originally modelled after the volunteer summer work camp programs conducted by the peace church agencies. The service ideology which permeated this worthwhile operation was carried over, perhaps a bit too uncritically, into CPS. According to McNeal ("Catholic Conscientious Objection," p. 233), President Roosevelt expressed himself as favoring a program of alternative service under military direction while negotiations were under way. This undoubtedly spurred the peace leaders to more concerted efforts on behalf of their proposal. As it worked out, though their plan for camp autonomy carried the day, in theory at least, the actuality of CPS was closer to what Roosevelt had in mind.
2. These factual data are taken from Lawrence S. Wittner, *Rebels Against War: The American Peace Movement, 1941–1960* (New York: Columbia University Press, 1969) and the Selective Service special monograph cited earlier. The latter source reveals a slight variance in the total of men assigned to CPS. ". . . it is estimated that between 70,000 and 75,000 military liable registrants, aged 18 through 44 years, filed claims of conscientious objection during the 6½ years of Selective Service operations during World War II." Of these, 11,950 are reported as having been assigned to CPS and another 1,624 assigned to camp but convicted for violations of the conscription law for refusing to go (*Conscientious Objection*, 1: 127).
3. As noted in the Introduction, the French diary is included in the Jane Addams Peace Library deposit at Swarthmore College.
4. From the withdrawal statement prepared for and approved by the Catholic members of the Alexian, Rosewood, and Trenton units. The complete text was published in the January-March (1945) issue of the *Catholic C.O.*
5. McNeal, "Catholic Conscientious Objection," p. 225.
6. One former camper recalls Mass being offered at Stoddard on only two or three occasions.
7. The Alexian unit (CPS #26) was officially approved March 3, 1942; the men must have been transferred there shortly after that date.
8. Here, too, a former camper who had been at Stoddard and who was kind enough to review an early draft of this chapter enters a mild demurrer on this count. "Thirty years have diminished my memory, but I don't think I really thought the new setting would make much difference. In my ignorance of life, the dissension in camp and the loafing on the project during the spring and summer of 1941 had been profoundly disturbing. I must have been deeply

masochistic not to have made some attempt to leave the camp for some other camp or unit." This comment assumes added significance in the fact that this camper was one of the eight who had volunteered to save the Catholic camp in the first place.

4. Days in the Life

1. Wittner, *Rebels Against War*, p. 160.
2. Boston and Maine passenger service is a thing of the past, and the only bus now arrives in Warner late in the evening on the outbound run and departs early in the morning. Since there are no motels or tourist home facilities, an overnight stay is out of the question. As for highway travel, Warner is now by-passed by an interstate expressway, reduced to little more than a quick glimpse of a steeple and a cluster of buildings seen at a distance.
3. William E. Stafford, *Down in My Heart* (Elgin, Ill.: The Brethren Press, 1947), p. 89.
4. Wittner, *Rebels Against War*, p. 74.
5. Ibid, pp. 72, 73.
6. Ibid, p. 74.
7. Stafford, *Down in My Heart*, pp. 28–29.
8. Ibid, p. 84.

6. The Men: A Gallery of Characters

1. The Luzon brothers and Richard Wysacki were special victims of "Mother Pat's" charade. Convinced the inspection was the preliminary to a possible opening of a new hospital unit in New York City, the former hastened to remove their collection of pin-ups from the wall behind their bunks. When the Mother Superior made her rounds, these archdisrupters and Wysacki, the most outspoken atheist in camp, stood at their places in reverential docility, to the great delight of those who had instigated the farce.
2. Roger Tennitt, writing in the April 1942 issue of *Salt*, provides one illustration of how individuals of more liberal persuasion dealt with the problem. He writes, "What can we do? you say. Hitler is bad and we are good. He is so bad that we must destroy him or we shall be destroyed. But I say that this has some truth but is not a truth. It is not a truth because to destroy is against the truth of good . . . the truth of kindness and love that is beautiful. And you say that wars have been always here . . . wars make history. And I say that history has been made in spite of wars. Man has progressed because of man's goodness to man rather than man's might over his fellows. How can we gain from hate . . . hate which is a necessity of war. To hate is to lose everything. Life is love which is beautiful."
3. A reader of a preliminary draft of this chapter enters a mild disclaimer that deserves to be noted.

   I think that many CO's were highly, even naively, idealistic. It was jarring to encounter deeply selfish, conniving, uncommitted, and fraudulent poseurs in our midst. I don't think that many were there "to celebrate our alienation" so much as "to celebrate our affirmation of very precious values." Was it too much to expect conscientiousness *of those who apparently defined themselves and were socially defined by that crucial index? . . .*

I tried to distinguish the neurotic and eccentric from the cunning and calculating "outsiders." After careful efforts at appraisal, I know that I responded to them differently then, and I think that my response would be the same today— sans *regret.*

The point is well taken and, of course, the question (Why weren't we more kind?) relates primarily to the authentic oddballs and not to the dissemblers or the disrupters. But there is a troubling fact (to be discussed later) that may have a significant bearing on this qualification as well. *All* of the Warner campers I have identified here as disrupters would ultimately be discharged from CPS on psychoneurotic grounds, a fact which might entitle them to a measure of retroactive sympathy on this score.

7. *Issues and Controversies*

1. Apparently this was not the first time this happened. The Selmon diary shows that such general weather day assignments were made on December 22 and 31 and, perhaps, on other occasions as well. Those particular days, however, show the men recorded "P" (on project) on the work sheets; the January 14 and 15 dates show "SD" (special detail). The earlier occasions probably involved such essential duties as shoveling snow from the walks and bringing in firewood. The January episodes were viewed more as made-work assignments to "keep the boys busy."

2. Sterner had been designated for this post before this particular controversy erupted and had spent the preceding month attending a Camp Directors' training course in Washington. He was not in camp at the time of the three meetings discussed here. As perhaps the most outgoing of the active Catholics at Warner—the reader will recall the earlier reference to him as the camp jock—he would not have been an unpopular choice. Nevertheless, as one more example of an arbitrary decision taken without consulting the campers, Sterner's selection could not completely resolve the basic issue.

3. This pattern, it may be well to note, had been well established even before this particularly unfortunate series of meetings. Thus, a meeting held to establish a Christmas furlough policy recorded a 13 to 7 tally; a week or so later, after a directive from Selective Service had injected a new limiting factor, the decision was reconsidered and a new plan was adopted, this time by an 8 to 7 vote. Since the camp roster listed approximately sixty members at that time, the level of participation is graphic testimony to the apathy and disenchantment that then prevailed. Similarly, the voting results show how far the camp had moved from the will-of-the-group ideal.

4. The ACCO unit at the Rosewood State Training School for the mentally deficient (Owings Mills, Maryland) was ultimately approved, but not before the camp personnel had been transferred to the AFSC camp at Oakland, Maryland. This Rosewood unit was to serve as a means of reestablishing the corporate witness begun at Stoddard and Warner. At best, however, it reunited a

minority of the Warner men, the bulk of whom were shortly to be transferred from the Oakland camp to a new AFSC camp located at Trenton,
North Dakota.

5. This allowance is not to be confused with compensation for work performed.
   Unfortunately the point is often missed. Thus McNeal speaks of the Catholic
   men at Rosewood receiving "a salary of $15.00 a month." At no time did
   they or anyone else in CPS receive a salary. At Rosewood the men did receive a monthly allowance, beginning at five dollars a month and late in the
   program increasing to the fifteen dollar figure, but they would never have
   considered this as pay for the work they were obliged to perform.
6. Wittner, *Rebels Against War*, p. 82.
7. *New York Journal American*, 30 August 1942.
8. Selective Service System, *Conscientious Objection*, 1:176.
9. Ibid, pp. 232-3.
10. A detailed review of the resistance movement in CPS, with special reference
    to the situation at Germfask and other government camps is provided in
    chapter 12 of the Selective Service monograph. Ibid,. pp. 229-51.
11. Ibid, p. 227.

8. *Events, High Spots and Galas*

1. Going to a movie was no small thing, as the writer can testify from his own
   experience. On my first trip to Concord, a month or so after I arrived at
   camp, the high point of the weekend was seeing *Bambi*, the best of the three
   movies available. In George's case, he saw *The Black Swan*, "a horse opera
   with ships substituting for the horses"—at that a better choice than mine,
   which I described in a letter as "too juvenile for words."
2. Another possibility suggested for an ACCO unit was the mental hospital at
   Augusta, Maine. That stirred even less interest.

9. *Exodus and Aftermath*

1. The bishop's letter is included in the Selective Service files in the National
   Archives in Washington. Unfortunately, the chancery files for the period in
   question do not include any letters of criticism that may have been addressed to him or any responses to such letters; therefore it is not possible
   to ascertain how much Bishop Peterson may have been under pressure from
   his flock to dissociate himself from Camp Simon and its affairs. It should be
   noted in this connection that, despite the virtually unanimous support for
   the war effort on the part of American Catholics and the tone of the more
   enthusiastic episcopal statements encouraging such support, it overstates the
   case for him to say that the Catholic Church as such had ever defined the
   performance of military service in World War II as "an essential duty."
2. Selective Service System, *Conscientious Objection*, 1:297.
3. Ibid, pp. 301-2.
4. Ibid.
5. The hearing, it seems, was concerned primarily with Kosch's defense of the
   point system that had been developed for the demobilization of men from

CPS, but the often antagonistic questions raised by several Congressmen (who felt the proposal was overly generous) led into these broader issues as well. The text of this July 8, 1945, hearing is provided in General Letter 124 issued by the NSBRO on July 13.

6. Selective Service System, *Conscientious Objection,* 1: 297. A summary of the procedures involved in determining whether an assignee was to be approved for medical discharge is provided on pages 298-99 of the monograph.

10. The Final Reckoning

1. The question: "Looking back on WWII, would you do it over again? (Any second thoughts about being a CO? Any second thoughts about accepting alternate service? Do you think now that your CPS experience or your opposition to the war was 'worth' the personal difficulties it may have caused?)"

2. The question: "What is your present over-all impressions of the men at Warner? (Do you think most of them were sincere—or merely trying to avoid an unpleasant or dangerous situation? Some would insist that COs as a category tend to be disproportionately susceptible to personality maladjustments or other forms of 'deviance'—do you think there was any evidence of this at Warner?)"

3. This is no coincidence. Ludlow was one of the framers of the statement of withdrawal signed by Arthur Sheehan as Executive Secretary of the ACCO. The genesis of the move is worth describing. Shortly before, in large part as a reflection of the sentiment prevailing among the men in its camps, the AFSC had announced its intention to end participation in the CPS program in March 1946. The Catholic men at the ACCO's Rosewood unit took this as an opportunity to agitate for an immediate withdrawal and circulated a draft statement to the Catholics at the Alexian unit in Chicago and the Warner remnants at two Western camps. The statement was adopted by a 3 to 1 majority, with all except the Alexian group voting unanimously in its favor. "Pro" and "Con" arguments, along with the text signed by Sheehan, were published in the January-March 1946 issue of the *Catholic C.O.* The Ludlow quotation is from his "Pro" commentary.

4. A summary report of prison activities, as well as CPS, is provided in an excellent cooperative project edited and produced by Robert Cooney and Helen Michalowski, *The Power of the People* (Culver City, Ca.: The Peace Press, 1977). Chapter 5, "World War II and the Pacifist Community," is particularly relevant to this study though it, too, fails to take any notice of the ACCO withdrawal—or, for that matter, the ACCO.

5. Except for the missing factor of religious agency administration, the ill-fated Ecology Corps project of the Vietnam period seems to have been modelled quite closely upon CPS. Originally developed as a volunteer opportunity, these forestry units soon deteriorated into a kind of warehousing operation such as favored by General Hershey. Eric Wright in *CCCO News Notes*, no. 2 (1972) describes the experience of the California Ecology Corps as "a dream shattered." The article is an extensive summary of various inequities and false assurances, but its most significant point for the present discussion is the statement, "The CEC which California originally stated would be

staffed by volunteers only, has become the cesspool into which are thrown COs who cannot find or obtain approval for work of their own choosing."

6. Pius XII, radio message on the fourth anniversary of the outbreak of war (September 1, 1943).

7. The January and February 1942 issues of the *Catholic Worker* featured the text of a letter written by the single even moderately well-known objector, Ben Salmon, to President Wilson in October 1918. At the time of writing he was in Fort Douglas, Washington, "the eleventh penal institution in which I have taken up my abode in consequence of refusal to kill." His was a shocking record of injustice which began with a nine-month sentence for failure to register; while that was being appealed (with Salmon under $2,500 bond, certainly a substantial amount in those days), he was arrested by military authorities and charged with "desertion from the army and propaganda" for which he was sentenced to twenty-five years in military confinement on August 10, 1918. Shortly thereafter he was offered a "First Class sergeancy" which he refused. Apparently he was granted some kind of executive clemency somewhere along the line, for, according to the *Worker*'s explanatory note, he died in freedom in Chicago eight years later.

8. A useful summary discussion of American Catholic peace activities and organizations between the two world wars, including the Catholic Worker and the CAIP is Patricia McNeal, "Origins of the Catholic Peace Movement," *Review of Politics* 35, no. 3 (July 1973) : 346–74.

9. It began, in fact, as a page in the regular monthly paper. Once it was on its own, the periodical carried the usual appeals for contributions to keep it going. This was enhanced in 1944–1945 by personal letters addressed to prominent Catholics, stressing the importance of expressing the journal's minority point of view even if the individual addressed did not share it. This special appeal brought a few contributions from Catholics who were not already in the pacifist fold. It also brought less encouraging responses. One well-known author of religious biographies wrote expressly to thank the editors for giving him the opportunity to refuse to support a position for which he had no sympathy whatsoever.

10. Among the best known examples are Franz Jaegerstaetter and Father Max Josef Metzger, both of whom were executed for refusing to support Hitler's wars. See Gordon C. Zahn, *In Solitary Witness: The Life and Death of Franz Jaegerstaetter* (New York: Holt, Rinehart & Winston, 1964) for a documented account of the former.

11. McNeal, "Catholic Conscientious Objection," p. 224.

12. Again, a documented survey of that record may be found in my *German Catholics and Hitler's Wars: A Study in Social Control* (New York: Sheed & Ward, 1962). The extensive discussion, not always favorable, stirred by the publication of this book helped to bring the issue to Catholics of all stations in this country and abroad. If, as I like to think, it contributed to the changes being discussed here, that would deserve to be counted as a Warner contribution.

13. On May 17, 1968, Fathers Daniel and Philip Berrigan and seven others invaded the Catonsville, Maryland, draft board offices, removed some files, and burned them with homemade napalm. This action had been preceded several

months before by Philip and three others who had invaded a Baltimore office and poured blood on files, and would be followed by a number of similar actions in Chicago, Milwaukee, and other widely scattered locales. For a
moving statement of the rationale behind these actions, see Daniel Berrigan,
The Trial of the Catonsville Nine (Boston: Beacon Press, 1970).

14. Christian Geissler, "Auschwitz, Hiroshima und die Hoffnungen des Men-
schen," *Werkhefte* 15 (July 1961): 229–35.

Library of Congress Cataloging in Publication Data
Zahn, Gordon Charles, 1918-
Another part of the war.
1. World War, 1939-1945—Conscientious ob-
jectors—United States. 2. Camp Simon.
3. World War, 1939-1945—Catholic Church.
I. Title.
D810.C82Z33   940.53'162   78-53181
ISBN 0-87023-259-2